Springer Texts in Business and Economics

Springer Texts in Business and Economics (STBE) delivers high-quality instructional content for undergraduates and graduates in all areas of Business/Management Science and Economics. The series is comprised of self-contained books with a broad and comprehensive coverage that are suitable for class as well as for individual self-study. All texts are authored by established experts in their fields and offer a solid methodological background, often accompanied by problems and exercises.

More information about this series at http://www.springer.com/series/10099

Lutz Kruschwitz • Andreas Löffler

Stochastic Discounted Cash Flow

A Theory of the Valuation of Firms

OPEN

Springer

Lutz Kruschwitz
Free University of Berlin
Berlin, Germany

Andreas Löffler
Department of Finance, Accounting, Taxation
Free University of Berlin
Berlin, Germany

ISSN 2192-4333 ISSN 2192-4341 (electronic)
Springer Texts in Business and Economics
ISBN 978-3-030-37080-0 ISBN 978-3-030-37081-7 (eBook)
https://doi.org/10.1007/978-3-030-37081-7

This book is an open access publication.

This Springer imprint is published by the registered company Springer Nature Switzerland AG.
The registered company address is: Gewerbestrasse 11, 6330 Cham, Switzerland

Preface

We are very pleased that Springer was ready to publish a revised version 13 years after the release of the first edition of this book. The following items have been changed:

- The way we dealt with the problem of transversality in the first edition never really got us satisfied. We now believe that we have found a way to deal with this issue much more convincingly than before.
- The same applies to sections where we discuss companies that can go bankrupt. We have incorporated new findings where they seemed important to us.
- We have extended the problems and included the sample solutions in the text; a separately available Solution Manual no longer appeared up to date to us.
- The book is now open access. Such a feature did not exist a decade ago, and we are extremely pleased that Springer makes possible this form of publication today.
- Last but not least, we would like to draw the reader's attention to the fact that the title of the book has changed—seemingly only slightly. For us authors, however, this is an important matter. We have found that the words "Discounted Cash Flow" are too reminiscent of the literature aimed at practitioners whose job is to find simple ad hoc solutions to the many problems of company valuation. We are academics and see our mission in finding logically stringent answers to complicated questions. This is sometimes quite far away from what practitioners have to cope with. Unlike practitioners, we cannot accept "sticking tax rates to capital costs in any arbitrary way" or ignore the probabilistic basis of risk and uncertainty. Rather, we want to concentrate on the scientific foundations of calculation under uncertainty and focus on the stochastic questions of valuation. Unfortunately, it then follows that we will inevitably have to ignore some practically important details in our analysis. But then, the title should not fake what the book does not deliver. Therefore, from now on, the book is called "Stochastic Discounted Cash Flow."

Undoubtedly, empirical questions of company valuation are currently in vogue. However, we sincerely hope that there will be a return to analytical questions in the not too distant future.

Berlin, Germany
November 2019

Lutz Kruschwitz
Andreas Löffler

Acknowledgements

We started the work on the subject in 2002. A first draft of the manuscript was published as discussion paper of the University of Hannover. Scott Budzynski translated this first draft and it was subsequently used for several courses in Hannover as well as in Berlin. We thank our students who carefully read the manuscript and helped us to eliminate a lot of mistakes. Further thanks go out to Dominica Canefield, Erik Eschen, Inka Gläser, Matthias Häußler, Anthony F. Herbst, Jörg Laitenberger, Petra Pade from GlobeGround, Marc Steffen Rapp, Stephan Rosarius, Christian Schiel, Andreas Scholze, Saskia Wagner, Martin Wallmeier, Stefan Weckbach, Jörg Wiese, Elmar Wolfstetter, and Eckart Zwicker for helpful comments. Arnd Lodowicks and Thorsten Rogall contributed two financial policies in the corporate tax chapter.

We would like to thank the *Verein zur Förderung der Zusammenarbeit von Lehre und Praxis am Finanzplatz Hannover e.V.* Their generous support made our work much easier. We thank our wives Ingrid Kruschwitz and Constanze Stein, who never complained when we sat up the whole night in front of our computers.

Berlin, Germany

Lutz Kruschwitz
Andreas Löffler

Contents

List of Figures

List of Symbols

$\widetilde{A}$	Amount of retained earnings
$\widetilde{Accr}$	Accruals
$\widetilde{CF}$	Cash flow
$\widetilde{D}$	Market value of debt
$\underline{\widetilde{D}}$	Book value of debt
Div	Dividend
d^u	Dividend-price ratio of unlevered firm
$\underline{\widetilde{e}}$	Increase in subscribed capital
$\widetilde{E}$	Market value of equity
$\underline{\widetilde{E}}$	Book value of equity
$\mathrm{E}[\cdot]$	(Conditional) expectation
$\widetilde{EBIT}$	Earnings before interest and taxes
$\widetilde{FCF}$	Free cash flow
$\widetilde{FCF}^l$	Free cash flow of levered firm
$\widetilde{FCF}^u$	Free cash flow of unlevered firm
$\vert\mathcal{F}_t$	Information in t
$\widetilde{GCF}$	Gross cash flow before tax
$\widetilde{I}$	Interest
$\widetilde{Inv}$	Investments
k	Cost of capital of untaxed firm
$\widetilde{k}^D$	Cost of debt
$k^{E,l}$	Cost of equity of levered firm
$k^{E,u}$	Cost of equity of unlevered firm
$\widetilde{k}^{\varnothing}$	WACC, type 1
$\widetilde{l}$	Leverage ratio to market values
$\underline{\widetilde{l}}$	Leverage ratio to book values
$\widetilde{L}$	Debt-equity ratio to market values
$\underline{\widetilde{L}}$	Debt-equity ratio to book values
$\widetilde{R}$	Debt repayment
r_f	Riskless interest rate
τ	Tax rate
$\widetilde{Tax}$	Tax payment
$\widetilde{Tax}^l$	Tax payment of levered firm
$\widetilde{Tax}^u$	Tax payment of unlevered firm
$\widetilde{V}^l$	Market value of levered firm
$\widetilde{V}^u$	Market value of unlevered firm
$\underline{\widetilde{V}}$	Book value of unlevered firm
$\widetilde{WACC}$	WACC, type 2

List of Definitions

List of Theorems

List of Assumptions

List of Rules

1 Introduction: A Stochastic Approach to Discounted Cash Flow

A new scientific truth does not best gain acceptance by convincing and instructing its opponents, but much more so in that its opponents gradually die out and the upcoming generation is entrusted with the truth from the beginning.
Max Planck, Autobiography

The valuation of firms is an exciting topic. It is interesting for economists engaged in either practice or theory, particularly for those in finance. Amongst practitioners, it is investment bankers and public accountants, who are regularly confronted with the question of how a firm is to be valued. The discussion about shareholder value (starting with Rappaport) indicated that one cannot tell from the numbers of traditional accounting alone whether the managers of a firm were primarily successful or did poorly. Instead, the change in the value of the firm is used in order to try and determine exactly this. That suffices for the practitioner's interest. The reasons why academics involve themselves with questions of valuation of firms are different.

If you look more closely at how finance theoreticians use to determine the value of a firm, you quickly realize that firms are not seen by them primarily as institutions that acquire production factors and manufacture either products or services. The actual side of economic activities is not looked at in any more detail. Instead, the income which the financiers, the owners in particular, can attain is the question of interest. The ways in which firms contribute to fulfilling consumer needs are of secondary importance. What is decisive is the amount of payments and its distribution among the owners and creditors. The income a company can earn determines its value. In the end, a firm is nothing more than a risky asset, or a portfolio of assets. The valuation of firms deals with nothing else than the question as to what economic value future earnings have today. It can be principally summed up as: the more the better, the earlier the more desirable, and the more certain the more valuable.

L. Kruschwitz, A. Löffler, *Stochastic Discounted Cash Flow*,
Springer Texts in Business and Economics,
https://doi.org/10.1007/978-3-030-37081-7_1

The literature on valuation of firms recommends logical, quantitative methods, which deal with establishing today's value of future free cash flows. In this respect, the valuation of a firm is identical with the calculation of the discounted cash flow, which is often only given by its abbreviation, DCF. There are, however, different coexistent versions that seem to compete against each other. Entity approach and equity approach are thus differentiated. Acronyms are often used, such as APV (adjusted present value) or WACC (weighted average cost of capital), whereby these two concepts are classified under the entity approach.

We see it as very important to systematically clarify the way in which these different variations of the DCF concept are related. Why are there several procedures and not just one? Do they all lead to the same result? If not, what are the economic differences? If so, for what purpose are different methods needed? And further: do the known procedures suffice? Or are there situations where none of the concepts developed up to now delivers the correct value of the firm? If so, how is the appropriate valuation formula to be found? These questions are not just interesting for theoreticians; even the practitioner who is confronted with the task of marketing his or her results has to deal with them.

When the valuation of risky assets is discussed by theoreticians, there are certain standards that get in the way of directly carrying over the results onto the problems of practical valuation of firms. Theory-based economists usually concentrate on specific details of their object of examination and leave out everything else which they consider to be less important at the moment. There have been models in which—for purposes of simplification—it is supposed that the firm to be valued will survive for exactly 1 year. Or you find models in which it is required for convenience's sake that the firm goes on forever. But in return for that, it yields cash flows which remain the same and it does not have to pay taxes. In yet other models, it is assumed that although a very simple tax is brought to bear on the business level, the shareholders are, however, spared any taxation. It is supposed in further models that the price of an asset follows a stochastic process, which the evaluator can describe very accurately and over which he or she is methodically (mathematically) in total control. Such simplifications and specializations are part and parcel of theoretical work. They are not only usual but extremely advantageous. They are, however, not always appropriate for means of practical valuation of firms. And this is the reason why considerable efforts must be made to move in the direction away from the fundamental theoretical understanding, which derives from assumptions demanding a great deal of simplification. Instead, a move should be made towards valuation equations that are either not based on such a great deal of simplification or else based in part on far-reaching simplifications.

The article by Modigliani and Miller represents, for instance, an important basis for traditional DCF theory. Two things are characteristic for this contribution: first, a very simple corporate income tax is depicted; second, the leverage ratio of the firm is measured in market values. If you now have to value a German firm, for example, the results from Modigliani and Miller cannot simply be applied. Instead, you have to carry out appropriate adjustments. First, the German system of business taxation is somewhat more complicated. And second, it could be that the managers of the firm have decided in favor of a financing policy in which the leverage ratio is measured on balance sheet basis. The question must then be asked, "how are the formulas to be changed?" The theoretical literature so far offers no clear path to follow.

If the theory does not provide an answer, practitioners are left with no other choice than to ad hoc adjust the valuation equations according to their judgement so that they do justice to the present situation as far as they are convinced. For the practitioner, the theory can only be a guideline to go by anyway. They are used to taking matters into their own hands in order to make the theory at all useable.

The theoreticians are not under the same time constraints as the practitioners. They are obligated to the truth, not their mandates. This is the reason it is not allowed for them to simply change valuation equations ad hoc, which were developed under the specific circumstances of a model, if the original conditions no longer prevail. They must instead abide by the rules, which make it possible to check to see if its assertions are correct. As a first step, the new conditions are to be described in an orderly way. On this basis and that of further contradiction-free assumptions, the theoretician must try to derive the valuation equation relevant for this case with the help of logical and mathematical operations. It is only in observing these conventions that they have the right to recommend a specific valuation equation as appropriate. And it is only in observing these rules that a third party has the possibility to check whether a valuation procedure in fact deserves the predicate "suitable." We are convinced that whoever does otherwise risks being accused of having no scientific ground to stand on.

We will attempt in this book to stick to the line of thought just described. We will thus not ad hoc draw up valuation equations, but rather call to mind the theoretical groundwork upon which these were gotten. We see no other serious alternative in this matter. Readers who take the trouble to follow along with us will indeed be rewarded with a lot of discoveries, which are at once formally precise and also economically interesting.

In closing, we want to get a little more concrete regarding the "long way round" that we have propagated and impart what we regard as particularly characteristic of our methodology. More than anything else there are four points, which differentiate our depiction of the DCF concept from that of the literature up until now:

No arbitrage Certain paradigms dominate finance theory today. These include, for instance, expected utility, the concept of perfect markets, the postulate that the markets are free of arbitrage, and the equilibrium concept, just to name a few. No reality-grounded theoretician would maintain that any of these are empirically representative. We are well aware that managers and investors do not always behave rationally. This presents the basis for an interesting development, which is today referred to as behavioral finance. The investors' assumption of homogenous expectations is characteristic of perfect markets. It is clear to us that in reality the market participants are working with asymmetric information. Principal–agent models, which take exactly that into consideration, have made a lot of headway in finance theory in the last 40 years.

But as far as the development of valuation equations is concerned, finance theoreticians have only been successful when they have strictly followed the guidelines of the neoclassical paradigm. And this paradigm is based without ifs, ands, or buts on the assumption that there is no free lunch in the market. Although we are in reality observing arbitrageurs, theoreticians have never attempted to make these arbitrage opportunities the object of independent theories. On the contrary, the principle of no free lunch represents the indispensable cornerstone of the neoclassical paradigm. That is why all valuation equations in this book are based on this condition. We are sure that this principle has not always been consequently paid attention to by other authors regarding the issue of valuation of firms and we will make that pointedly clear at the appropriate spot.

Cost of capital Cost of capital is definitely one of the key concepts in finance. Surprisingly, there is no definition of this term to be found in the literature that is precise enough that it can be used with logical operations to get valuation equations in particular in a multiperiod context. Since we regard cost of capital as a central term, we have chosen to begin our considerations with its clarification. But then, several statements that are considered in the literature to be obviously true have to be proven by us.

Data given As far as we can perceive, the information that the evaluator has on the firm to be valued plays no systematic role within the DCF literature. But it is in fact exactly this that can decide how the evaluator is to calculate. That is why we will always very precisely describe what information is supposed to be available when we develop a valuation equation.

Uncertainty of Cash Flows We have found that when evaluating a company, many practitioners attach little or no importance to the stochastic structure of future cash flows. Practitioners are much more likely to limit themselves to estimating the expectations of cash flows. If we were to fully understand the significance of this, then valuation concepts explicitly based on the stochastic structure of payment patterns are ruled out.

We are thus concentrating on models, where the expectation of the cash flows is of central interest and extraneous information about the distribution of cash flows is left out. That will play an important role in our analysis.

The first version of our book has been published some 10 years ago. Since then we have worked continuously on the subject and added new insights to the second edition. We removed mistakes and typos, added a new chapter on transversality and were able to enrich our findings on default. New literature was also included. Some of our ideas have since then found its way into textbooks (see, among others, Fan and Yo (2017, p. 346 ff.)), although we still think that a systematic and concise approach as we prefer it is still missing.

In the first edition of the book we marked all random variables with a tilde, i.e., $\widetilde{X}$. Today, such a notation clearly looks old-fashioned, typographically complex, and in the modern literature the use of the tilde is discouraged. Notwithstanding this fact, we decided to mark random variables with a tilde and this mainly for didactic reasons. Otherwise, it would require some time for the inexperienced reader to notice that an equation like

$$E[X \cdot Y] = X \cdot E[Y]$$

needs several assumptions for being correct.

We have provided extensive supplementary material for those who want to use this book for teaching. You find slides and additional material on our website http://www.wacc.info/.

Reference

Fan J, Yo Q (2017) The elements of financial econometrics. Cambridge University Press, Cambridge (UK)

Basic Elements: Cash Flow, Tax, Expectation, Cost of Capital, Value

2

2.1 Fundamental Terms

Valuation is being talked about everywhere. Finance experts, CPAs, investment bankers, and business consultants are discussing the advantages and disadvantages of discounted cash flow (DCF) methods since years. This book takes part in the discussion, and intends to make a theoretical contribution to it.

Those who get involved with the DCF approach will inevitably run into a number of reoccurring terms. It is typically said that the valuation of a firm involves the discounting

- of its future payment surpluses
- after consideration of taxes
- using the appropriate cost of capital.

Three things must obviously be clarified: firstly, it must be understood what payment surpluses are; secondly, a proper understanding of the taxes taken into consideration is needed; and thirdly, information about the cost of capital is required.

The payment surpluses, which are to be discounted, are also called cash flows. Nowhere in the literature this term is clearly defined. So one can be certain that no two economists speaking about cash flows will have one and the same thing in mind. The reader of this book might expect that we will go into elaborate detail on how cash flows are determined. We will disappoint these hopes. Essentially, we will be limiting ourselves to working out the difference between gross cash flows and free cash flows.

It is relatively clear what one means when speaking of taxes while doing a business valuation. The lawmakers leave no doubt as to which payments are due to him. Furthermore, it is known to all those involved in business valuation that taxes on profit are to be taken into particular consideration. Finally, every evaluator

L. Kruschwitz, A. Löffler, *Stochastic Discounted Cash Flow*,
Springer Texts in Business and Economics,
https://doi.org/10.1007/978-3-030-37081-7_2

knows that there are such taxes on the corporate as well as on the private level of business. In Germany, for instance, one must think about corporate and trade tax on the business level, and about income tax on the level of the financiers. This book is not, however, intended for readers who are interested in the details of a particular national tax system. Therefore, we do not plan to individually present the British, German, or US tax systems. On the contrary, we will base our considerations on a stylized tax system. Some readers may have different expectations regarding this point as well.

As a rule it remains rather unclear in business valuation what is meant by cost of capital. Even those who consult the relevant literature will not find, in our opinion, any precise definition of the term. This brings us head-on with the question as to what cost of capital is.

Every theory of business valuation is based on a model. Such a model possesses characteristics which we will describe here. In the following sections, we will deal with cash flows, taxes, and cost of capital in some more detail.

2.1.1 Cash Flows

To make use of a DCF approach, the evaluator must estimate the company's future cash flows. This leads to two clearly separate problems. The first question asks what it actually is that must be estimated ("What are cash flows?"), and the other concerns their amount ("How are future cash flows being estimated?"). The first question is a matter of definition, whereas the second involves a prognosis. We are concentrating on the first issue.

Gross Cash Flow By gross cash flows we understand the payment surpluses, which are generated through regular business operations. They can either be paid to the financiers, or kept within the company, and so be realized as investments. When referring to the financiers, we are speaking about the shareholders on the one hand, and the debt holders on the other. The payments to the financiers involve either interest repayments or debt service, or dividends and capital reductions. In the case that taxes have not yet been deducted from the gross cash flow, we are speaking about gross cash flow before taxes, see Table 2.1.

Table 2.1 From EBIT to gross and free cash flow

	Earnings before interest and taxes (EBIT)
+	Accruals
=	Gross cash flow before taxes
–	Corporate income taxes
–	Investment expenses
=	Free cash flow
–	Interest and debt service
–	Dividend and capital reduction
=	Zero

Those who need to determine the gross cash flow for an already past accounting year of an existing business normally fall back upon the firm's annual financial statements. They study balance sheets, income statements and, most likely, cash flow statements as well. The way in which one needs to deal with these individually depends heavily upon which legal provisions were used to draw up the annual reports, and on how the existing law structures in place were used by the managers of the firm. It makes a big difference if we are looking at a German corporation, which submits a financial statement according to the total cost format, and in doing so follows the IFRS (International Financial Reporting Standards), or if it concerns a US American company, which concludes according to the cost of sales format and pays heed to the US-GAAP (Generally Accepted Accounting Principles). No uniform procedure can be described for calculating the gross cash flow of the past business year for both firms. Thus, we may justify why we will not elaborate here on the determination of gross cash flows.

Free Cash Flow Companies must continually invest if they want to stay competitive. These investments are usually subdivided into expansion and replacement investments. Expansion investments ensure the increase of capacities and are indispensable if the firm should grow. The replacement investments, in contrast, ensure the furtherance of the status quo. They are, hence, usually fixed according to the accruals. We are working under the assumption that the firm being valued is intending on making investments in every period. Sensibly enough, those are only investment projects that are attractive from an economic perspective.

We refer to the difference between gross cash flow after taxes and the amount of investment as the firm's free cash flow. This amount can be paid out to the firm's financiers, namely the shareholders and the creditors.

Projection of Cash Flows The practically engaged evaluator must spend a considerable amount of her precious time on the prognosis of future cash flows: we already mentioned that it is not the historical payment surpluses that matter to the firm being valued, but rather the cash flows that it will yield in the future. The work of theoretically based finance experts is generally of limited use for this important activity. We will not be discussing practical questions related to the prognosis of cash flows in this book at all.

2.1.2 Taxes

Income-, Value-Based- and Sales Tax As a matter of fact, a company is not dealing with only one single type of tax. We usually distinguish between income taxes (for example, personal income tax), value-based taxes (for example, real-estate tax), and sales taxes (for example, value-added tax and numerous others). For the purposes, which we are aiming towards in this book, the sales taxes do not play any significant role—they simply depict a component of the cash flow and are otherwise of no further interest. Value-based taxes are also not usually discussed in-depth within the framework of literature on valuation of firms. We follow this convention and are concentrating largely just on income taxes.

Business- and Personal Tax Income tax is imposed on the firm level, as well as upon the shareholder level. In the first case we will speak about a corporate income tax, and in the second about personal income tax. In the USA, a corporate income tax is to be thought of with business tax; in addition, income tax accrues on the shareholder level (on the federal and local levels).

Our readers should not expect that we will go into detail on either the US American or other national tax systems. In this book we do not intend to treat the particularities of national tax laws with their immeasurable details. We have two reasons for this. For one, national tax laws are subject to constant changes. Every such change would require a new edition of the book. We are concerned here with a general theory, which is able to deal with the principle characteristics of tax law. Secondly, we would thus not only have to deal with the integration of one single tax law into the DCF approach, but rather of the tax laws of every important industrial nation around the world. This would, however, overstep the intended breadth of the book.

Those who identify the value of a firm with the marginal price from the viewpoint of a normal person will have no other alternative than to consider the business as well as the personal taxes.[1]

Features of a Tax In order to more exactly identify a tax, three characteristics are to be kept in mind, which can be observed in every type of tax. Thus, the next pertinent question is, who must pay the taxes: this is the tax subject. The tax base expresses how the object of taxation is quantified. And finally, the tax scale describes the functional relation between the tax due and the tax base. We are characterizing the corporate income tax and the personal income tax as well in the following with regard to the three named characteristics.

Tax Subject The tax subject describes who has to pay the taxes. In the case of the corporate income tax it is the firm, which is to be valued, while the object of taxation are the business activities of the firm. In the case of the personal income tax it is the financiers (owner as well as debt holder) who are the tax subject. The object of taxation are then the income streams from the firm or other activities particularly on the capital market.

Tax Base The corporate income tax is calculated according to an amount that is commonly referred to as profit. If one thinks of the US American corporate income tax, one effectively envisages the tax profit. Regarding the personal income tax the gross income minus some expenses form the tax base.

[1]In Germany that corresponds to the viewpoint of the profession of chartered accountants, see Institut der Wirtschaftsprüfer in Deutschland (2008).

Tax Scale If the tax scale is applied to the tax base, the tax due is established. Linear and nonlinear scale functions are usually observed. We will be working with a linear tax scale and take neither allowances nor exemption thresholds into consideration. The tax due is ascertained by multiplying the tax base by a tax rate, which we assume is independent of the tax base.

Such an assumption is obviously unrealistic. We do not know any income tax worldwide where the tax scale is certain, an allowance (as small as possible) causes the tax function to be nonlinear. In the recent past there has been done some research on nonlinear tax scales and valuation but the number of pertinent papers can be counted on the one hand. Hence, we will uphold linearity.

What is more, we will assume that the tax rate at the time of valuation is known and absolutely unchangeable! That is a far-reaching assumption, and we are entirely aware of the resulting limitations. We feel that uncertain tax rates have not been discussed in the literature until now, besides in isolated cases, and not at all in the DCF approaches to date. There is a gulf here between theory and practice that we will not be able to bridge over in this book. The practice-orientated reader will regard our course of action as rather far off from reality. In this book, we will later speak a lot about certain and uncertain tax advantages. If we state this here, and then later follow through on it, the manager may suspect—not unjustifiably—the most important source of uncertainty to be future unknown tax rates. Regardless, all known DCF approaches rule out just this source of uncertainty before we even begin. We still have a wide field of research ahead of us.

2.1.3 Cost of Capital

We do not know if this book's reader is particularly interested in a precise definition of cost of capital. We are convinced that for a theoretical debate of the DCF methods, it is of considerable importance. We would be happy, if our reader would be understanding of this, or would at least develop such an understanding in reading the book.

Cost of Capital as Returns In order to make our considerations more understandable, let us leave out uncertainty. The company that is to be valued may promise certain cash flows for the future, which we denote by $FCF_1, FCF_2, \ldots$. We will gain a preliminary understanding of the notion of cost of capital, when we ask about the role the cost of capital should play. It serves for the determination of the company's value. For this purpose the certain cash flows are discounted with the (probably time-dependent) cost of capital. A valuation equation would look, for example, like the following:

$$V_0 = \frac{FCF_1}{1+k_0} + \frac{FCF_2}{(1+k_0)(1+k_1)} + \ldots, \tag{2.1}$$

where $k_0, k_1, \ldots$ are the cost of capital of the zeroth, first, and all further periods and V_0 is the company's value at time $t = 0$. In the course of our book, we will see that we repeatedly need an equation for the future value of firm V_t at $t > 0$. It would be convenient if Eq. (2.1) could be used analogously at later times. For that we had

$$V_t = \frac{FCF_{t+1}}{1+k_t} + \frac{FCF_{t+2}}{(1+k_t)(1+k_{t+1})} + \ldots . \tag{2.2}$$

And one obviously gains a computational provision from which such future business values are established.

By assuming $V_{n\to\infty} = 0$ Eq. (2.2) can be used to infer the relation

$$k_t =_{\text{Def}} \frac{FCF_{t+1} + V_{t+1}}{V_t} - 1, \tag{2.3}$$

that gives us a basis for a precise definition of the cost of capital as future return. The economic intuition of such a definition is most easily revealed if one imagines that an investor at time t acquires an asset for the price V_t. At time $t+1$, this asset may yield a cash flow (a dividend) of FCF_{t+1} and immediately afterwards be sold again for the price of V_{t+1}. The return of such an action is then precisely given through the definition (2.3).

Obviously, the definition of the cost of capital (2.3) and the application of the valuation Eq. (2.2) for all times $t = 0, 1, \ldots$ are two statements, which are logically equivalent to each other. If it is decided to understand cost of capital as return in the sense of definition (2.3), then the valuation statement (2.2) is straightforward. The inversion is true as well: starting out from the valuation statement (2.2), it is implied that the suitable cost of capital are indeed the returns. This simple idea will be the red thread throughout our presentation.

Cost of Capital as Yields Let us suppose for a moment that it is possible at time t to pay a price $P_{t,s}$ and in return to earn nothing else than a dividend in amount of FCF_s (in which $s > t$). If under $\frac{1}{(1+\kappa_{t,s})^{s-t}}$ the price of a monetary unit is understood that is to be paid at time t and which is due at time s, then we designate $\kappa_{t,s}$ as yield. The following relations are valid for such yields:

$$P_{t,t+1} = \frac{FCF_{t+1}}{1+\kappa_{t,t+1}}$$

$$P_{t,t+2} = \frac{FCF_{t+2}}{(1+\kappa_{t,t+2})^2}$$

$$\vdots$$

The value of a firm at time t, which promises dividends at times $s = t + 1, \ldots$, could be (again assuming $V_{n\to\infty} = 0$) written in the form

$$V_t = \frac{FCF_{t+1}}{1 + \kappa_{t,t+1}} + \frac{FCF_{t+2}}{(1 + \kappa_{t,t+2})^2} + \ldots . \tag{2.4}$$

But to the contrary of the valuation Eq. (2.2), the formal structure of (2.4) cannot be used at time $t + 1$. The yields of time t will certainly be different from the yields one period later, i.e.,

$$V_{t+1} = \frac{FCF_{t+2}}{1 + \underbrace{\kappa_{t+1,t+2}}_{\stackrel{?}{=}\kappa_{t,t+1}}} + \frac{FCF_{t+3}}{(1 + \underbrace{\kappa_{t+1,t+3}}_{\stackrel{?}{=}\kappa_{t,t+2}})^2} + \ldots$$

For our purpose it is only appropriate to understand cost of capital as returns and not as yields.

Those who are used to work with empirical data will not hesitate to agree with our definition of the term. At any rate, in all empirical examinations known to us, returns are always determined when cost of capital should be calculated. It is much more difficult to estimate yields or discount rates (to say nothing of risk-neutral probabilities which will be introduced shortly). Therefore, defining cost of capital as returns is suitable.

The question must now be asked how the concept of cost of capital can be defined under uncertainty. We will first be able to answer this question more exactly in a later section of the book.

2.1.4 Time

In order to illustrate a basic idea of the DCF model, let us use an agricultural analogy: a cow is worth as much milk as it gives. For businesses and their market value, that means a firm's market value is orientated on future payment surpluses. If this is accepted, then the question arises as to how long a firm stays alive.

Life span So long as nothing to the contrary is known, one cannot go wrong in assuming that the firm will be around for more than a year. Such a vague supposition is of little help. As a rule it can be said that firms are set up for the long-run, and that most investors involved in the purchase of companies—and who fall back on procedures of business valuation for this means—have an investment horizon, which clearly overstretches 1 year. However, we are running in circles, because whether we assume the business will survive for more than a year, or think that it will remain active until "however long," the picture is still pretty unclear.

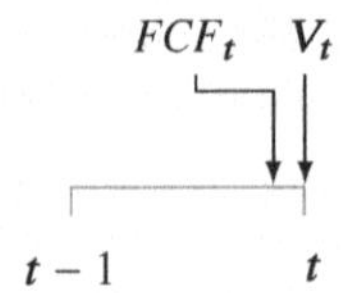

Fig. 2.1 Prices are always ex cash flow

Coming to a head, we question whether it should be suggested in business valuation that firms either have a finite life span, or are eternally active. It seems rather bizarre at first glance to conceive that firms live infinitely.

Regardless, there are worthwhile arguments in favor of the fiction of the eternally living company. When valuing a firm, which only has a limited life span, its end-date must be determined. An exact answer—apart from very few exceptions—would be impossible. Moreover, on the last day of the firm's history, a residual value will be paid to the owners. If you wanted to answer the question as to how the firm's residual value is to be determined, you would have to fall back upon the subsequent payments to be attained—that certainly does not fit into our assumption anymore that the world is just about to end. That is why an exact calculation of the residual value would likewise not succeed. If it can also be shown that it makes no difference worth mentioning whether you operate under the premises of a business life span of, let us say, 30 years, or that the business is incessantly active, then the fiction of an perpetually active firm, albeit objectively false, can be justified for the sake of convenience.[2]

What we want to get across to our readers is to the effect that we are working on the basis of an investment horizon of many periods, and do not yet want to conclusively commit to either a finite (denoted by T) or an infinite horizon. Since in actuality, were our theory really to be put into practice, we should suggest an infinite planning horizon.

Trade- and Payment Dates It is necessary to specify the trade- and payment dates of our model. An investor, who owns a share gets the cash flow at just the right second before t (see Fig. 2.1). If she sells this security at t, then the buyer always pays a "price ex cash flow." Although this arrangement is fully normal within the framework of the DCF approach, we explicitly stress it here. It leads to not being able to illustrate particular trading strategies in our model. For dividend stripping, for instance, a share would have to be bought immediately before the dividend payment—a comportment our model does not allow.

Continuous or Discrete Time We have decided that the firm to be valued, will be observed over a time frame of several periods. But should our model now be continuous time or discrete time?

[2]If cost of capital in the amount of 10% and constant cash flows are implied, then the first 30 years explain virtually 95% of the firm's total value.

In order to make the difference between both types of models clear, let us look at a firm with a finite life span of T years. If we use a time-screen, in which there are only times $t = 0$ (today), $t = 1$ (1 year from today), ..., $t = T$ (T years from today), then the model's framework is discrete. We could, without question, divide up each year into quarters, months, weeks, or even days. In the last case, we would run the time index t from 0 to 365 T, and since the days are countable, we would still be dealing with a discrete model. The more minutely we choose to divide up the time, that many more sub-periods there are in a year. But only after we let the number of annual sub-periods grow beyond all limits, so that the number of time intervals can no longer be counted, would we be looking at a continuous time model.

After we have gotten a good enough idea as to where the difference between discrete time and continuous time models lies, we turn back again to the question as to which type of model we should choose. In so doing, we find out that we do not have any criteria by which we can ascertain the advantages and disadvantages of one type or another.

One could get the idea that this continuous modeling is unpractical, since just as the cow cannot be continually milked, neither can a firm pay out dividends incessantly. So, let us instead say that the cow is milked once a day, and a corporation pays dividends once a year, for instance. Such intermittent events can, however, be included within a continuous time model, as well as a discrete time model. We must think of something else.

In the modern finance literature, continuous time models have experienced a notable boom. They are much more popular than discrete models. But the mathematical tools required in the continuous time models are by far more demanding compared to those, which can be used in discrete time models. From our experience, new economical understanding in valuation of firms is not gained through the assumption of a continuous time world. In this book we always apply the framework of a discrete time model. This is purely and solely for practical reasons.

Distinguishing the current time $t = 0$ (present) from the future $t = 1, 2 \ldots, T$, the ending time T as seen from today's perspective can or cannot be infinitely far off. The length of a time interval is not dependent upon the situation in which our model will be used. Intervals of 1 year are typically the case.

2.1.5 Problems

1. Let the world end the day after tomorrow, $T = 2$. Assume that $FCF_2 = 100$ is certain, but $\widetilde{FCF}_1$ is uncertain with $\mathrm{E}\left[\widetilde{FCF}_1\right] = 100$. The riskless rate is $r_f = 5\%$. We now show that yields and cost of capital cover different economic terms.
   (a) Assume that the yield for the first cash flow is $\kappa_{0,1} = 10\%$. Evaluate the company and determine the cost of capital k_0.

(b) Assume that the cost of capital for the first cash flow is $k_0 = 10\%$. Evaluate the company and determine the yield $\kappa_{0,1}$.

2. The reference point of our definition of yields was given by the time t. If we would have used time $t+1$ the corresponding equation would read

$$P_{t+1,t+2} = \frac{FCF_{t+2}}{1+\kappa_{t+1,t+2}}.$$

Prove that there is an opportunity for the investor to get infinitely rich (a so-called arbitrage opportunity) if

$$\left(1+\kappa_{t,t+1}\right)\left(1+\kappa_{t+1,t+2}\right) = \left(1+\kappa_{t,t+2}\right)^2$$

does not hold.

2.2 Conditional Expectation

As the evaluator of a firm, we find ourselves at time $t = 0$, that is, in the present. The valuation of firms is taking place today, and it is not necessary to worry about how our knowledge about the object of valuation will increase over time. Although we cannot, so to speak, move ourselves out of the present, let us still consider what we know today, and what we will know in the future. We do not clarify how our knowledge is increasing, but rather only how the additional knowledge is dealt with and what consequences that has for the valuation of a company. This requires the understanding of uncertainty and the notion of conditional expectation.

2.2.1 Uncertainty and Information

We begin with the hardly surprising announcement that the future is uncertain. How now? For the variables analyzed by the evaluator, it means that today it still is not known what those variables will be. It is not known how many liters of milk the cow will produce tomorrow. It cannot exactly be said what the cash flow of the firm to be valued will be in 3 years. Instead, there exist many possibilities. We also speak of events, which can influence the amount of the cash flows. Uncertainty in relation to the cash flow is marked by adding a tilde to its symbol,

$$\widetilde{FCF}_t.$$

This type of notation is certainly out of fashion: In many papers and almost all textbooks random variables are nowadays not identified by a particular symbol like the tilde. From a typographical point of view this increases readability. But we believe that for someone who must learn the difference between a random value and a deterministic number it is of great help if the random variable has a clear and visible label. There are transformations that are allowed with deterministic numbers and that fail with random variables[3]—without a unique label this can lead to serious errors. Therefore, we will persist on using the tilde.

States of Nature This representation leaves us in the dark as to what the interested variable is dependent upon. In fact, it is so that we foresee various possible states of nature. Such states could be described, for example, through product's market shares, or unemployment quotas or other variables. The cash flow would then be dependent upon however defined state variables denoted by ω. If we do not refer to the entire random variable but to the cash flow in one particular state, we use the notation

$$\widetilde{FCF}_t(\omega).$$

There are theoretical as well as practical reasons for our not making use of this detailed notation in the following, but instead only using the more simple spelling.

So we will make no statements in our theory at all about whether the number of the possible future states is finite or infinite. Rather, we simply leave it open, as to whether the state space is discrete or continuous. The formal techniques for dealing with continuous state spaces are more complicated than the instruments needed for the analysis of a discrete state space. We are trying to avoid wasting energy as much as possible here.

From our experience, every evaluator gives up making statements about future states of the world. One tries in practice to determine the expectations of the established quantities. And anticipated cash flows, or anticipated returns, are approximately estimated in such a way so that they do not need to rely upon the state-contingent quantities. Then why should we not try to avoid these details in our theory?

For both these reasons, we will in the future hold back the contingency of uncertain variables from states of the world, and will not further clarify the structure of the uncertainty.

Notation In order to make ourselves understood, we must introduce a few mathematical variables into the discussion. In so doing, we will use the notation common in current finance literature. The reader who is not used to this, may possibly ask at first why we did not try for a less exacting notation. The formal notation that we are now going to introduce, does in fact take some time to get used to, but is in no way so complicated that one should get scared off. It presents a straightforward and very compact notation for the facts, which need to be described in clarity. We therefore ask our readers to make the effort to carefully comprehend our notation. We promise on our part to make every possible effort to present the relations as simply as they are.

[3]For example, see footnote 10 in Sect. 2.3.2.

Let us now concentrate on, for example, the cash flow, which the firm will yield at time $t = 3$, so $\widetilde{FCF}_3$. The evaluator will know something more about this uncertain cash flow at time $t = 2$ than at time $t = 1$. When we are speaking about the expected cash flow from the third year and want to be precise, we must explain which state of information we are basing ourselves on. We denote the prospective on-hand information at time $t = 1$ as $\mathcal{F}_1$. The expression

$$\mathrm{E}\left[\widetilde{FCF}_3|\mathcal{F}_1\right]$$

describes how high the evaluator's expectations will be about the cash flow of time $t = 3$ from today's presumption of the state of information at time $t = 1$. If the investor uses her probable knowledge at time $t = 2$, she will have a more differentiated view of the third year's cash flow. This differentiated view is described through the conditional expectation

$$\mathrm{E}\left[\widetilde{FCF}_3|\mathcal{F}_2\right].$$

How is that to be read? The expression describes what the investor today believes she will know about the cash flow at time $t = 3$ in 2 years. So you see, what at first glance appears to be a somewhat complicated notation, allows for a very compact notation of facts. Facts, that anyone can only painstakingly present verbally. Mathematically, the expression

$$\mathrm{E}\left[\widetilde{FCF}_t|\mathcal{F}_s\right]$$

is the conditional expectation of the random variable $\widetilde{FCF}_t$, given the information at time s.

Classical Expectation What differentiates a classical expectation from a conditional one? With the classical expectation, a real number is determined that gives back the average amount of a random variable. Here, however, it is with the limitation that certain information about this random variable is already available. The information, for example, could relate to whether a new product was successful, or proved to be a flop. Now the investor must determine the average amount of a random variable (we are thinking of cash flows) according to the scenario—twice in our example—to establish the conditional expectation. The conditional expectation will no longer be a single number like in the classical expectation. Instead, it depicts a quantity, which itself is dependent upon the uncertain future: according to the market situation (success or flop), two average cash flows are conceivable. Summing up this observation, we must consider the following: the conditional expectation itself can be a random variable! This differentiates it from the classical expectation, which always depicts a real number.

In our theory of business valuation, we will often be dealing with conditional expectations. One or another reader may thus possibly be interested in getting a clean definition and being told about important characteristics of this mathematical concept in detail. We will now disappoint these readers, as we do not intend to explain in further detail what conditional expectations are. Much rather, we will just describe how they are to be used to calculate with. There is one simple reason as to why we are holding back. We have, until now, avoided describing the structure of the underlying uncertainty in detail. If we now wanted to explain how a conditional expectation is defined, we would also have to show how an expectation is calculated altogether and what probability distributions are. But we do not need these details for business valuation. A few simple rules suffice. The entire mathematical apparatus can be left in the background. Likewise, if you want to be a good car driver, you do not have to get involved with the physics of the combustion engine or acquire knowledge about the way transmissions function. It is enough to read the manual, learn the traffic signs, and get some driving experience. Experts must forgive us here for our crude handling.[4]

2.2.2 Rules

In the following, we will present five simple rules for calculating conditional expectations. You should make good note of these, as we will be using them again and again.

What is the connection between the conditional expectation and the classical expectation? Our first rule clarifies this.

Rule 1 (Classical Expectation) At time $t = 0$, the conditional expectation and the classical expectation coincide,

$$\mathrm{E}\left[\widetilde{X}|\mathcal{F}_0\right] = \mathrm{E}\left[\widetilde{X}\right].$$

The rule shows that the conditional expectation is dealing with a generalization of the classical expectation that comprises more information and other times than the present can take into consideration.

The second rule concerns the linearity, which is supposedly known to our readers for the classical expectation.

Rule 2 (Linearity) For any real numbers a, b and any random variables $\widetilde{X}$ and $\widetilde{Y}$, the following equation applies

$$\mathrm{E}\left[a\widetilde{X} + b\widetilde{Y}|\mathcal{F}_t\right] = a\,\mathrm{E}\left[\widetilde{X}|\mathcal{F}_t\right] + b\,\mathrm{E}\left[\widetilde{Y}|\mathcal{F}_t\right].$$

[4]For those who would like to know more, in the last section we give recommendations for further reading.

For technical reasons we need a further rule, which concerns real numbers. We know that these quantities correspond to their expectations. That should now also be true when we are working with conditional expectations.

Rule 3 (Certain Quantity) For the certain quantity 1 we have

$$\mathrm{E}\left[1|\mathcal{F}_t\right] = 1.$$

An immediate conclusion from this rule affects all quantities, which are not risky. On grounds of the linearity (Rule 2) the following is valid for real numbers X,

$$\mathrm{E}\left[X|\mathcal{F}_t\right] = X\ \mathrm{E}\left[1|\mathcal{F}_t\right] = X. \tag{2.5}$$

It should be kept in mind that condition $\mathcal{F}_t$ is not dealing with the information, which we will in fact have at this time. Much rather, it is dealing with the information that we are alleging at time t. The fourth rule makes use of our idea that as time advances, we get smarter.

Rule 4 (Iterated Expectation) For $s \leq t$ it always applies

$$\mathrm{E}\left[\mathrm{E}\left[\widetilde{X}|\mathcal{F}_t\right]|\mathcal{F}_s\right] = \mathrm{E}\left[\widetilde{X}|\mathcal{F}_s\right].$$

The rule underlines an important point of our methodology, although it is supposedly the hardest to understand. Nevertheless, there is a very plausible reason behind it. We repeatedly emphasized that we continually find ourselves in the present and are speaking only of our conceptions about the future. The actual development in contrast is not the subject of our observations. Rule 4 illustrates that.

Let us look at our knowledge at time s. If s comes before t, this knowledge comprises the knowledge that is already accessible to us today, but excludes beyond that the knowledge that we think we will have gained by time t. We should know more at time t than at time s: We are indeed operating under the idea, that as time goes on, we do not get more ignorant, but rather smarter. If our overall knowledge is meant to be consistent or rational, it would not make sense to have a completely different knowledge later on if it is built on our today's perceptions of the future.

If we wanted to verbally describe rule 4, we would perhaps have to say the following: "When we today think about what we will know tomorrow about the day after tomorrow, we will only know what we today already believe to know tomorrow."

Rule 5 (Expectation of Realized Quantities) If a quantity $\widetilde{X}$ is realized at time t, then for all other $\widetilde{Y}$

$$\mathrm{E}\left[\widetilde{X}\,\widetilde{Y}|\mathcal{F}_t\right] = \widetilde{X}\ \mathrm{E}\left[\widetilde{Y}|\mathcal{F}_t\right].$$

Rule 5 illustrates again our methodology that we stay in the present thinking about the future. At time t we will know how the random variable $\widetilde{X}$ will have materialized. $\widetilde{X}$ is then no longer a random variable, but rather a real number. When we then establish the expectation for the quantity $\widetilde{X}\widetilde{Y}$, we can extract $\widetilde{X}$ from the expectation, just as we do so with real numbers: $\widetilde{X}$ is known at time t. Rule 5 means, if with the state of information $\mathcal{F}_t$ we know the realization of a variable we can treat it in the conditional expectation like a real number: with the conditional expectation known quantities are like certain quantities.

2.2.3 Example

The Finite Case To make the handling of conditional expectations and our rules more understandable, let us look at an example. Concentrate on Fig. 2.2.

We are dealing here with a company, which will bear 3 years of payments to its owners. The payments, however, cannot be predicted with certainty.

1. In the first year ($t = 1$), two situations are conceivable, which we want to designate as "up" or "down," as the case may be. From now on we will be using the terms "up" and "down" not with respect to the actual cash flow movements. Rather, up means that the cash flow of the next period is stated at the top of the original value in our figure. Hence, up does not mean that the cash flow increases (as, for example, is clearly visible from $t = 2$ to $t = 3$ with the cash flow 110 going up to 96.8).

Fig. 2.2 Binomial tree in the finite example

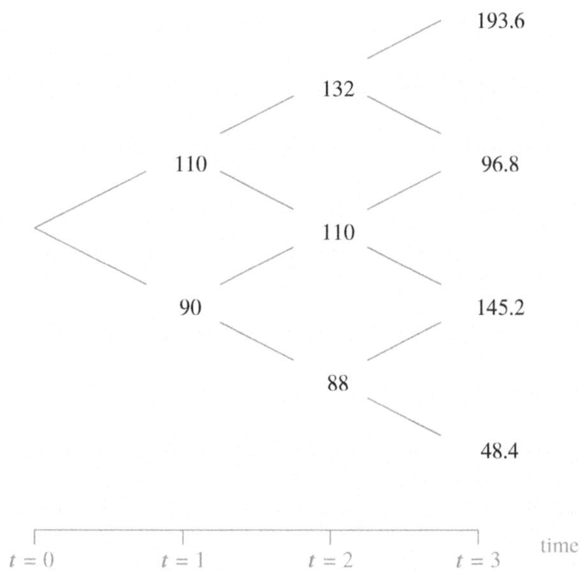

If the development is up, then the payment amounts to 110, otherwise to 90. Both states are equally possible.[5]

2. In the second year ($t = 2$), three states are probable.
   - If we operate in $t = 1$ from up, the development can again proceed up or down. Should chance see to it that the sequence is up–up (abbreviated uu), then the cash flow in the second year amounts to 132. If the development happens, in contrast, to read up–down (abbreviated ud), then the owners only get a payment of 110.
   - But if the movement in $t = 1$ was down, then things could either turn up, or they could again be down. The development down–up leads at time $t = 2$ to payments in the amount of 110, in the case of down–down, the owners only receive 88.

   The three states can also be described differently: Chance twice ensures an unforeseeable development.
   - If it goes up twice, then the cash flow amounts to 132. The probability for this comes to $0.5^2 = 25\%$.
   - If it, in contrast, only goes up once, then the owners get a payment in the amount of 110. Since there are two ways of ending up with this state, their probability comes to $2 \cdot 0.5 \cdot (1 - 0.5) = 50\%$.
   - If, finally, it never goes up, then there is a cash flow of only 88, and the probability for that is $(1 - 0.5)^2 = 25\%$.
3. In the last year ($t = 3$) four states are possible, which can be reached as follows:
   - The development proceeds up three times. That leads to a cash flow of 193.6, and namely with a probability of $0.5^3 = 12.5\%$.
   - It only goes up twice.[6] There are three possible ways for moving into the state with the payment of 96.8, which is why the possibility for this is $3 \cdot 0.5^2 \cdot (1 - 0.5)^1 = 37.5\%$.
   - The development is now only up once. There are also three ways of reaching this state, which is why its probability is $3 \cdot 0.5^1 \cdot (1 - 0.5)^2 = 37.5\%$, and namely with a payment in the amount of 145.2.
   - Finally, it can also always go down. That leads to a cash flow of 48.4, and namely with a probability of $(1 - 0.5)^3 = 12.5\%$.

We could now determine the conditional expectations for every period and in so doing check our rules. As an example let us concentrate on the third-year cash flow

[5] In case the actual development will yield a value neither 90 nor 110 our model was wrongly specified. Any decision based on this wrong model will be misleading.

[6] We continue to use the term "up" even if the path is $udu = (110, 110, 96.8)$ and the cash flow in this case in particular goes down from $t = 2$ to $t = 3$.

and the conceptions, that we will probably have of it at time $t = 1$. It is thus dealing with the expression

$$\mathrm{E}\left[\widetilde{FCF}_3|\mathcal{F}_1\right].$$

At time $t = 1$, two states can have entered in. Let us at first look at the case that we had an up development. From here, three developments are conceivable, namely

- twice up: cash flow 193.6 with probability 25%,
- once up: cash flow 96.8 with probability 50%,
- never up: cash flow 145.2 with probability 25%.

The conditional expectation for the up condition at time $t = 1$ is then

$$0.25 \cdot 193.6 + 0.5 \cdot 96.8 + 0.25 \cdot 145.2 = 133.1\,.$$

Now, we still have the case to look at that at time $t = 1$ we experienced a down development. Three developments are again conceivable from here that by an analogous procedure lead to

$$0.25 \cdot 96.8 + 0.5 \cdot 145.2 + 0.25 \cdot 48.4 = 108.9\,.$$

From that we finally end up with

$$\mathrm{E}\left[\widetilde{FCF}_3|\mathcal{F}_1\right] = \begin{cases} 133.1, & \text{if the development in } t = 1 \text{ is up,} \\ 108.9, & \text{if the development in } t = 1 \text{ is down.} \end{cases}$$

At this point we discover that $\mathrm{E}\left[\widetilde{FCF}_3|\mathcal{F}_1\right]$ is a random variable, since at time $t = 0$ it still cannot be known which of the two conditions will manifest at time $t = 1$.[7]

Let us now direct our attention to the unconditional expectation of the random variables $\widetilde{FCF}_3$. We can get it directly from

$$0.125 \cdot 193.6 + 0.375 \cdot 96.8 + 0.375 \cdot 145.2 + 0.125 \cdot 48.4 = 121.$$

[7] The attentive reader will ascertain that the conditional expectation of the cash flow $\widetilde{FCF}_3$ and the $\widetilde{FCF}_1$ are in a close relation to each other. In our payment example, $\mathrm{E}\left[\widetilde{FCF}_3|\mathcal{F}_1\right] = 1.1^2 \cdot \widetilde{FCF}_1$ is namely valid, since $1.1^2 \cdot 110 = 133.1$ and $1.1^2 \cdot 90 = 108.9$. This characteristic is not arbitrarily chosen and will be analyzed more thoroughly in Sect. 3.1.2.

It is, moreover, possible to determine the expectation of the random variables $\mathrm{E}\left[\widetilde{FCF}_3|\mathcal{F}_1\right]$. In order to show that we come to the same result this way, we again have to use our rules. But, we can limit ourselves here to the iterated expectation (rule 4) as well as the classical expectation (rule 1). The following must apply:

$$\begin{aligned} \mathrm{E}\left[\mathrm{E}\left[\widetilde{FCF}_3|\mathcal{F}_1\right]\right] &= \mathrm{E}\left[\mathrm{E}\left[\widetilde{FCF}_3|\mathcal{F}_1\right]|\mathcal{F}_0\right] && \text{rule 1} \\ &= \mathrm{E}\left[\widetilde{FCF}_3|\mathcal{F}_0\right] && \text{rule 4} \\ &= \mathrm{E}\left[\widetilde{FCF}_3\right]. && \text{rule 1} \end{aligned}$$

And the result is in fact

$$0.5 \cdot 133.1 + 0.5 \cdot 108.9 = 121 \ .$$

With that we would like to bring the examination of our rules through the payment example to a close.

The Infinite Case An essential difference from our example that we have been looking at until now is that the firm will now live on indefinitely. We want to suppose that the cash flows follow a binomial process according to Fig. 2.3. Seen from time t onward, the cash flows can move up through time $t+1$ with either factor u or move down with factor d, in whereby we will speak of an upward movement in the first case and a downward movement in the second case.

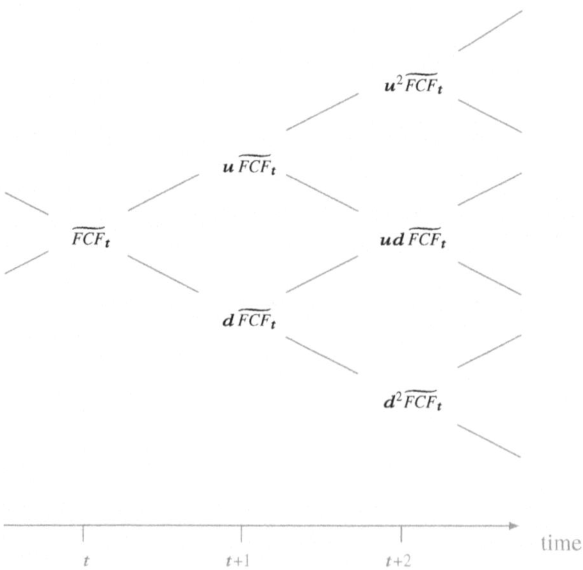

Fig. 2.3 Part of the binomial tree of the infinite example

For two consecutive times, the following is always valid:

$$\widetilde{FCF}_{t+1} = \begin{cases} u\,\widetilde{FCF}_t & \text{if the development in } t = 1 \text{ is up,} \\ d\,\widetilde{FCF}_t & \text{if the development in } t = 1 \text{ is down.} \end{cases}$$

We will specify neither u nor d in more detail. We only suppose that they are not dependent upon time and positive. The conditional probabilities at state ω and time $t+1$ with which the upward and downward movement occur will be denoted by $P_{t+1}(u|\omega)$ and $P_{t+1}(d|\omega)$. These probabilities do not depend on time $t+1$ and state ω, hence, we suppress both variables from now on.

If under the given assumptions we determine the conditional expectation of a cash flow $\widetilde{FCF}_{t+1}$ at time t, then the following applies

$$\begin{aligned} \mathrm{E}\left[\widetilde{FCF}_{t+1}|\mathcal{F}_t\right] &= \left(P_{t+1}(u|\omega)\,u\,\widetilde{FCF}_t + P_{t+1}(d|\omega)\,d\,\widetilde{FCF}_t\right) \\ &= \underbrace{(u\,P(u) + d\,P(d)}_{=:1+g}\,\widetilde{FCF}_t. \end{aligned}$$

The variable g is thus not dependent on time. Out of this we can immediately derive the relation

$$\begin{aligned} \mathrm{E}\left[\widetilde{FCF}_t|\mathcal{F}_s\right] &= \mathrm{E}\left[\ldots\,\mathrm{E}\left[\widetilde{FCF}_t|\mathcal{F}_{t-1}\right]\ldots|\mathcal{F}_s\right] \\ &= (1+g)\ldots(1+g)\widetilde{FCF}_s \\ &= (1+g)^{t-s}\widetilde{FCF}_s \end{aligned} \tag{2.6}$$

for $s \leq t$ on the basis of rule 4. We will always, for the subsequent examples, be working from the basis $FCF_0 = \mathrm{E}[\widetilde{FCF}_1] = 100$ and assume that all parameters have been so chosen that $g = 0$ is valid. It is also said in this case that the cash flows form a martingale.

2.2.4 Problems

1. Look at the example in Fig. 2.4. Assume that the cash flows satisfy

$$\widetilde{FCF}_t = \mathrm{E}\left[\widetilde{FCF}_{t+1}|\mathcal{F}_t\right].$$

   (This particular property of cash flows will become important in the next chapter.) Assume that the up- and down-movements occur with the same probability. Fill in the gaps.
2. The following problem shows that expectations under different probability measures cannot be changed arbitrarily.

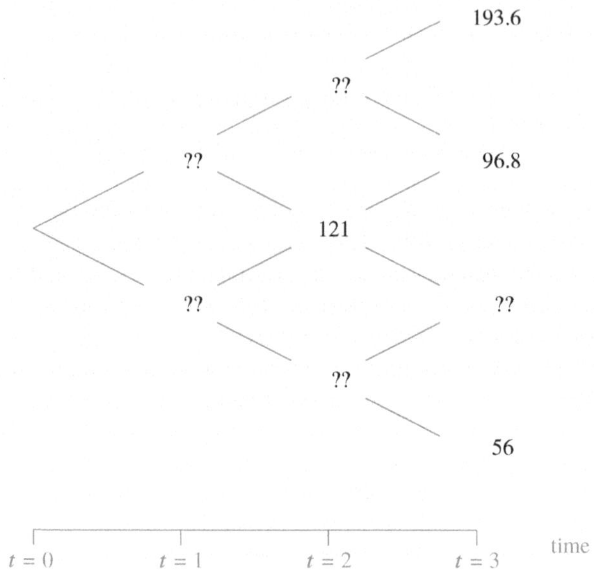

Fig. 2.4 Cash flows in future periods of Problem 1

Go back to the solution of the last problem (see again Fig. 2.4). Let there be two different probabilities: P assigning the same probability to the up- and down-movements and Q that assigns 0.1 to the up- and 0.9 to the down-movement. Verify that

$$\mathrm{E}\left[\mathrm{E}_Q\left[\widetilde{FCF}_2|\mathcal{F}_1\right]|\mathcal{F}_0\right] = \mathrm{E}_Q\left[\mathrm{E}\left[\widetilde{FCF}_2|\mathcal{F}_1\right]|\mathcal{F}_0\right].$$

This particular property of probabilities will be necessary when showing that cost of capital are also discount rates. But be careful if the binomial tree distinguishes between up–down and down–up as shown in Fig. 2.5. Verify that in case of Fig. 2.5

$$\mathrm{E}\left[\mathrm{E}_Q\left[\widetilde{FCF}_2|\mathcal{F}_1\right]|\mathcal{F}_0\right] \neq \mathrm{E}_Q\left[\mathrm{E}\left[\widetilde{FCF}_2|\mathcal{F}_1\right]|\mathcal{F}_0\right].$$

3. The following problem shows that for any cash flows with constant expectations

$$\mathrm{E}\left[\widetilde{FCF}_1\right] = \mathrm{E}\left[\widetilde{FCF}_2\right] = \mathrm{E}\left[\widetilde{FCF}_3\right] = FCF_0$$

a binomial model can be established where the conditional expectations of these cash flows satisfy an assumption that was mentioned in Problem 1:

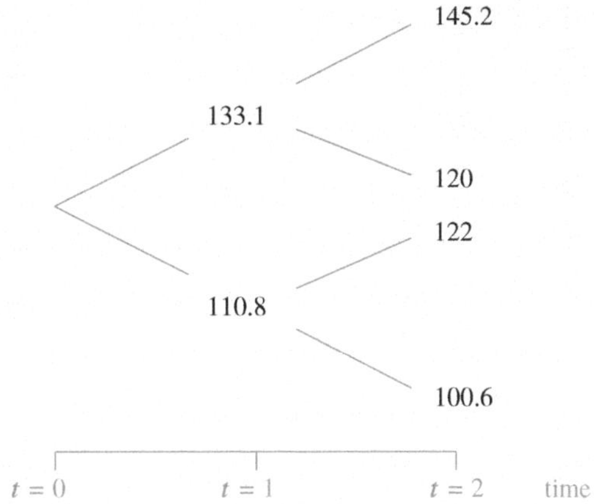

Fig. 2.5 Cash flows in future periods of Problem 2

Consider a binomial tree where up- and down-movements occur with the same probability. Let two arbitrary numbers u,d be given such that (this will ensure $g = 0$)

$$\frac{1}{2}u + \frac{1}{2}d = 1, \qquad u > d > 0.$$

Show that the cash flows following the binomial tree in Fig. 2.3 satisfy

$$\mathrm{E}\left[\widetilde{FCF}_3|\mathcal{F}_2\right] = \widetilde{FCF}_2,$$

$$\mathrm{E}\left[\widetilde{FCF}_2|\mathcal{F}_1\right] = \widetilde{FCF}_1,$$

$$\mathrm{E}\left[\widetilde{FCF}_1|\mathcal{F}_0\right] = FCF_0\,.$$

4. Consider a trinomial tree as in Fig. 2.6. Three movements are possible: "up," "middle," and "down." They occur with the same probability and furthermore (we use u, d, and m as in Fig. 2.6)

$$u\,d = m^2.$$

What further assumptions on u,m,d are necessary so that in this example

$$\mathrm{E}\left[\widetilde{FCF}_2|\mathcal{F}_1\right] = \widetilde{FCF}_1$$

holds?

Fig. 2.6 Trinomial tree of cash flows

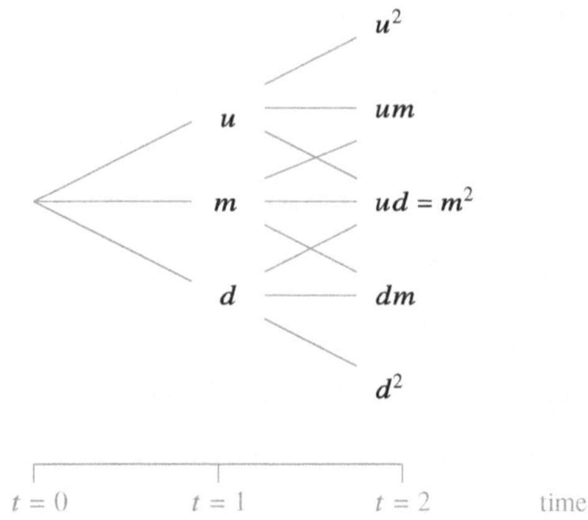

2.3 A First Glance at Business Values

In the following section, we will introduce a generalized form of a business valuation concept, which we will regularly use in this book. The connections between business values and cost of capital that will be discussed in this section are to be understood as general in so far as we both want to and still can leave it open as to whether we are analyzing levered or unlevered firms. That is why our procedure still does not demand too polished a use of symbols at this point.

2.3.1 Valuation Concept

Every theory is based on assumptions. This is also not different for a theory of business valuation. A central assumption on which further expositions are built up is the following.

Assumption 2.1 (No Free Lunch) *The capital market is free of arbitrage.*

This assumption is usually specified in finance with the help of an extravagant formalism. We would like to do away with that here, since the effort far outweighs the usefulness and the following does not require such details. We limit ourselves to illustrating the assumption. Arbitrage free means, in loose terms, that no market participant is in the position to make earnings from nothing. Anyone, who has some cash inflows will put up with cash outflows. We will go into the conclusions of this assumption in somewhat more detail.

No Arbitrage and Equilibrium If we assume that the capital market does not allow for a free lunch, we are quite sure that this assumption is indisputable. One is usually convinced that arbitrage opportunities can hold only briefly and will be exploited sooner or later so that they disappear. For us, this assumption is straightforward. But, we do not assume that there is an equilibrium on the capital market and we explicitly stress that the existence of an equilibrium is far stronger than the assumption of an arbitrage free market. Any (general) equilibrium will be free of arbitrage, but not vice versa!

The central building block of our theory of business valuation is the so-called *fundamental theorem of asset pricing*. It can be derived from the concept of no arbitrage. We will not go through the trouble of proving the theorem. But to at least make it plausible, we introduce alternative valuation concepts. While doing so, we limit ourselves for simplicity's sake to the one-period case.

Valuation (in the One-Period Case) Under Certainty Imagine a capital market in which only claims for certain payments are traded that are due in $t = 1$. You can think of a firm, which pays dividends at time $t = 1$ in the amount of FCF_1. It is obvious how these securities are to be valued when the capital market is arbitrage free. The certain cash flows are discounted with the riskless interest rate. If we denote the interest rate with r_f, then equation

$$V_0 = \frac{FCF_1}{1 + r_f} \tag{2.7}$$

must be valid. Otherwise, one could end up with a strategy that practically comes down to operating a private money pump. And that would be in opposition to the assumption of no free lunch.

If, for instance, the left-hand side of the equation was smaller than the right-hand side, an investor could take out a loan today with the interest rate r_f and acquire the firm for the price V_0. The sum of all payments at time $t = 0$ would amount to zero. At time $t = 1$, she would retain the cash flows and pay back the loan. And the now remaining account balance would presumably be positive,

$$FCF_1 - \left(1 + r_f\right) V_0 > 0.$$

That is an arbitrage opportunity, and it is exactly such results that we would like to exclude with the Assumption 2.1.[8]

Valuation (in the One-Period Case) Under Uncertainty Future payments are indeed not certain in the world we are looking at. We must thus ask, in what way it can be managed to generalize the relation described in Eq. (2.7). There are three different ways, the last of which deserves our particular attention, to incorporate risk into valuation.

[8]We could make a completely analogous argumentation, if the left-hand side of Eq. (2.7) was larger than the right-hand side.

Certainty Equivalent If the cash flows payable at time $t = 1$ are uncertain, you could ask about that certain payment at time $t = 1$, which the investor finds just as attractive as the risky cash flows. Such a payment is called a certainty equivalent. The certainty equivalent will be discounted with the riskless rate, instead of the expected payments at time $t = 1$. The certainty equivalent itself must be determined with the help of a utility function. According to our knowledge, this formulation is rather seldom incurred in practice.

To illustrate the procedure through an example, let us again look at our firm. There are two states of nature in the future. We concentrate solely on the payments due at time $t = 1$. Assume then

$$\widetilde{FCF}_1 = \begin{cases} 110 & \text{if the development in } t = 1 \text{ is up,} \\ 90 & \text{if the development in } t = 1 \text{ is down.} \end{cases}$$

Assume further, that the two relevant states of nature are equally probable and the riskless interest rate is $r_f = 5\%$.

The certainty equivalent is now that payment S_1 for which the preference relation

$$S_1 \sim (110, 90 : 50\%, 50\%)$$

has been met. The certain payment S_1 is just as attractive as a lottery, in which one gets 110 or 90, respectively, with the same probability. That corresponds in the expected utility representation to equation

$$u(S_1) = \mathrm{E}\left[u\left(\widetilde{FCF}_1\right)\right],$$

from which, according to the application of the reverse function, we get

$$S_1 = u^{-1}\left(\mathrm{E}\left[u\left(\widetilde{FCF}_1\right)\right]\right).$$

If $u(x) = \sqrt{x}$ is now the utility function, then the certainty equivalent in our example amounts to

$$S_1 = \left(0.5 \cdot \sqrt{110} + 0.5 \cdot \sqrt{90}\right)^2 \approx 99.75.$$

From that we finally get,

$$V_0 = \frac{S_1}{1 + r_f} = \frac{99.75}{1 + 0.05} = 95.00.$$

Cost of Capital There is the much more widely spread technique in the valuation practice of raising the riskless interest rate with a risk premium. The sum of both quantities is the cost of capital. In equation (2.7) we then adjust the denominator and not the numerator.

If the risk premium is named z, then the value of the firm in our example results from

$$V_0 = \frac{\mathrm{E}\left[\widetilde{FCF}_1\right]}{1 + r_f + z},$$

and one would come to the same result using the relevant numbers here with a risk premium of $z \approx 0.264\%$ as with the certainty equivalent method, since

$$V_t = \frac{0.5 \cdot 110 + 0.5 \cdot 90}{1 + 0.05 + 0.00264} = \frac{100}{1.05264} = 95.00.$$

Risk-Neutral Probabilities With this third formulation, the riskless interest rate r_f is further used to discount with. In the numerator we find an expectation of the risky cash flow. But the expectation is not calculated with the actual estimated subjective probabilities. Instead of that, risk-adjusted probabilities are used, which are also called risk-neutral.

In our example the subjective probabilities for the up, or, as the case may be, down development come to 50% in each case. It is plain to see that one can express risk aversion with measuring up with a lesser weight and down with a heavier weight.

If the expectation calculated on the basis of risk-neutral probabilities is denoted by $\mathrm{E}_Q[\cdot]$, then the valuation formula in our example runs

$$V_0 = \frac{\mathrm{E}_Q\left[\widetilde{FCF}_1\right]}{1 + r_f}.$$

It can be shown that with the relevant numbers here a risk-neutral probability of 48.75% for up leads to the same result as both concepts already described, since

$$V_0 = \frac{0.4875 \cdot 110 + 0.5125 \cdot 90}{1 + 0.05} = \frac{99.75}{1.05} = 95.00.$$

Several different terms have been used in the literature for this third way. Equivalent martingale measure is also often spoken of, instead of risk-neutral probability.

We now turn to the second approach in more detail and will then be dealing with the last approach.

2.3.2 Cost of Capital as Conditional Expected Returns

Discount Rates and Expected Returns In order to get a preliminary notion of cost of capital under uncertainty, let us take a glance in the textbooks. It is often said that cost of capital is an expected return. For example, Copeland et al. (2005, p. 557) use the expression "rate of return" instead of "cost of capital," in order to present the valuation concept for a firm. Brealey et al. (2020, p. 228) write explicitly, that the "cost of capital … is the expected rate of return demanded by investors in the firm's common stock." de Matos (2001, p. 43) also explains that the cost of capital involves expected returns.

However, we also then find the suggestion within the literature to bring the notion of the cost of capital to life somewhat differently. This concerns the idea that the cost of capital should be suitable as discount rate for future cash flows. Brealey et al. (2020, p. 39), for instance, speak of the cost of capital as those figures with which cash flows are to be discounted. There is a related remark in Miles and Ezzell (1980, p. 722), for example, where it is said that "at any time k, ρ is the appropriate rate for discounting the time i expected unlevered cash flow in period j where ρ is referred to as the unlevered cost of capital."

It is not recommended to simply equate expected returns and discount rates. This warning does not easily stand to reason with the critical reader. This will, however, change from now on.

Conditional Expected Returns How can our definition of the cost of capital be generalized, if the future is uncertain? We shift to time $t > 0$. The evaluator will have some notions as to the returns at this time. In addition, she sets the reflux one period later in proportion to the employed capital. When the evaluator does this on the basis of the information at time t, then the employed capital $\widetilde{V}_t$ is not uncertain for her any more. The evaluator can now treat the employed capital like a real number, granted that she always assumes the state of information at time t. The evaluator considers the conditional expectation of the reflux $t+1$ against the employed capital $\widetilde{V}_t$. Through this understanding of the term cost of capital, a derivation of the valuation equation analogous to (2.1) will be possible. To this end, the following definition of the cost of capital is appropriate.

Definition 2.1 (The Firm's Cost of Capital) The cost of capital $\widetilde{k}_t$ of a firm is the conditional expected return

$$\widetilde{k}_t := \frac{\mathrm{E}\left[\widetilde{FCF}_{t+1} + \widetilde{V}_{t+1} | \mathcal{F}_t\right]}{\widetilde{V}_t} - 1.$$

Before we move on, we must, however, take note that our cost of capital definition has a possible disadvantage. Look at numerators and denominators separately. In the numerator of Definition 2.1, the expectations of payments at time $t+1$ stand under the condition that the evaluator possesses the state of information of time t. One cannot simply assume that these expectations are certain. It is much more likely that these conditional expectations at time t are uncertain, and thus depict random variables. If these random variables are now divided by $\widetilde{V}_t$, the result is another random variable again, regardless whether $\widetilde{V}_t$ is certain or uncertain. But that means that the cost of capital, as it is so defined, constitutes a random variable. Future expected returns from equity as well as debt are all of a sudden uncertain, and that most surely comes as no great surprise for the manager either. Unfortunately, one cannot discount today with quantities, the realization of which is not known at time $t = 0$. So, we have a definition of the cost of capital that is not suitable for our intended purpose here!

Deterministic Cost of Capital We will only make it out of this dilemma, if we make an assumption on an heroic scale. One which purports that cost of capital, as defined in Definition 2.1, *should* be certain. We are plainly and simply taking it for granted that the cost of capital is certain, and will later show that it also makes a suitable discount rate. In other words, those who comprehend the cost of capital as conditional expected return, and assume that it is a certain quantity, may also use them as discount rate.

Our critical colleagues may want to object at this point that the knowledge of future anticipated returns in the valuation of firms depicts all too heroic of an assumption; one which cannot actually be met in real life. To that, we can only answer that it does indeed involve a very large assumption. Only, without this assumption, no one, not even our critics, can prove a valuation equation analogous to Eq. (2.1).[9] Thus seen, although the assumption is admittedly heroic, it is also indispensable for a theory of business valuation. Those who principally reject it, must also renounce the determination of firms' market values through the use of a DCF approach. Regrettably, we have no other choice in the matter.

The attentive reader will still recall the objection mentioned in the previous section. We had noticed that "time will tell." If we already insinuate that the cost of capital is certain at time $t = 0$, then we have taken it for granted that an enormous amount of knowledge is to be gained. Everything that can be ascertained about cost of capital is already known today. At this point we repeat the statement that there is no business to be done without the assumption of certain cost of capital.

Attempts at Other Definitions We would like to point out with all clarity that our definition of cost of capital cannot be made more simple. At first glance nothing seems to speak against buying into Eq. (2.3) and to consider the fact that we are now dealing with uncertainty through an (unconditional) expectation: expression

$$k_t \overset{?}{=} \mathrm{E}\left[\frac{\widetilde{FCF}_{t+1} + \widetilde{V}_{t+1}}{\widetilde{V}_t} - 1\right]$$

would then describe the cost of capital.

[9]One should never say never: We are currently working on a project where cost of capital can be stochastic without violating basic principles of finance. See Kruschwitz and Löffler (2019).

As an academic, you have the freedom to choose your terms as you like. Definitions of cost of capital can be neither true nor false. They are at best suitable or unsuitable. And the preceding definition is by all means unsuitable. To allow for an equation of the form

$$V_0 = \frac{\mathrm{E}\left[\widetilde{FCF}_1\right]}{1+k} + \frac{\mathrm{E}\left[\widetilde{FCF}_2\right]}{(1+k)^2} + \dots$$

to be obtained it is necessary to detach $\widetilde{V}_t$ from the expectation above. But this is impossible for a random variable due to Jensen's inequality.[10]

Even a more refined approach, such as in equation

$$k_t \stackrel{?}{=} \frac{\mathrm{E}\left[\widetilde{FCF}_{t+1} + \widetilde{V}_{t+1}\right]}{\mathrm{E}\left[\widetilde{V}_t\right]} - 1$$

does not lead to the kind of results with which we can be satisfied. True, if k_t is constant through time, this is easily converted to the following important equation:

$$V_0 = \frac{\mathrm{E}\left[\widetilde{FCF}_1\right]}{1+k} + \frac{\mathrm{E}\left[\widetilde{FCF}_2\right]}{(1+k)^2} + \dots .$$

But we had more in mind for our definition of cost of capital. We were not just thinking about a computational rule, which allows for the current business value to be determined. More importantly, it should be possible to determine future business values. While calculation of V_0 can now be managed with this definition of cost of capital, we cannot, however, get an equation in the form of

$$\widetilde{V}_t = \frac{\mathrm{E}\left[\widetilde{FCF}_{t+1}|\mathcal{F}_t\right]}{1+k} + \frac{\mathrm{E}\left[\widetilde{FCF}_{t+2}|\mathcal{F}_t\right]}{(1+k)^2} + \dots$$

from the definition, since the cost of capital always depicts unconditional expectations. This definition of cost of capital also turns out to be unsuitable for our purposes.

Let us summarize. With a DCF approach, cost of capital is, sensibly enough, taken as conditional expected returns. This idea will be the red thread throughout our presentation. As already stated, we will still assume in the following that the cost

[10] For a random variable $\widetilde{V}_t$ that is not deterministic

$$\frac{1}{\mathrm{E}\left[\widetilde{V}_t\right]} \neq \mathrm{E}\left[\frac{1}{\widetilde{V}_t}\right]$$

holds due to Jensen's inequality. A similar result will apply to our attempted definition of cost of capital.

of capital does not involve random, but rather deterministic quantities. We cannot get any valuation equation without this assumption.

2.3.3 A First Valuation Equation

In order to derive the valuation equation, we will use our rules for conditional expectations for the first time. Although this calculation is rather simple, we want to deal with it in some detail. Our intention in doing so is to get our readers more comfortable with the formal usage of the rules.

Theorem 2.1 (Market Value of the Firm) *When the cost of capital k_t is deterministic, then the firm's value at time t amounts to*

$$\widetilde{V}_t = \sum_{s=t+1}^{T} \frac{\mathrm{E}\left[\widetilde{FCF}_s|\mathcal{F}_t\right]}{(1+k_t)\dots(1+k_{s-1})}.$$

The reader used to the product symbol Π might prefer the expression

$$\widetilde{V}_t = \sum_{s=t+1}^{T} \frac{\mathrm{E}\left[\widetilde{FCF}_s|\mathcal{F}_t\right]}{\prod_{\sigma=t}^{s-1}(1+k_\sigma)}$$

as more compact.

To prove this statement, let us reformulate Definition 2.1 of the cost of capital to

$$\widetilde{V}_t = \frac{\mathrm{E}\left[\widetilde{FCF}_{t+1} + \widetilde{V}_{t+1}|\mathcal{F}_t\right]}{1+k_t}.$$

The above equation is recursive, as $\widetilde{V}_t$ is a function of $\widetilde{V}_{t+1}$. If we use the appropriate relation between $\widetilde{V}_{t+1}$ and $\widetilde{V}_{t+2}$, the result is

$$\widetilde{V}_t = \frac{\mathrm{E}\left[\widetilde{FCF}_{t+1} + \frac{\mathrm{E}\left[\widetilde{FCF}_{t+2}+\widetilde{V}_{t+2}|\mathcal{F}_{t+1}\right]}{1+k_{t+1}}|\mathcal{F}_t\right]}{1+k_t}.$$

Because the cost of capital is deterministic and the conditional expectation is linear, we can reformulate this expression with the help of Rule 2 (linearity) to

$$\widetilde{V}_t = \frac{\mathrm{E}\left[\widetilde{FCF}_{t+1}|\mathcal{F}_t\right]}{1+k_t} + \frac{\mathrm{E}\left[\mathrm{E}\left[\widetilde{FCF}_{t+2}|\mathcal{F}_{t+1}\right]|\mathcal{F}_t\right]}{(1+k_t)(1+k_{t+1})} + \frac{\mathrm{E}\left[\mathrm{E}\left[\widetilde{V}_{t+2}|\mathcal{F}_{t+1}\right]|\mathcal{F}_t\right]}{(1+k_t)(1+k_{t+1})}.$$

Rule 4 (iterated expectation) allows us to notate the expectation in a more simple form,

$$\widetilde{V}_t = \frac{\mathrm{E}\left[\widetilde{FCF}_{t+1}|\mathcal{F}_t\right]}{1+k_t} + \frac{\mathrm{E}\left[\widetilde{FCF}_{t+2}|\mathcal{F}_t\right]}{(1+k_t)(1+k_{t+1})} + \frac{\mathrm{E}\left[\widetilde{V}_{t+2}|\mathcal{F}_t\right]}{(1+k_t)(1+k_{t+1})} .$$

If we continue this procedure through time T, we get

$$\widetilde{V}_t = \frac{\mathrm{E}\left[\widetilde{FCF}_{t+1}|\mathcal{F}_t\right]}{1+k_t} + \ldots + \frac{\mathrm{E}\left[\widetilde{FCF}_T|\mathcal{F}_t\right]}{(1+k_t)\ldots(1+k_{T-1})} + \frac{\mathrm{E}\left[\widetilde{V}_T|\mathcal{F}_t\right]}{(1+k_t)\ldots(1+k_{T-1})}.$$

On account of the transversality, the last term disappears, giving us

$$\widetilde{V}_t = \sum_{s=t+1}^{T} \frac{\mathrm{E}\left[\widetilde{FCF}_s|\mathcal{F}_t\right]}{(1+k_t)\ldots(1+k_{s-1})} .$$

Under the particular prerequisite, that we are to look at the value of the firm at time $t = 0$, it follows out of Theorem 2.1 in relation to Rule 1 (classical expectation)

$$V_0 = \sum_{s=1}^{T} \frac{\mathrm{E}\left[\widetilde{FCF}_s\right]}{(1+k_0)\ldots(1+k_{s-1})}$$

and finally in the particular case of time-invariant cost of capital

$$V_0 = \sum_{t=1}^{T} \frac{\mathrm{E}\left[\widetilde{FCF}_t\right]}{(1+k)^t} .$$

q.e.d.

2.3.4 Fundamental Theorem of Asset Pricing

The idea of an equivalent martingale measure has to do with offering the evaluator other probabilities for the states of nature and thus making her world risk-neutral. That this method is always successful, that there always exist probabilities in which the valuation can be made risk-neutral, is the content of the (first) fundamental theorem of asset pricing.

The fundamental theorem maintains that the investor's subjective probability can be replaced by another probability measure Q. We denote the new expectations with E_Q. The following statement is valid for them.

Theorem 2.2 (Fundamental Theorem of Asset Pricing) *If the capital market is free of arbitrage, then conditional probabilities Q can be chosen to the extent that* *the following equation is valid:*

$$\widetilde{V}_t = \frac{\mathrm{E}_Q\left[\widetilde{FCF}_{t+1} + \widetilde{V}_{t+1}|\mathcal{F}_t\right]}{1+r_f} .$$

The fundamental theorem is valid for all conceivable financial claims, for equities as well as debts, for levered as well as unlevered firms.

In Theorem 2.1, we were able to gain a preliminary equation for the valuation of firms out of the definition of the cost of capital. In a completely analogous way, we could show that with the help of risk-neutral probabilities a valuation equation can also be proven. It runs

$$\widetilde{V}_t = \sum_{s=t+1}^{T} \frac{\mathrm{E}_Q\left[\widetilde{FCF}_s|\mathcal{F}_t\right]}{\left(1+r_f\right)^{s-t}} , \tag{2.8}$$

and does not need a new proof.

If we compare the fundamental Theorem 2.2 with Eq. (2.7), we then determine similarities and differences: here as there, we are discounting with the riskless interest rate. Instead of certain payments, we now deal with their conditional expectations. The risk of future payments comes into the equation in so far as we are not working with the subjective probabilities for future states of nature, but rather instead with the so-called risk-neutral probabilities. It deals with a third way, other than certainty equivalents and cost of capital, of incorporating risk into the valuation equation. Again and again throughout this book we will see that the fundamental theorem can be put to practical use.

Risk Neutrality Before we turn to the practical application of the concept, we want to answer the question as to why the probabilities used here are termed as riskless whatsoever. We will make use here as well of our rules for conditional expectations.

For this purpose, we reformulate the fundamental theorem. It goes as

$$1+r_f = \frac{\mathrm{E}_Q\left[\widetilde{FCF}_{t+1} + \widetilde{V}_{t+1}|\mathcal{F}_t\right]}{\widetilde{V}_t} .$$

We know according to Rule 5 (expectation of realized quantities), that the value of the firm at time t is already known and therefore may also be included within the conditional expectation, without changing the result,

$$1+r_f = \mathrm{E}_Q\left[\left.\frac{\widetilde{FCF}_{t+1} + \widetilde{V}_{t+1}}{\widetilde{V}_t}\right|\mathcal{F}_t\right] .$$

The one on the left-hand side is certain. On the grounds of rule 3 (certain quantities), we can replace it with its expectation,

$$r_f = \mathrm{E}_Q\left[\frac{\widetilde{FCF}_{t+1} + \widetilde{V}_{t+1}}{\widetilde{V}_t}\middle|\mathcal{F}_t\right] - \mathrm{E}_Q\left[1|\mathcal{F}_t\right] .$$

Lastly, we use Rule 2 (linearity) and get

$$r_f = \mathrm{E}_Q\left[\frac{\widetilde{FCF}_{t+1} + \widetilde{V}_{t+1}}{\widetilde{V}_t} - 1\middle|\mathcal{F}_t\right] .$$

This presentation of the fundamental theorem allows for a clear economic interpretation. We look to the returns as an argument for the conditional expectation. An investor attains these if she acquires a security at time t, receives the cash flows one period later and immediately afterwards again sells the security. The statement of the last equation then reads that the conditional expected return of this strategy is always riskless, if the risk-neutral probabilities are fallen back upon instead of the subjective probabilities. The designation "risk-neutral probability" for Q relates back to this characteristic.

Flat Term Structure Look again at the fundamental Theorem 2.2. The riskless interest rate in this equation has no time index t. We have implicitly insinuated with it that the riskless interest rates are constant over time. This limitation is not necessary and can be easily dropped. If the term structure is not flat, then the riskless interest rate simply attains a time index, and the statement of the fundamental theorem remains further valid.

Uniqueness of Q The question arises whether the mentioned probability Q is unique and what consequences can be drawn if several risk-neutral probabilities exist. We do not want to go into detail here, but the following can be said. For the existence of the risk-neutral probability measure it is completely sufficient that the market is free of arbitrage. The assertion that any claim, so complicated as it may be, is also traded (in this case the market is called complete), is not necessary to prove the fundamental theorem of asset pricing. Admittedly, in this case of an incomplete market one can show that Q need not to be unique. But this is not a problem at least for valuation, since every "possible" probability will lead to one and the same price of the firm.

It is, however, a problem if the firm to be valued is not or not yet traded on the market. In this case the fundamental theorem may not yield one particular value but instead a range of possible prices of the firm. Therefore, a second assumption that is also necessary for DCF valuation is the following.

Assumption 2.2 (Spanning) *The cash flows of an asset to be valued can be perfectly duplicated at the capital market.*

Let us discuss this assumption. Again we suppress the formalism required to formulate it in a mathematically precise manner. The assumption requires that the possible cash flow of the company, complicated as it may be, can also be achieved by holding a (possibly involved) portfolio of assets, bonds, derivatives, or any other assets from the capital market. Instead of buying the company, the investor could turn to the capital market and would receive not only a similar, but also the same distribution of cash flows.

It might be questionable, why the investor at all would now buy the company if she can invest in a portfolio of equities and bonds. But we do not care for determining an investor's optimal portfolio (this would require an examination of her utility function). Instead we are decided to value a company by trying to replicate the company's cash flows by a portfolio of traded assets. We stress explicitly here that in this book valuation is a comparison of a company with the capital market. Spanning is necessary to perform this comparison.

2.3.5 Transversality and Infinite Life Span

We are working under the assumption in any case that the value of the business closes in on zero, as the firm's end approaches. In the case of a firm with a finite life span, it is a very obvious, even trivial, statement. Beyond time T, the cash flows do not flow any more, which is why the value of the firm must disappear. But we also need an analogous business value characteristic when we have a firm with an infinite life span as our basis. In the formally orientated literature, the so-called transversality is spoken of when the discounted business value is heading towards zero with the advance of time. If transversality is not accepted, the danger arises of getting entangled in serious contradictions.[11]

If transversality is responsible for a vanishing firm value if time goes to infinity, it is by no means clear how this condition should be formulated appropriately. One could, for example, use the risk-neutral probability measure and stipulate that

$$\lim_{T\to\infty} \frac{\mathrm{E}_Q\left[\widetilde{V}_T\right]}{(1+r_f)^T} = 0 .$$

[11]If, for example, a firm that is being looked at finds enough valuable investments over an infinite period, no free cash flows are generated in this case. Since the firm's free cash flow is always at zero, the firm's value (if the transversality condition is not taken into consideration) will also be zero—although the firm is certainly worth more than nothing.

But also the use of the subjective probability could be a possibility. In the first edition of this book we indeed used the specification

$$\lim_{T\to\infty} \frac{\mathrm{E}\left[\widetilde{V}_T\right]}{(1+k)^T} = 0\,.$$

Meanwhile, we have figured out that this approach will get us nowhere and that Eq. (2.9) provides the required results.[12]

Assumption 2.3 (Transversality) *If the life span of a firm goes to infinity ($T \to \infty$), then we have almost-everywhere*

$$\lim_{T\to\infty} \frac{\mathrm{E}_Q\left[\widetilde{V}_T|\mathcal{F}_t\right]}{(1+r_f)^{T-t}} = 0 \qquad \forall t\,. \tag{2.9}$$

Clearly, this is a mathematical limit. But it is far from easy to interpret a limit correctly in this case. This is because we do not deal with real numbers here but with a limit of random variables, i.e., a limit of functions. Recall that the conditional expectations $\mathrm{E}_Q\left[\widetilde{FCF}_T|\mathcal{F}_t\right]$ may be uncertain. Now we must take note that there is no one and only definition of a limit of functions. Instead, there are several concepts at hand.[13]

One can show that the so-called almost-everywhere convergence is appropriate. On this basis we state that a sequence of random variables X_t "converges" to a random variable X if the following is true: For every state we ask whether

$$\lim_{T\to\infty} \widetilde{X}_t(\omega) = \widetilde{X}(\omega)$$

holds. By fixing the state ω we are no longer dealing with sequences of random variables, but instead with sequences of numbers. Based on this fact we can be certain whether a limit exists and equals a number $\widetilde{X}(\omega)$. However, we do not know how large the set of all such states ω is. Therefore we say that $\widetilde{X}_t$ *converges almost-everywhere* to $\widetilde{X}$ if the set of such states has probability one. Put differently: "It is certain that the sequence $\widetilde{X}(\omega)$ converges for every ω to $\widetilde{X}(\omega)$."

---

[12] See in particular Kruschwitz and Löffler (2013).

[13] Convergence can be pointwise, almost-everywhere, in L^2 or in probability, etc. (see Stoyanov (2013, section 14) for an overview of different convergence concepts for random variables, their interrelations and numerous counterexamples). Notice that further an assumption is necessary that establishes a lower bound K of all cash flows at any time and any state. This lower bound can be arbitrary but need to be a finite number. We believe that this assumption is of technical nature that is not an important economic restriction. The following considerations are—in parts literally—taken from Kruschwitz and Löffler (2013).

Valuation equation (2.11)

Transversality (2.9) and Fundamental theorem (2.10)

Fig. 2.7 Transversality is necessary to use a valuation equation with infinite lifetime and accomplish unique enterprise values

In that sense transversality includes the condition (2.9) for an almost-everywhere convergence.

Transversality is not only a technical condition but can be interpreted in an economic meaningful way. Let us assume for a moment that transversality would not be satisfied. Then the fundamental theorem[14]

$$\widetilde{V}_t = \frac{\mathrm{E}_Q\left[\widetilde{FCF}_{t+1} + \widetilde{V}_{t+1}|\mathcal{F}_t\right]}{1+r_f} \tag{2.10}$$

will even with given cash flows not yield a *unique* value of the company. Instead, there exists an infinite number of variables $\widetilde{V}_t$ that will satisfy the fundamental theorem and could be acknowledged as "value of the company." There is not one but an infinite number of such "values." The valuation of a company using the fundamental theorem is doomed to fail. Transversality is in this sense indispensable.

Figure 2.7 illustrates the interplay between transversality and fundamental theorem on the one hand and a unique firm value on the other hand. Transversality ensures that the fundamental theorem (2.10) and the valuation equation

$$\widetilde{V}_t = \sum_{s=t+1}^{\infty} \frac{\mathrm{E}_Q\left[\widetilde{FCF}_s|\mathcal{F}_t\right]}{(1+r_f)^{s-t}} \tag{2.11}$$

are equivalent even in the case of infinitely living firms. Those, who presume the fundamental theorem can utilize the valuation equation and vice versa if transversality holds. Exactly this is the meaning of Fig. 2.7.

Let us summarize. The transversality condition 2.3 is necessary if we want to value companies that stay on forever. Forgoing this assumption will lead to inconsistent results.

Notwithstanding we want to emphasize that we do not believe in companies living forever. The main reason for dealing with these peculiar firms is the fact that this assumption simplifies our considerations very much.

[14]For details see Kruschwitz and Löffler (2013, theorem 2).

2.3.6 Problems

1. Consider the return

$$\widetilde{r}_s := \frac{\widetilde{FCF}_{s+1} + \widetilde{V}_{s+1}}{V_s} - 1.$$

Assume that cost of capital (conditional expected returns) are deterministic. Show using only the rules of this chapter that for $s_1 > s_2 > t$ always

$$\mathrm{E}\left[\widetilde{r}_{s_1}\widetilde{r}_{s_2}|\mathcal{F}_t\right] = \mathrm{E}\left[\widetilde{r}_{s_1}|\mathcal{F}_t\right]\mathrm{E}\left[\widetilde{r}_{s_2}|\mathcal{F}_t\right].$$

This is also known as independence of returns.

2. Consider the infinite example from Fig. 2.3. Assume that the cost of capital k are constant. Prove that

$$\widetilde{V}_{t+1} = \begin{cases} u\,\widetilde{V}_t & \text{if up,} \\ d\,\widetilde{V}_t & \text{if down.} \end{cases}$$

Show furthermore that (analogous to (2.6))

$$\mathrm{E}\left[\widetilde{V}_t|\mathcal{F}_s\right] = \widetilde{V}_s.$$

Hint Remember $g = 0$.

3. Assume that cost of capital k are deterministic and constant. The firm is infinitely living ($T \to \infty$). Assume that the expected cash flows pursue constant growth

$$\mathrm{E}\left[\widetilde{FCF}_{t+1}\right] = (1+g)^t\,C$$

for deterministic and constant g with $-1 < g < k$ and $C > 0$. Find a simple formula for the value of the firm V_0 using Theorem 2.1. What happens if $g \geq k$?

4. This problem will show that without transversality the value of a company might not be unique. To this end assume that we have an infinite number of company values $\widetilde{V}_t$ and a sequence of cash flows $\widetilde{FCF}_t$ such that the recursion

$$\widetilde{V}_t = \frac{\mathrm{E}_Q[\widetilde{V}_{t+1} + \widetilde{FCF}_{t+1}|\mathcal{F}_t]}{1+r_f}$$

is satisfied. Transversality shall not hold. Show that the new sequence $\widetilde{V}_t^* := \widetilde{V}_t + C(1+r_f)^t$ with an arbitrary number $C \neq 0$ is also a "valid firm value" in the sense that this $\widetilde{V}_t^*$ also satisfies the valuation equation.

5. The following problem is based on Froot and Obstfeld (1991). Let us assume that the cash flows follow a white noise process, i.e.,

$$\widetilde{FCF}_t = \widetilde{FCF}_0 + \varepsilon_t,$$

where ε_t are iid and $\mathrm{E}_Q[\varepsilon_t] = g$. Show that then

$$\widetilde{V}_t := \frac{\widetilde{FCF}_0 + g}{r_f}$$

are the corresponding firm values because they satisfy the following two characteristics
(a) The recursion equation holds, i.e., $(1 + r_f)\widetilde{V}_t = \mathrm{E}_Q[\widetilde{V}_{t+1} + \widetilde{FCF}_{t+1}|\mathcal{F}_t]$.
(b) For every t the transversality condition $\lim_{T\to\infty} \frac{\mathrm{E}_Q[\widetilde{V}_T|\mathcal{F}_t]}{(1+r_f)^{T-t}} = 0$ holds.

2.4 Further Literature

The concept of the conditional expectation goes back to the work of the Russian mathematician Kolmogorov from the 1930s and is found in every textbook on probability theory. The presentation given in the textbook from Williams (1991) is worth reading. Although it deals only with discrete time, this textbook also gives a very good introduction to the theory of martingale measure. This also applies to Shreve (2004a). Those who want to read more about continuous time models can turn to Karatzas and Shreve (1991), Musiela and Rutkowski (2005), Revuz and Yor (1999) or Shreve (2004b). Though all books are written for students majoring in mathematics.

The fundamental theorem of asset pricing was gradually recognized in several papers and is based on works from Beja (1971), Harrison and Kreps (1979), and Back and Pliska (1991). A proof can also be found in the textbook Musiela and Rutkowski (2005) and in Revuz and Yor (1999).

The definition and determination of cash flows are dealt with in-depth in every textbook on balance sheet analysis; Koller et al. (2015) is a good reference. The topic of the prognosis of future cash flows is unfortunately very often left out, Welch (2014, chapter 20) is a notable exception.

Rapp (2006) and Laitenberger (2006) discuss the question whether a suitable definition of cost of capital can be found that does not need the restriction of nonrandom returns.

Niemann (2004) analyzes uncertain tax rates and their impact on neutrality of tax systems. An overview about national tax codes can be found in Koller et al. (2010, pp. 357–380). (The 2015 edition does not contain a chapter on national tax codes anymore.)

In Husmann et al. (2006) it is shown how several national tax codes can be implemented into our model.

Transversality is extensively discussed in Kruschwitz and Löffler (2013). A lot of examples, counterexamples as well as proofs can be found there.

Asymmetric taxation with respect to valuation was discussed in Schaefer (1982), Dybvig and Ross (1986), Ross (1987), Dermody and Rockafellar (1991), and recently Becker and Löffler (2016).

References

Back K, Pliska SR (1991) On the fundamental theorem of asset pricing with an infinite state space. J Math Econ 20:1–18

Becker M, Löffler A (2016) Arbitrage and nonlinear tax scales, No. 205. arqus diskussionsbeitrag. Arbeitskreis Quantitative Steuerlehre

Beja A (1971) The structure of the cost of capital under uncertainty. Rev Econ Stud 38:359–368

Brealey RA, Myers SC, Allen F (2020) Principles of corporate finance, 13th edn. McGraw-Hill, New York

Copeland TE, Weston JF, Shastri K (2005) Financial theory and corporate policy, 4th edn. Pearson, Addison-Wesley, Boston

de Matos JA (2001) Theoretical foundations of corporate finance. Princeton University Press, Princeton

Dermody JC, Rockafellar RT (1991) Cash stream valuation in the face of transaction costs and taxes. Math Financ 1:31–54

Dybvig P, Ross SA (1986) Tax clienteles and asset pricing. J Financ 41:751–62

Froot KA, Obstfeld M (1991) Intrinsic bubbles: the case of stock prices. Am Econ Rev 81:1189–1214

Harrison JM, Kreps DM (1979) Martingales and arbitrage in multiperiod securities markets. J. Econ. Theory 20:381–408

Husmann S, Kruschwitz L, Löffler A (2006) WACC and a generalized tax code. Eur J Financ 12:33–40

Institut der Wirtschaftsprüfer in Deutschland (2008) IDW Standard: Grundsätze zur Durchführung von Unternehmensbewertungen [IDW S 1] (Stand: 02.04.2008). Die Wirtschaftsprüfung (Suppl) 3:68–89

Karatzas I, Shreve SE (1991) Brownian motion and stochastic calculus, 2nd edn. Springer, New York

Koller T, Goedhart M, Wessels D (2010) Valuation: measuring and managing the value of companies, 5th edn. John Wiley & Sons, Hoboken

Koller T, Goedhart M, Wessels D (2015) Valuation: measuring and managing the value of companies, 6th edn. John Wiley & Sons, Hoboken

Kruschwitz L, Löffler A (2013) Transversality and the stochastic nature of cash flows. http://ssrn.com/paper=2373744

Kruschwitz L, Löffler A (2019) Stochastic discounting revisited. Mimeo. Freie Universität Berlin

Laitenberger J (2006) Rendite und Kapitalkosten. Z Betriebswirt 76:79–101

Miles JA, Ezzell JR (1980) The weighted average cost of capital, perfect capital markets, and project life: a clarification. J Financ Quant Anal 15:719–730

Musiela M, Rutkowski M (2005) Martingale methods in financial modelling, 2nd edn. Springer, Berlin

Niemann R (2004) Tax rate uncertainty, investment decisions, and tax neutrality. Int Tax Public Financ 11:265–281

Rapp MS (2006) Die arbitragefreie Adjustierung von Diskontierungssätzen bei einfacher Gewinnsteuer. Z Betriebswirtsch Forsch 58:771–806

Revuz D, Yor M (1999) Continuous martingales and Brownian motion, 3rd edn. Springer, Berlin

Ross SA (1987) Arbitrage and martingales with taxation. J Polit Econ 95:371–393

Schaefer SM (1982) Taxes and security market equilibrium. In: Sharpe WF, Cootner CM (eds) Financial economics: essays in honor of Paul Cootner, Prentice-Hall, Englewood Cliffs, pp 159–178

Shreve SE (2004a) Stochastic calculus for finance I: the binomial asset pricing model. Springer, New York

Shreve SE (2004b) Stochastic calculus for finance II: continuous-time models. Springer, New York

Stoyanov JM (2013) Counterexamples in probability, 3rd edn. Dover Publications, New York

Welch I (2014) Corporate finance, 3rd edn. Ivo Welch

Williams D (1991) Probability with martingales. Cambridge University Press, Cambridge

Corporate Income Tax: WACC, FTE, TCF, APV 3

There is a variety of problems in the valuation of firms. That is why the evaluator has to make some simplifications in order to come up with a result. That also goes for the theory of valuation. We will take the first step in assuming that the firm has no debt. In simplifying with this assumption, we shall see that a number of economic problems can be discussed. In the next step we will turn to indebted firms.

3.1 Unlevered Firms

Whoever has to value levered firms, also has to be able to value unlevered firms. Both are mutually conditional.

By itself, this claim does not shed any light. It should be understood that if a levered firm is spoken of without naming any further details, then that remains unclear. Are we dealing with a heavily or only moderately levered firm? Will the firm's debt increase, or are the responsible managers planning to reduce the firm's credit volume? In contrast to a levered firm in which this must all be explained in detail, the circumstances of an unlevered firm are clear and simple. When we speak of an unlevered firm, we mean a firm, which will not have debts today, nor anytime in the future. Of course it is difficult to believe that there are actually such firms in our world. But this—no doubt fully correct assessment—does not matter here. All we want to state is that what we mean by an unlevered firm is completely straightforward, while by a levered firm it is not so clear without further information.

Cost of Capital and Leverage A firm's cost of capital essentially depends upon two influences: firstly, the firm's business risk, and secondly, its indebtedness. It is fundamentally valid that the greater the risk is and the greater the firm's debt-equity ratio is, that much higher the expected returns are. And if we make the connection between this law and the considerations of the preceding paragraph, then the cost

L. Kruschwitz, A. Löffler, *Stochastic Discounted Cash Flow*,
Springer Texts in Business and Economics,
https://doi.org/10.1007/978-3-030-37081-7_3

of capital of an equity-financed firm is straightforward, while the cost of capital of an indebted firm is dependent upon the level of debt. Of course this is all only valid so long as we keep all other influences upon the cost of capital—particularly the business risk and the tax rate—constant.

The indebted firm's cost of capital is needed in order to be able to correctly value it. To put it more exactly: the cost of capital is needed of a firm, which has two things in common with the firm to be valued. These regard, namely, its business risk and its debt. If you want to determine this cost of capital by using empirical data from the capital market, you typically get into the following situation. You go to the trouble of finding a firm that belongs to the same, or at least very similar risk class (comparison firm) and estimate the expected value of the returns, which the financiers receive. In doing so you almost always have to observe that the comparison firm is financed differently than the firm to be valued. But if the debt now has an influence on the amount of the cost of capital, the comparison firm's cost of capital cannot simply be applied to the firm to be valued. As we already made clear, indebted firms are not necessarily comparable even when they belong to the same risk class. And it is exactly here that the equity-financed firm comes into play as reference firm.

The indebted firm, this will become clear in a moment, is under any circumstances more valuable than an equity-financed company with identical cash flows. Hence, raising debt will serve as a leverage that can increase the firm's value. In this case one also speaks of a leverage effect caused by debt. That is why we will use the expressions indebted and levered as well as equity-financed and unlevered as synonyms.

Unlevering and Relevering In order to determine the cost of capital of the firm to be valued, the comparison firm's cost of capital is to be adjusted because of the reasons described here. Academics, who are involved with the theoretical side of valuation of firms, have to develop functional equations, which allow for the cost of capital of the—levered—comparison firm to be converted into the unlevered firm's cost of capital. If they are successful, then the equations can be used to infer the reference firm's cost of capital from the comparison firm's cost of capital (unlevering), but also to infer the cost of capital of the firm to be valued from the reference firm's cost of capital (relevering).

And thus the circle is complete: whoever wants to value a levered firm, must also be able to value an unlevered firm. The academics are then naturally required to live up to the expectations placed on them and must actually be in the position to develop the necessary adjustment equations. Should they fail at this, then the discounting of levered firms' cash flows with the appropriate cost of capital must simply be forgotten.

Notation In the first chapter of this book, we spoke of free cash flows and firm values without troubling ourselves with how the firms are financed. Now we are concentrating on firms, which are completely equity-financed. Therefore, the relevant symbols get an appropriate index. We use a superior u for unlevered firms. We will, for instance, designate the free cash flows after corporate income taxes of such firms with $\widetilde{FCF}_t^u$, and the firm values with $\widetilde{V}_t^u$. Notice that since only cash flows after taxes can be paid to the owners of the firm, $\widetilde{FCF}_t^u$ will denote free cash flows after corporate income tax. Unlevered firms have only one single group of financiers. For the returns that the owners are expecting we will use the symbol $\widetilde{k}_t^{E,u}$.

3.1.1 Valuation Equation

We assume in the following that it is possible to successfully come up with the required adjustment equations and will actively attempt to do so ourselves as best we can. Under this condition, the cost of capital of the totally equity-financed firm can be considered to be known. We assume that the evaluator knows the unlevered firm's conditional expected free cash flows $\mathrm{E}\left[\widetilde{FCF}_s^u|\mathcal{F}_t\right]$ for time $s = t+1, \ldots, T$.

Definition 3.1 (Cost of Capital of the Unlevered Firm) Cost of capital $\widetilde{k}_t^{E,u}$ of an unlevered firm are conditional expected returns

$$\widetilde{k}_t^{E,u} := \frac{\mathrm{E}\left[\widetilde{FCF}_{t+1}^u + \widetilde{V}_{t+1}^u|\mathcal{F}_t\right]}{\widetilde{V}_t^u} - 1.$$

The reader should notice that we use the cash flows after corporate income tax in our definition of cost of capital. Therefore, $k_t^{E,u}$ are variables after corporate income tax, too. The question, how we can defer from these any cost of capital before tax is not our concern, since we do not investigate how the value of a company changes with a changing of the tax rate. Although possibly time dependent, our tax rates are fixed once and for all today. Nevertheless, if anyone tries to determine the cost of capital before tax he cannot operate on grounds of our theory since it does not tell anything about how the value of a firm changes with the tax rates.

The valuation of the unlevered firm is absolutely unproblematic under these conditions.

Theorem 3.1 (Market Value of the Unlevered Firm) *If the cost of capital of the unlevered firm $k_t^{E,u}$ are deterministic, then the value of the firm, which is only financed with owners' equity, amounts at time t to*

$$\widetilde{V}_t^u = \sum_{s=t+1}^{T} \frac{\mathrm{E}\left[\widetilde{FCF}_s^u|\mathcal{F}_t\right]}{\left(1+k_t^{E,u}\right)\ldots\left(1+k_{s-1}^{E,u}\right)}.$$

We do not have to further involve ourselves here with the proof of the assertion. We already handled it in a generalized form in Sect. 2.3.3 and do not need to bore our readers here by repeating ourselves.[1]

3.1.2 Weak Auto-Regressive Cash Flows

In Theorem 3.1 we determined a valuation equation for unlevered firms that the evaluator can only use if she knows the cost of equity of the unlevered firm. This condition can only very rarely be counted upon in practice. If the required conditions to use the theorem are not met, then the valuation is anything but a trivial problem.

Cash Flows of the Unlevered Firm You can only get further in such a situation if the adjustment equation already mentioned above is available. The derivation of such an equation is, however, only possible if the appropriate suppositions are met. In the following sections of this book we will develop adjustment equations for demanding cases. Our results are indeed based on a special condition regarding the structure of the unlevered firm's free cash flows after taxes. From now on we will assume that the cash flows form a so-called weak auto-regressive process.[2] The reader may rest assured that without recourse to this assumption, development of correct adjustment formulas is doomed to fail.

Assumption 3.1 (Weak Auto-Regressive Cash Flows) *There are real numbers* $g_t > -1$ *such that*

$$\mathrm{E}\left[\widetilde{FCF}_{t+1}^{u}|\mathcal{F}_t\right] = (1+g_t)\,\widetilde{FCF}_t^{u}$$

is valid for the unlevered firm's cash flows after taxes.

We must assume that g_t is greater than -100% in order to prevent cash flows from having oscillating signs which would be rather unrealistic. It is not necessary to assume that g_t is positive, so shrinking cash flows are not excluded with Assumption 3.1.

[1] The valuation equation

$$\widetilde{V}_t^{u} = \sum_{s=t+1}^{T} \frac{\mathrm{E}_Q\left[\widetilde{FCF}_s^{u}|\mathcal{F}_t\right]}{(1+r_f)^{s-t}}$$

can also be gotten analogously without needing a new proof.

[2] We use the term *weak* auto-regressive to distinguish it from a simple auto-regressive model. Here a growth factor g_t will occur that has to be time-independent with auto-regressive processes. Furthermore, our increments are uncorrelated, not necessarily independent.

Uncorrelated (Additive) Increments In order to understand this assumption, we firstly look at the increments of the cash flow process. In formal notation we thus have

$$\widetilde{FCF}^{u}_{t+1} = (1 + g_t)\,\widetilde{FCF}^{u}_{t} + \varepsilon_{t+1}. \tag{3.1}$$

g_t is a deterministic amount that is already known in $t = 0$. What does our assumption on weak auto-regressive cash flows imply for the increments ε_{t+1}? It will imply that these increments have expectation zero and are uncorrelated to each other (sometimes called "white noise" although this in fact refers to independent increments).

It is not immediately recognizable that this assumption really implies uncorrelated noise terms. In order to prove that, we have to carry out a little calculation. In doing so, we will again make use of the rules for conditional expectations. We first of all show that the noise terms' expectation disappears,[3]

$$\begin{aligned}
\mathrm{E}\left[\varepsilon_{t+1}\right] &= \mathrm{E}\left[\varepsilon_{t+1}|\mathcal{F}_0\right] && \text{Rule 1}\\
&= \mathrm{E}\left[\mathrm{E}\left[\varepsilon_{t+1}|\mathcal{F}_t\right]|\mathcal{F}_0\right] && \text{Rule 4}\\
&= \mathrm{E}\left[\mathrm{E}\left[\widetilde{FCF}^{u}_{t+1} - (1+g_t)\widetilde{FCF}^{u}_{t}|\mathcal{F}_t\right]|\mathcal{F}_0\right] && \text{by (3.1)}\\
&= \mathrm{E}\left[\mathrm{E}\left[\widetilde{FCF}^{u}_{t+1}|\mathcal{F}_t\right] - (1+g_t)\,\mathrm{E}\left[\widetilde{FCF}^{u}_{t}|\mathcal{F}_t\right]|\mathcal{F}_0\right] && \text{Rule 2}\\
&= \mathrm{E}\left[\mathrm{E}\left[\widetilde{FCF}^{u}_{t+1}|\mathcal{F}_t\right] - (1+g_t)\widetilde{FCF}^{u}_{t}|\mathcal{F}_0\right] && \text{Rule 5}\\
&= \mathrm{E}\left[0|\mathcal{F}_0\right] && \text{Assumption 3.1}\\
&= 0\,.
\end{aligned}$$

Now we come to the proof that the noise terms are uncorrelated. We look at two points in time $s < t$ and have to show that the covariance $\mathrm{Cov}[\varepsilon_s, \varepsilon_t]$ disappears. We already know that the noise terms' expectations are zero. And so from the covariance it immediately follows:

$$\begin{aligned}
\mathrm{Cov}[\varepsilon_s, \varepsilon_t] &= \mathrm{E}\left[\varepsilon_s\varepsilon_t\right] - \mathrm{E}\left[\varepsilon_s\right]\mathrm{E}\left[\varepsilon_t\right]\\
&= \mathrm{E}\left[\varepsilon_s\varepsilon_t\right]\,.
\end{aligned}$$

From the rules as well as from the definition of noise term it follows:

$$\begin{aligned}
\mathrm{Cov}[\varepsilon_s, \varepsilon_t] &= \mathrm{E}\left[\varepsilon_s\varepsilon_t\right]\\
&= \mathrm{E}\left[\varepsilon_s\varepsilon_t|\mathcal{F}_0\right] && \text{Rule 1}
\end{aligned}$$

[3]We abstain from using the tilde for the random variable ε.

$$
\begin{aligned}
&= \mathrm{E}\left[\mathrm{E}\left[\varepsilon_s \varepsilon_t | \mathcal{F}_s\right] | \mathcal{F}_0\right] && \text{Rule 4} \\
&= \mathrm{E}\left[\varepsilon_s \, \mathrm{E}\left[\varepsilon_t | \mathcal{F}_s\right] | \mathcal{F}_0\right]. && \text{Rule 5}
\end{aligned}
$$

Now we concentrate on the conditional expectation, which comes up in the last equation and get the following from the rules as well as the fact that cash flows are weak auto-regressive:

$$
\begin{aligned}
\mathrm{E}\left[\varepsilon_t | \mathcal{F}_s\right] &= \mathrm{E}\left[\widetilde{FCF}_t^u - (1+g_{t-1})\widetilde{FCF}_{t-1}^u | \mathcal{F}_s\right] \\
&= \mathrm{E}\left[\mathrm{E}\left[\widetilde{FCF}_t^u - (1+g_{t-1})\widetilde{FCF}_{t-1}^u | \mathcal{F}_{t-1}\right] | \mathcal{F}_s\right] && \text{Rule 4} \\
&= \mathrm{E}\left[\mathrm{E}\left[\widetilde{FCF}_t^u | \mathcal{F}_{t-1}\right] - (1+g_{t-1})\widetilde{FCF}_{t-1}^u | \mathcal{F}_s\right] && \text{Rule 2, 5} \\
&= 0. && \text{Assumption 3.1}
\end{aligned}
$$

The covariance disappears, which is exactly what we wanted to show. q.e.d.

Independent (Additive) Increments Until now, we have proven that the vanishing expectation of the noise terms ε_{t+1} as well as their uncorrelation results from the Assumption 3.1. You may get the impression that the reverse is true as well. This is not the case. For reasons of order, we have to ascertain that it is the condition

$$
\mathrm{E}\left[\varepsilon_{t+1} | \mathcal{F}_t\right] = \mathrm{E}\left[\varepsilon_{t+1}\right] (= 0),
$$

which is logically sufficient to weak auto-regressive cash flows.

To understand this condition, we refer to the fact that numerous financial models work on the assumption that a firm's free cash flows would follow a random walk. What does that mean? It means that the cash flows possess increments, which are independent from each other and distributed identically. The noise terms ε_{t+1} have an expectation of zero, are distributed identically and are mutually independent.

This is a big assumption, far bigger than the one we made. The independence of the noise terms implies, for instance, that the increments of the cash flow in t is not connected to the cash flows from years 1 to $t-1$. If we have been looking at continuously growing cash flows in the last few years, that by no means suggests that this growth will remain in year t. You cannot draw any conclusions in the least from the development of the years 1 to $t-1$ for the year t! Uncorrelation in contrast does not pose such a strong challenge.

While uncorrelation excludes only a linear relation, independence negates every single causal relation: In our notation independence is equivalent to

$$
\mathrm{E}\left[f(\varepsilon_{t+1}) | \mathcal{F}_t\right] = \mathrm{E}\left[f(\varepsilon_{t+1})\right]
$$

for any function $f(x)$.[4] Compare this to the equation above, where f needs only to be linear. If the equation does not hold for any linear function, then there may well be any other nonlinear functional relation f. Independent random variables have always correlation zero, but uncorrelated random variables are—apart from normally distributed random variables—not independent from each other. This again makes clear that in the assumption on weak auto-regressive cash flows we are dealing with a weaker formulation. We are not insinuating any random walk with regard to the cash flows within the framework of our theory, but are instead working on the basis of the less demanding uncorrelated growth.

Multiplicative Versus Additive Increments Understanding auto-regressive cash flows is not an easy task. In the previous section, we looked at additive increments of cash flows in order to find an appropriate way of interpretation. But the additive context is by no means compelling. We could have used a multiplicative link as well. In the following, we will briefly discuss this and show that the result does not change at all. So, whether we go the additive or a multiplicative path is pure taste. A multiplicative relation is defined by

$$\widetilde{FCF}^u_{t+1} = (1 + g_t)\,\widetilde{FCF}^u_t\,(1 + \varepsilon_{t+1})\,. \tag{3.2}$$

First, we will check which properties of the error terms ε_t guarantee that the cash flows turn out to be weak auto-regressive once again. By inserting Assumption 3.1 in the definition we get

$$\begin{aligned}(1 + g_t)\widetilde{FCF}^u_t &= \mathrm{E}[\widetilde{FCF}^u_{t+1}|\mathcal{F}_t] && \text{Assumption 3.1}\\ &= (1 + g_t)\cdot\widetilde{FCF}^u_t\cdot(1 + \mathrm{E}[\varepsilon_{t+1}|\mathcal{F}_t]) && \text{Rule 5.}\end{aligned}$$

This means that

$$\mathrm{E}[\varepsilon_{t+1}|\mathcal{F}_t] = 0$$

is sufficient and necessary for weak auto-regression. Differences between additive and multiplicative increments only play a role when the distributions of the error terms come into play. However, these differences are not important in the following. The result can also be seen by taking the logarithm on both sides of Eq. (3.2),

$$\log\left(\widetilde{FCF}^u_{t+1}\right) = \log\left((1 + g_t)\widetilde{FCF}^u_t\right) + \log\left(1 + \varepsilon_{t+1}\right).$$

[4]See, for example, Ingersoll jr. (1987, p. 15). Also compare Problems 3 and 4.

In a multiplicative model the logarithms of the cash flows follow an additive model with $\log(1 + \varepsilon_{t+1})$ representing the error terms.[5] Based on these considerations we will restrict ourselves on additive error terms from now on.

Justification of Weak Auto-Regressive Cash Flows Every economic theory is based on assumptions. The numerous jokes usually told about us economists are based on the fact that we occasionally apply unrealistic, odd conditions. Economists who would like to be taken seriously must put up with the question as to whether their assumptions are justifiable. May we actually insinuate in good conscience that the Assumption 3.1 is met in terms of a firm's free cash flows? Isn't this assumption perhaps totally "far-fetched"?

From our experience, practically engaged evaluators normally do not deal at all with the question as to which distribution laws uncertain future cash flows follow. On the contrary they limit themselves to estimating the expectations of these future cash flows. It can now be shown that there are always state spaces with upwards and downwards movements like that analogous to Fig. 2.2 for whatever sequence of expectations you like. Assumption 3.1 is thus met in this model.[6] But that does not mean anything else than that an evaluator working with estimated expectations of cash flows can operate upon the basis that—so to speak behind the scenes—there is always a state space that corresponds to the Assumption 3.1. All in all, that is why we hold the assumption on weak auto-regressive cash flows to be practically acceptable.

The question can be raised at this point as to why exactly the unlevered firm's cash flows should be weak auto-regressive. It is obvious that our Assumption 3.1 is arbitrary and it does not make any sense to hide that. Couldn't we have just as well replaced our assumption with the condition that the free cash flows of a levered firm are weak auto-regressive? Could this levered firm be chosen in just any way, or would it have to be a firm with a particular financing policy? We must give a clear answer to the questions raised here: Varying results would be gotten in any case for the valuation equations, which we will be developing in the following. What is more, we think the following ascertainment is important: If it were to be supposed that a levered firm has weak auto-regressive cash flows, then it would not necessarily follow that the free cash flows of a firm with a different financing policy have this same characteristic as well.[7]

---

[5] See Problem 1.

[6] The proof demands some rather involved calculations, which we would spare ourselves here. Whoever takes the trouble and turns back to our example from Fig. 2.2, will determine that the assumption on weak auto-regressive cash flows is valid for the cash flows in this example. Also Problem 3 was devoted to that calculation.

[7] Problem 1 is devoted to this point.

Conclusions from Weak Auto-Regressive Cash Flows: Dividend-Price Ratio If cash flows are weak auto-regressive, then it can be proven that the unlevered firm's value is a multiple of the free cash flow. To put it differently, the unlevered firm must always show a deterministic dividend-price ratio. This result is well-known in the case of a perpetual rent from the Williams/Gordon-Shapiro formula.

Theorem 3.2 (Williams/Gordon-Shapiro Formula) *If the cost of capital is deterministic and cash flows are weak auto-regressive, then for the value of the unlevered firm*

$$\widetilde{V}_t^u = \frac{\widetilde{FCF}_t^u}{d_t^u}$$

holds for deterministic and positive $d_t^u > 0$ *which will be called dividend-price ratio.*

We have banned the proof for this theorem to the appendix.

The last proposition shows that the expected capital gains of the unlevered firm rate is deterministic

$$\frac{\operatorname{E}\left[\widetilde{V}_{t+1}^u|\mathcal{F}_t\right] - \widetilde{V}_t^u}{\widetilde{V}_t^u} = \frac{\left(d_{t+1}^u\right)^{-1}\operatorname{E}\left[\widetilde{FCF}_{t+1}^u\right]}{\left(d_t^u\right)^{-1}\widetilde{FCF}_t^u} - 1 = \frac{d_t^u(1+g_t)}{d_{t+1}^u} - 1$$

and is zero in particular if the dividend-price ratio is constant and the growth rate is zero.

Conclusions from Weak Auto-Regressive Cash Flows: Discount Rates We had already made it clear in the introduction that for the case under certainty, the returns and not the yields present the appropriate means of determining the value of cash flows. Now we take up the question as to the relation which exists between returns and discount rates. Let us take a look in order to get a certain idea of the free cash flows of any year you like. Without further assumptions on the capital market, we cannot act as if a claim to this single cash flow will be traded. Otherwise, the owner of a share would have claims to dividends, so to speak, but not to the share price of the security. Nevertheless, the question that we want to ask ourselves is: what price should an investor pay at time $t < s$ for an isolated free cash flow $\widetilde{FCF}_s^u$?

Although we have not precisely developed the basic elements of the arbitrage theory, we may make use of the fundamental theorem in terms of an analogous argument. If we can actually value levered as well as unlevered firms with this principle, then this should also be possible for the claim to an isolated cash flow. This cash flow is valued by constituting the expectation in terms of the risk-neutral probability and then discounting it with the riskless rate,[8]

$$\frac{\mathrm{E}_Q\left[\widetilde{FCF}^u_s|\mathcal{F}_t\right]}{(1+r_f)^{s-t}}\ .$$

The above expression gives the value of the free cash flows $\widetilde{FCF}^u_s$ at time t. It is immediately noticeable that this valuation formula, albeit extremely elegant, is totally useless: we know next to nothing about the probability measure Q. We will now turn our attention to a second outcome, which can be gotten from the fact that cash flows are weak auto-regressive. If cash flows are weak auto-regressive, then there is another way to value them which is of interest to us. In order to let that become clear, we must precisely define the term discount rate, which has until now been only vaguely introduced. For that we will make use of a few preliminary considerations.

Under the discount rate κ_t we understand that number, which allows the price of the cash flow $\widetilde{FCF}^u_{t+1}$ at time t to be determined. According to our statements up to present, the discount rate κ_t shall serve as an instrument to value the single cash flow $\widetilde{FCF}^u_{t+1}$, or using the subjective probabilities we must have

$$\frac{\mathrm{E}\left[\widetilde{FCF}^u_{t+1}|\mathcal{F}_t\right]}{1+\kappa_t}=\frac{\mathrm{E}_Q\left[\widetilde{FCF}^u_{t+1}|\mathcal{F}_t\right]}{1+r_f}\ . \tag{3.3}$$

Yet, this consideration alone is not sufficient for our purposes. We do not simply want to make use of the discount rates to value cash flows, which are each one single period away from the time of valuation. If we are, for instance, dealing with the valuation of the cash flow $\widetilde{FCF}^u_{t+2}$ at time t, then we want to manage this task with two discount rates, namely with κ_t as well as with κ_{t+1} in just such a way that

$$\frac{\mathrm{E}\left[\widetilde{FCF}^u_{t+2}|\mathcal{F}_t\right]}{(1+\kappa_t)(1+\kappa_{t+1})}=\frac{\mathrm{E}_Q\left[\widetilde{FCF}^u_{t+2}|\mathcal{F}_t\right]}{\left(1+r_f\right)^2} \tag{3.4}$$

is valid. But now it is not so unmistakably clear whether κ_t is serving the valuation of the cash flow $\widetilde{FCF}^u_{t+1}$ or the cash flow $\widetilde{FCF}^u_{t+2}$. And we can also no longer assume that the discount rate κ_t from Eq. (3.3) agrees with κ_t from Eq. (3.4).[9] We will thus suggest a definition for the discount rates that takes the cash flows to be valued into consideration and which requires a somewhat more complicated notation.

[8]We already mentioned that it can be shown with advanced mathematical methods that this procedure is in fact permissible with regard to all conceivable payment claims.

[9]See Problem 10 for the last remark.

Definition 3.2 (Discount Rates of the Unlevered Firm) Real numbers $\kappa_t^{t\to s}, \kappa_{t+1}^{t\to s} \dots$ are called discount rates of the cash flow $\widetilde{FCF}_s^u$ of the unlevered firm at time t, if they satisfy

$$\frac{\mathrm{E}_Q\left[\widetilde{FCF}_s^u|\mathcal{F}_t\right]}{(1+r_f)^{s-t}} = \frac{\mathrm{E}\left[\widetilde{FCF}_s^u|\mathcal{F}_t\right]}{\left(1+\kappa_t^{t\to s}\right)\dots\left(1+\kappa_{s-1}^{t\to s}\right)} .$$

We stress that this is only one of many conceivable definitions. We could, for instance, also define the discount rates as yields instead of the version we have chosen. If we do not do so, it is due solely to practical considerations.

We can, on the basis of definition (3.2), clarify the question as to whether the cost of capital $k^{E,u}$ prove to be appropriate candidates for discount rates of the unlevered cash flows. In answering this question we fall back upon the assumption that the cash flows of the unlevered firm are weak auto-regressive. Cost of capital does not then just only prove itself as appropriate discount rates. It has, much further, the pleasant characteristic that it is independent of the particular cash flow to be valued $\widetilde{FCF}_s^u$. This characteristic will later prove itself to be very helpful.

Theorem 3.3 (Equivalence of the Valuation Concepts) *If the cost of capital is deterministic and the cash flows of the unlevered firm are weak auto-regressive, then the following is valid for all times:* $s > t$

$$\frac{\mathrm{E}_Q\left[\widetilde{FCF}_s^u|\mathcal{F}_t\right]}{\left(1+r_f\right)^{s-t}} = \frac{\mathrm{E}\left[\widetilde{FCF}_s^u|\mathcal{F}_t\right]}{\left(1+k_t^{E,u}\right)\dots\left(1+k_{s-1}^{E,u}\right)} .$$

This is the same as to say that cost of capital are indeed discount rates regardless of $s > t \geq \tau$

$$\kappa_t^{s\to\tau} = k_t^{E,u} .$$

That this theorem follows from the met assumptions can hardly be so easily recognized. Since the proof would demand a fair amount of space and perhaps not even be of interest to every reader, we have banned it to an appendix.[10]

Critical readers could suspect that this theorem has to do with a simple application of the definition of the cost of capital. This would most definitely be a wrong conclusion and in order to make it more understandable, we would like to

[10]In the given theorem the cost of capital has a time index, which the riskless interest rate in contrast does not. We had already pointed out that we are supposing a flat term structure; it is no problem whatsoever, though, to generalize this theorem for the case of a non-flat term structure as well.

go into it in more detail. Just equating Eq. (2.8) with Theorem 3.1 leads us in terms of unlevered firms to the result

$$\widetilde{V}_t^u = \sum_{s=t+1}^{T} \frac{\mathrm{E}_Q\left[\widetilde{FCF}_s^u|\mathcal{F}_t\right]}{\left(1+r_f\right)^{s-t}} = \sum_{s=t+1}^{T} \frac{\mathrm{E}\left[\widetilde{FCF}_s^u|\mathcal{F}_t\right]}{\left(1+k_t^{E,u}\right)\ldots\left(1+k_{s-1}^{E,u}\right)}.$$

The preceding equation is of little surprise, as it only claims the equivalence of two different ways of calculation: either the risk-neutral probability and the riskless interest rate is used, or the evaluator applies the subjective probability and the (correspondingly) defined cost of capital. Since the cost of capital is now so defined that both expressions give identical values, there is no reason to worry about coming up with equal firm values.

Of surprise, however, is the declaration that not only do the sums agree in the last equation, but the summands as well. This is everything but obvious, as the simple example

$$4+6=3+7 \qquad \text{but } 4 \neq 3 \text{ and } 6 \neq 7$$

shows. The reader should keep both statements (i.e., the identity of the sums as well as the identity of the summands) clearly separate. Our statement is everything but self-evident and is thoroughly in need of a proof.

A First Look at Default Until now we had purposely not included the case in which the firm to be valued can go bankrupt. But as the company grows, the probability of going into default is increasing.

If the court in charge allows for the commencement of bankruptcy proceedings, the consequences for creditors, suppliers, employees, owners, and managers are determined in detail by the bankruptcy law. As a rule a liquidator is placed in charge of the business affairs and examines how each party's payment claims can best be settled. The liquidator makes suitable suggestions within a given time frame and tries to get the agreement of the creditors and the court.

There are principally three possibilities. You can try to rehabilitate the firm, that is, to re-establish the profitability through suitable restructuring measures. In order to do this, the creditors must be willing to renounce some of their claims. If that is not feasible, then the insolvent firm can be transferred over to a bail-out firm and the creditors are paid off by the sales proceeds. If such a solution is also not practical, then there is no other option than to close down and liquidate the firm. What then remains is the smaller the faster the breakup of the firm takes place.

In the following we only assume that in determining future cash flows as well as in laying down future financing and investment policies, all conceivable developments were taken into consideration. If all conceivable developments are being spoken of, then that also includes situations in which the firm goes into default or has gone into default.

Unlevered firms can go bankrupt if claims of tax authorities, employees, and the like are not satisfied. Formal insolvency proceedings are regulated differently from one jurisdiction to the other. However, most countries apply similar default triggers. Usually, illiquidity and over-indebtedness are typical default triggers. A company gets illiquid if its net cash flows (i.e., cash flows to equity or CFE) are negative. A company is over-indebted if the value of equity is negative (whereas market as well as book values are being used in this definition).[11] Similarly, e.g., the UK Insolvency Act initiates bankruptcy proceedings if a firm either does not have enough assets to cover its debts (i.e., the value of assets is less than the amount of the liabilities), or it is unable to pay its debts as they fall due.

Let us first concentrate on the case of an unlevered firm. It is tempting to suggest that an unlevered company is illiquid if the owners' net cash flows turn out to be negative or $\widetilde{FCF}_t^u(\omega) < 0$. But it is clearly apparent that this definition has its pitfalls when used in a DCF context. Why do we have to emphasize this? If net cash flows are positive, the company pays money to the owners. But if not, it is just the other way round: the owners pay money to the company if net cash flows appear to be negative. Now, if a sufficient amount of money is paid to the company, the firm is no longer illiquid. The owners simply rectify the unpleasant situation. Hence, if and only if the owners do not completely comply with their reserve liabilities, one can actually speak of a *lack of liquidity* of the company.

We hold the following: whenever the owners cannot or do not meet their funding obligations, the company effectively faces illiquidity.[12] However, the mere existence of negative net cash flows does not automatically imply such a run of events. We should therefore speak of the *danger of illiquidity* that arises if net cash flows turn out to be negative or $\widetilde{FCF}_t^u(\omega) < 0$.

Let us now turn to over-indebtedness as the second default trigger. How could this term be interpreted when we look at an unlevered firm? We will characterize such a situation by $\widetilde{V}_t^u(\omega) < 0$. If this condition is fulfilled, from the owner's point of view continuing the business would be out of the question. It would undoubtedly be appropriate to speak of "not continuable unlevered firms." However, for systematic reasons we use the terms "in danger of illiquidity" and "in danger of negative equity," provided the mentioned inequality is met.

The following proposition will show that now over-indebtedness and danger of illiquidity are in the case of unlevered firms merely equivalent. Both default triggers in fact turn out to coincide and it was too much of an effort to distinguish both cases. But it will turn out that in the case of a levered firm things will become much more complicated.

[11]According to German Bankruptcy Code (Insolvenzordnung), for example, a firm has to file for bankruptcy if illiquidity or over-indebtedness occurs.

[12]In principle, a third party could enter the scene and take the company's debt. But we want to exclude this case.

Theorem 3.4 (Default of the Unlevered Firm) *Consider an unlevered firm with weak auto-regressive cash flows. If the company is in danger of illiquidity at date t in some state, it will also be in danger of negative equity at the same date for the same state.*

This immediately follows from Proposition 3.2.

Notice that the market value of equity for corporations cannot be negative, since they have limited liability. The market value of non-corporations, say partnerships, can be negative though. This is the reason why we speak only of danger of insolvency instead of insolvency itself. Our theorem mainly discloses how a consistent valuation model even of an unlevered firm has to be built in order to avoid such logical contradictions.

We now have the basic elements of our theory on discounted cash flow. In the following sections it must be shown what can be done with these basic elements.

3.1.3 Example (Continued)

The Finite Case Beforehand we want to take up our example from Sect. 2.2.3 and establish the value of the unlevered firm. As we have seen the cash flows follow a weak auto-regressive development. In addition, we assume that the cost of capital of the unlevered firm is constant in time and amounts to 20%. According to Theorem 3.1, it is obvious what market value the unlevered firm has at time $t = 0$,

$$\begin{aligned} V_0^u &= \frac{\mathrm{E}\left[\widetilde{FCF}_1^u\right]}{1+k^{E,u}} + \frac{\mathrm{E}\left[\widetilde{FCF}_2^u\right]}{(1+k^{E,u})^2} + \frac{\mathrm{E}\left[\widetilde{FCF}_3^u\right]}{(1+k^{E,u})^3} \\ &= \frac{100}{1.2} + \frac{110}{1.2^2} + \frac{121}{1.2^3} \approx 229.75\,. \end{aligned}$$

Although the use of this calculation is perhaps not recognizable yet here, we want to determine the market value of the unlevered firm for time $t = 1$ as well. This is not clear, because we cannot yet know today, if the outcome at time $t = 1$ will result in the condition up or down. Depending upon the condition, we are discounting different cash flows. In the condition of up, we get[13]

$$\begin{aligned} \widetilde{V}_1^u(u) &= \frac{\mathrm{E}\left[\widetilde{FCF}_2^u(\omega|u)\right]}{1+k^{E,u}} + \frac{\mathrm{E}\left[\widetilde{FCF}_3^u(\omega|u)\right]}{(1+k^{E,u})^2} \\ &= \frac{121}{1.2} + \frac{133.1}{1.2^2} \approx 193.26\,, \end{aligned}$$

[13] $\widetilde{FCF}_2^u(\omega|u)$ (or $\widetilde{FCF}_2^u(\omega|d)$) denotes the cash flow at time $t = 2$ given that the first movement was up (or down).

while for the condition of down

$$\widetilde{V}_1^u(d) = \frac{\mathrm{E}\left[\widetilde{FCF}_2^u(\omega|d)\right]}{1+k^{E,u}} + \frac{\mathrm{E}\left[\widetilde{FCF}_3^u(\omega|d)\right]}{(1+k^{E,u})^2}$$

$$= \frac{99}{1.2} + \frac{108.9}{1.2^2} \approx 158.13$$

is what we get. With that we get altogether

$$\widetilde{V}_1^u \approx \begin{cases} 193.26, & \text{if the development in } t = 1 \text{ is up,} \\ 158.13, & \text{if the development in } t = 1 \text{ is down.} \end{cases}$$

Using the same technique the value of the unlevered firm at $t = 2$ is given by

$$\widetilde{V}_2^u \approx \begin{cases} 121.00, & \text{if the development is up–up,} \\ 100.83, & \text{if the development is up–down or down–up,} \\ 80.67, & \text{if the development is down–down.} \end{cases}$$

An additional result, which, however, is not required for the valuation of the unlevered firm but which will be used subsequently, is that the risk-neutral probability Q can be worked out. To this end we suppose a riskless interest rate of r_f =10% and consider a particular time, for example, $t = 3$. Due to Theorem 3.3, we have

$$\frac{\mathrm{E}_Q\left[\widetilde{FCF}_3^u|\mathcal{F}_2\right]}{1+r_f} = \frac{\mathrm{E}\left[\widetilde{FCF}_3^u|\mathcal{F}_2\right]}{1+k^{E,u}} .$$

Assume that state ω occurred at time $t = 2$. The last equation translates to

$$\frac{Q_3(u|\omega)\,\widetilde{FCF}_3^u(u|\omega) + Q_3(d|\omega)\,\widetilde{FCF}_3^u(d|\omega)}{1+r_f} =$$

$$= \frac{P_3(u|\omega)\,\widetilde{FCF}_3^u(u|\omega) + P_3(d|\omega)\,\widetilde{FCF}_3^u(d|\omega)}{1+k^{E,u}} .$$

The conditional Q-probabilities add to one

$$Q_3(u|\omega) + Q_3(d|\omega) = 1 .$$

The conditional P-probabilities of an up- or a down-movement each come to 0.5. From that we get, for example, at $\omega = dd$

$$Q_3(u|dd) \approx 0.4167, \qquad Q_3(d|dd) \approx 0.5833 .$$

Fig. 3.1 Conditional probabilities Q in the finite example

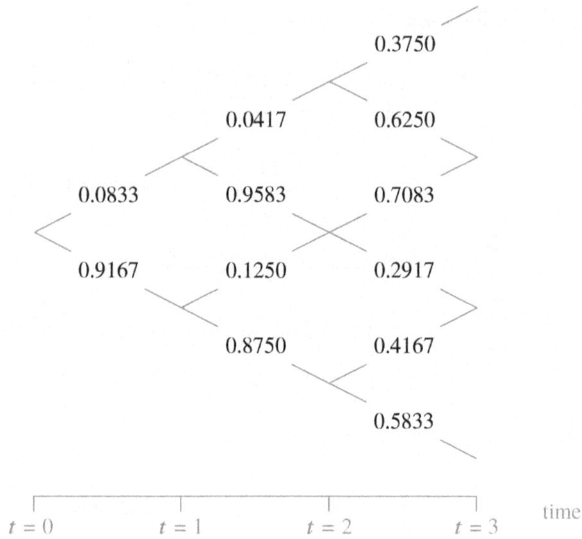

Using this idea at any time t and any available state ω we can finally determine all conditional probabilities. We have summarized our results in Fig. 3.1.

The Infinite Case Let the unlevered cost of capital be $k^{E,u} = 20\%$. Then the value of the unlevered firm is using rule 4 (remember $g = 0$)

$$\begin{aligned} V_0^u &= \sum_{t=1}^{\infty} \frac{\mathrm{E}\left[\widetilde{FCF}_t^u | \mathcal{F}_0\right]}{(1+k^{E,u})^t} \\ &= \sum_{t=1}^{\infty} \frac{\mathrm{E}\left[\widetilde{FCF}_1^u\right]}{(1+k^{E,u})^t} \\ &= \frac{\mathrm{E}\left[\widetilde{FCF}_1^u\right]}{k^{E,u}} \\ &= \frac{100}{0.2} = 500\,. \end{aligned}$$

As in the finite example we can evaluate the conditional up- and down-probabilities. To this end we assume that $r_f = 10\%$. Due to Theorem 3.3, we have at any time t

$$\frac{\mathrm{E}_Q\left[\widetilde{FCF}_{t+1}^u | \mathcal{F}_t\right]}{1+r_f} = \frac{\mathrm{E}\left[\widetilde{FCF}_{t+1}^u | \mathcal{F}_t\right]}{1+k^{E,u}}\,.$$

This is equivalent to

$$\frac{Q_{t+1}(u|\omega)\,\widetilde{FCF}^u_{t+1}(u|\omega) + Q_{t+1}(d|\omega)\,\widetilde{FCF}^u_{t+1}(d|\omega)}{1+r_f} = \\ = \frac{P_{t+1}(u|\omega)\,\widetilde{FCF}^u_{t+1}(u|\omega) + P_{t+1}(d|\omega)\,\widetilde{FCF}^u_{t+1}(d|\omega)}{1+k^{E,u}}$$

or

$$\frac{Q_{t+1}(u|\omega)\,u + Q_{t+1}(d|\omega)\,d}{1+r_f}\,\widetilde{FCF}^u_t(\omega) = \\ = \frac{P_{t+1}(u|\omega)\,u + P_{t+1}(d|\omega)\,d}{1+k^{E,u}}\,\widetilde{FCF}^u_t(\omega)\;.$$

The cash flow $\widetilde{FCF}^u_t(\omega)$ cancels. Furthermore the growth rate of the cash flows is zero ($g = 0$) and we arrive at

$$Q_{t+1}(u|\omega)\,u + Q_{t+1}(d|\omega)\,d = \frac{1+r_f}{1+k^{E,u}}\;.$$

The conditional Q-probabilities add to one

$$Q_{t+1}(u|\omega) + Q_{t+1}(d|\omega) = 1\;.$$

From that we get for the infinite example

$$Q_{t+1}(u|\omega) = \frac{\frac{1+r_f}{1+k^{E,u}} - d}{u-d}, \qquad Q_{t+1}(d|\omega) = \frac{u - \frac{1+r_f}{1+k^{E,u}}}{u-d}$$

regardless of t and ω.

This is an interesting result. The factors u and d cannot be chosen arbitrarily if the cost of capital are to be constant. Furthermore we can see that

$$d < \frac{1+r_f}{1+k^{E,u}} < u$$

must hold in order to ensure positive Q-probabilities. Any increase of the cost of capital enforces a decrease of the corresponding d.

3.1.4 Problems

1. The next two problems shall clarify the differences between additive and multiplicative increments. The error terms ε may be iid with values of 0.5 or −0.5, respectively, with 50% probability. In this case there is no growth, i.e., $g = 0$.
   (a) Consider additive increments. Assume that the cash flows follow the process
   $$\widetilde{FCF}_t^u = 1 + \varepsilon_1 + \varepsilon_2 + \ldots + \varepsilon_t .$$
   Show that under these conditions the cash flows form a binomial tree.
   (b) Now, look at multiplicative increments. Consider cash flows that follow the process
   $$\widetilde{FCF}_t^u = (1 + \varepsilon_1)(1 + \varepsilon_2) \cdots (1 + \varepsilon_t) .$$
   Show that the logarithmized cash flows are binomially distributed.
2. Let error terms ε be iid.
   (a) Consider additive increments that are normally distributed with expectation 0 and variance 1. The cash flows may follow the process
   $$\widetilde{FCF}_t^u = 1 + \varepsilon_1 + \varepsilon_2 + \ldots + \varepsilon_t .$$
   Show that $\widetilde{FCF}_t^u$ must be normally distributed with expectation 1 and variance t.
   (b) Switch to multiplicative increments that are lognormally distributed with expectation 0 and variance 1. The cash flows follow the process
   $$\widetilde{FCF}_t^u = (1 + \varepsilon_1)(1 + \varepsilon_2) \cdots (1 + \varepsilon_t) .$$
   Are the cash flows now lognormally distributed with expectation 1 and variance t?
3. Assume that cash flows follow a process as in (3.1). Show that
   $$0 = \mathrm{E}\left[\varepsilon_{t+1} | \mathcal{F}_t\right]$$
   is sufficient for the cash flows to be weak auto-regressive. Show furthermore that the noise terms are uncorrelated, i.e., for $s > t$
   $$\mathrm{Cov}\left[\varepsilon_s, \varepsilon_t\right] = 0 .$$
4. Consider the binomial tree from Fig. 3.2 (additive increments). Up- and down-movements have the same probability, notice that we not necessarily require $\widetilde{FCF}_2^u(ud) = \widetilde{FCF}_2^u(du)$.

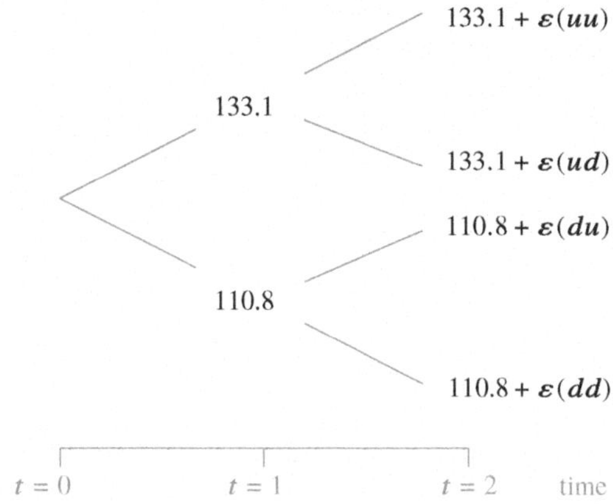

Fig. 3.2 Independent and uncorrelated increments in Problem 4

(a) Determine all possible distributions of the noise terms ε at time $t = 2$ such that

$$\mathrm{E}\left[\varepsilon_2|\mathcal{F}_1\right] = \mathrm{E}\left[\varepsilon_2\right] = 0$$

holds (uncorrelated additive increments).

(b) Determine all possible distributions of the noise terms ε at time $t = 2$ such that furthermore

$$\mathrm{E}\left[f(\varepsilon_2)|\mathcal{F}_1\right] = \mathrm{E}\left[f(\varepsilon_2)\right]$$

holds for any function $f(x)$ (independent additive increments).

5. Consider the binomial tree from Fig. 3.3. Up- and down-movements have the same probability, again we do not require $\widetilde{FCF}_2^u(ud) = \widetilde{FCF}_2^u(du)$. In this example the noise terms are multiplicative instead of additive.
   (a) Determine all possible distributions of the noise terms ε at time $t = 2$ such that

   $$\mathrm{E}\left[\varepsilon_2|\mathcal{F}_1\right] = \mathrm{E}\left[\varepsilon_2\right] = 0$$

   holds (uncorrelated multiplicative increments).
   (b) Determine all possible distributions of the noise terms ε at time $t = 2$ such that furthermore

   $$\mathrm{E}\left[f(\varepsilon_2)|\mathcal{F}_1\right] = \mathrm{E}\left[f(\varepsilon_2)\right]$$

   holds for any function $f(x)$ (independent multiplicative increments).

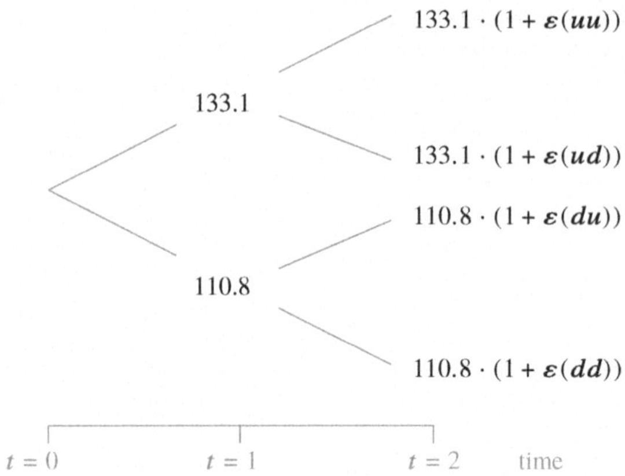

Fig. 3.3 Independent and uncorrelated increments in Problem 4

6. Let the dividend ratio at time t be defined as

$$\mathrm{div}_t := \frac{\mathrm{E}\left[\widetilde{FCF}^u_{t+1}|\mathcal{F}_t\right]}{\widetilde{V}^u_t}.$$

Show that it is deterministic for weak auto-regressive cash flows and determine it given the growth rate g_t and the dividend-price ratio d^u_t. Do the same for the capital gains ratio

$$\mathrm{gain}_t := \frac{\mathrm{E}\left[\widetilde{V}^u_{t+1} - \widetilde{V}^u_t|\mathcal{F}_t\right]}{\widetilde{V}^u_t}.$$

7. Assume that the cost of capital $k^{E,u}$ are deterministic and constant. The firm is infinitely living ($T \to \infty$). Assume that the cash flows of the unlevered firm are weak auto-regressive as in Assumption 3.1 for deterministic and constant g with $-1 < g < k^{E,u}$.
   (a) Find a simple formula for the value of the firm $\widetilde{V}^u_t$ analog to Theorem 3.1. Evaluate the capital gains and the dividend ratio for that case.
   (b) What happens to the firm value if $g \geq k^{E,u}$?
   (c) Show that the free cash flows are furthermore weak auto-regressive under Q as well, i.e.,

$$\mathrm{E}_Q\left[\widetilde{FCF}^u_{t+1}\right] = \left(1 + g^Q_t\right)\widetilde{FCF}^u_t.$$

   and determine g^Q_t.

8. A straightforward extension of weak auto-regressive cash flows would be that for every t

$$\mathrm{E}\left[\widetilde{FCF}^u_{t+1}|\mathcal{F}_t\right] = \widetilde{FCF}^u_t + X_t,$$

where X_t is a random variable satisfying

$$\mathrm{E}\left[X_t|\mathcal{F}_{t-1}\right] = \mathrm{E}_Q\left[X_t|\mathcal{F}_{t-1}\right] = 0$$

and furthermore X_t is uncorrelated to $\widetilde{FCF}^u_t$. Hence, this random variable is white noise and has no price at $t-1$. Several problems will be devoted to this special case.

(a) Assume that the firm will live forever ($T \to \infty$). Verify that the value of the company having constant cost of capital satisfies

$$\widetilde{V}^u_t = \frac{\widetilde{FCF}^u_t}{k^{E,u}} + \frac{X_t}{k^{E,u}},$$

and show that the variance of the firm value $\widetilde{V}^u_t$ is strictly greater than the variance of the corresponding cash flow $\widetilde{FCF}^u_t$ if $k^{E,u} < 100\%$.

(b) Verify that

$$\mathrm{E}\left[\widetilde{V}^u_{t+1}|\mathcal{F}_t\right] = \widetilde{V}^u_t$$

and hence the expected capital gains rate is zero.

(c) In this particular case the cost of capital may be used as discount rates (Theorem 3.3). Verify this by showing that

$$\frac{\mathrm{E}\left[\widetilde{FCF}^u_{t+1}|\mathcal{F}_t\right]}{1+k^{E,u}} = \frac{\mathrm{E}_Q\left[\widetilde{FCF}^u_{t+1}|\mathcal{F}_t\right]}{1+r_f}$$

and

$$\frac{\mathrm{E}\left[\widetilde{FCF}^u_{t+2}|\mathcal{F}_t\right]}{(1+k^{E,u})^2} = \frac{\mathrm{E}_Q\left[\widetilde{FCF}^u_{t+2}|\mathcal{F}_t\right]}{(1+r_f)^2}.$$

9. Another straightforward extension of weak auto-regressive cash flows would be to assume

$$\mathrm{E}\left[\widetilde{FCF}^u_{t+1}|\mathcal{F}_t\right] = \widetilde{FCF}^u_t + C$$

for constant $C \neq 0$ (see, for example, Feltham and Ohlson (1995) or Barberis et al. (1998), although they consider a different approach). Several problems will be devoted to this special case.

(a) Prove that the infinitely living unlevered firm having constant cost of capital satisfies

$$\widetilde{V}_t^u = \frac{\widetilde{FCF}_t^u}{k^{E,u}} + \frac{1+k^{E,u}}{(k^{E,u})^2}\,C\,.$$

Hint: You might want to use

$$\sum_{s=1}^{\infty} \frac{s}{(1+x)^s} = \frac{1+x}{x^2} \qquad \text{if } x > 0\,.$$

(b) Show that the expected capital gains rate of the unlevered firm is not zero.

(c) Show that

$$\mathrm{E}_Q\left[\widetilde{FCF}_{t+1}^u|\mathcal{F}_t\right] = \frac{1+r_f}{1+k^{E,u}}\,\widetilde{FCF}_t^u + \frac{r_f}{k^{E,u}}\,C$$

for the expectation of the cash flow under Q. Does Theorem 3.3 still hold?

10. The Definition 3.2 of a discount rate is cumbersome since it always refers to the time the cash flow is paid and the time the cash flow is valued as well. The aim of this problem is to show that even in simple cases if $\kappa_t^{r\to s}$ shall be independent from r and s, this can lead to a contradiction.

Consider cash flows that are independent from each other and identically distributed. In this case the conditional expectation

$$\mathrm{E}\left[\widetilde{FCF}_{t+1}^u|\mathcal{F}_t\right], \quad \mathrm{E}_Q\left[\widetilde{FCF}_{t+1}^u|\mathcal{F}_t\right], \ldots$$

will always be a real number.[14] Furthermore, the discount rate $\kappa_t^{r\to s}$ shall depend neither on r nor on s

$$\kappa_t^{r\to s} = \kappa_t\,.$$

(a) Show that the discount rates are equal to $r_f = \kappa_t$.

(b) Show that they cannot be equal if the expectations do not coincide, i.e.,

$$\mathrm{E}\left[\widetilde{FCF}_{t+1}^u|\mathcal{F}_t\right] \neq \mathrm{E}_Q\left[\widetilde{FCF}_{t+1}^u|\mathcal{F}_t\right].$$

[14] We do not go into detail here. You are asked to use our recommended literature if you want more explanation on this assertion on independent random variables.

3.2 Basics About Levered Firms

We now bring to a close the debate of unlevered firms and turn towards the truer-to-reality case of the levered firm. To do so we first of all need a clear separation between equity and debt.[15] In addition, we will work out in which the taxation of levered firms is different from the unlevered firm. These differences in taxation influence the value of the firm. And the degree of influence on value is dependent upon the type of financing policy the managers of the firm to be valued are operating under. In connection to the fundamental representation of this relation, we will analyze how numerous conceivable forms of financing policy effect value of firms and derive each appropriate valuation equation.

3.2.1 Equity and Debt

To come quickly to a needed result, we suppose that the firm to be valued is a corporation, where financiers can be divided into two groups. The financiers come up with capital, which the managers use to employ on risky investments. In return, the financiers get securities which we term debt or equity, as the case may be. Although we presume our choice of words is already sufficiently clear, we do, however, want to get down an important characteristic of the securities. We assume that equity and debt are traded on capital markets, that is, they can be bought and sold at any time. The securities thus have market prices, and we designate the market value of the equity at time t with $\widetilde{E}_t$, and the market value of the debt with $\widetilde{D}_t$. The tilde over the symbol makes it clear that a random variable is being dealt with. If we want to express that there are no random variables, we write D_t. Interest paid at time $t+1$ is $\widetilde{I}_{t+1}$.

The firm's generated net profit in total is uncertain and is distributed among the financiers so that debt financiers (creditors, debt holders) are taken care of first, while the equity financiers (owners, shareholders) have to make do with what possibly remains. Further financiers are not to be considered. The distribution rule is completely straightforward.

Notation In the equations that we have used until now, we were always dealing with free cash flows and values of firms. In the previous chapter, when unlevered firms were dealt with we added the index u to the symbols which we needed. Now we will use the index l, since levered firms are being dealt with. We thus write $\widetilde{FCF}^l_t$. For the equity cost of capital of the levered firms we will use the symbol $\widetilde{k}^{E,l}_t$.

We will have to introduce a whole range of other symbols. It will always be recognized when these symbols are used in the context of an unlevered firm by

[15] It is well known that a straightforward separation can bring considerable difficulties with it, if you want to undertake this within the context of all the financing contracts which occur in reality.

index u. If, on the other hand, a levered firm is being dealt with, we will make that clear with the index l.

The Firm'S Market Value, Debt-Equity Ratio, and Leverage Ratio The goal of our theory is the establishment of the market value of a firm. For the market value of the levered firm at time t, we use the symbol $\widetilde{V}_t^l$. The market value of the firm is equal to the sum of the equity's market value and the debt's market value,

$$\widetilde{V}_t^l := \widetilde{E}_t + \widetilde{D}_t .$$

Debt equity ratios and leverage ratios will play a big role in our further considerations. The debt ratio measures the proportion of debt to the market value of the firm,

$$\widetilde{l}_t := \frac{\widetilde{D}_t}{\widetilde{V}_t^l} , \tag{3.5}$$

while the leverage ratio (debt-equity ratio) is defined in the form

$$\widetilde{L}_t := \frac{\widetilde{D}_t}{\widetilde{E}_t} . \tag{3.6}$$

Even though we will use the debt ratios in later sections, we can also apply the leverage ratio. Since both quantities can easily be converted into each other this is not a limitation,

$$\widetilde{L}_t = \frac{\widetilde{l}_t}{1 - \widetilde{l}_t}$$

is valid. With these symbols we stress that all quantities are measured in market values.

Book Values In a few sections of this chapter the book value of equity and debt will be dealt with. These are those values, with which the owners' or creditors' claims are to be found in the balance books of the firm to be valued. As symbols for debt and equity for book values, we use $\underline{\widetilde{D}}_t$ and $\underline{\widetilde{E}}_t$, respectively. The sums of equity and debt at time t are written in the form

$$\underline{\widetilde{V}}_t^l := \underline{\widetilde{E}}_t + \underline{\widetilde{D}}_t .$$

We will notate

$$\underline{\widetilde{l}}_t := \frac{\underline{\widetilde{D}}_t}{\underline{\widetilde{V}}_t^l} \tag{3.7}$$

for the debt ratio measured in book values, and

$$\underline{\widetilde{L}}_t := \frac{\underline{\widetilde{D}}_t}{\underline{\widetilde{E}}_t}$$

for the correspondingly measured leverage ratio. Again, debt ratio and leverage ratio can easily be converted into each other.

3.2.2 Earnings and Taxes

In the foundational chapter of this book, we gave a preliminary introduction of gross cash flows and free cash flows. The terms developed there were perfectly adequate to come up with valuation equations for firms where the financing policy was not set in detail (Chap. 2) or which were totally financed with equity (Sect. 3.1). Now we are supposed to be dealing with levered firms, which forces us to bring more structure to the terms.

Tax Equation In order to understand the relevant relationships, we again present the ascertaining of free cash flows from Fig. 2.1, but now with a more detailed notation that will be used in this chapter, see Fig. 3.4. Interest on debt is of course only accrued by levered firms. If we add it to the earnings before taxes (EBT), then we get the earnings before interest and taxes (EBIT). If we add accruals, we arrive at the gross cash flow before taxes, also called EBITDA. If we finally deduct the investment expenses and deduct taxes as well, then we get the free cash flow. This cash flow is fully distributed to the owners of the company.

As was announced earlier, we are limiting ourselves in this chapter to a business tax and leave out the income tax on the shareholder's level of the company. The tax base of the profit taxes is the earnings before taxes (EBT)

$$\widetilde{Tax} = \tau \cdot \widetilde{EBT}. \tag{3.8}$$

Fig. 3.4 From earnings before taxes (EBT) to free cash flow (FCF)

	Earnings before taxes	$\widetilde{EBT}$
+	Interest	I
=	Earnings before interest and taxes	$\widetilde{EBIT}$
+	Accruals	$\widetilde{Accr}$
=	Gross cash flow before taxes	$\widetilde{GCF}$
−	Corporate income taxes	$\widetilde{Tax}$
−	Investment expenses	$\widetilde{Inv}$
=	Free cash flow	$\widetilde{FCF}^l$

The tax equations should be valid independent of the sign of the tax base. If the tax base is positive, the firm has to pay taxes; if it is, on the other hand, negative, then the firm gets a return in the amount of the tax due. We will not give more realistic models of loss set-off or loss carryback rules than that.

In order to describe the difference between the levered and the unlevered firm we will assume that their investment policies coincide.

Assumption 3.2 (Identical Gross Cash Flows) *The gross cash flows before taxes as well as the accruals and investment expenses of the unlevered firm do not differ from those of the levered firm.*

Hence, the EBIT must be just as large for the firm financed by equity as it is for the firm financed by debt. In Fig. 3.4 the third and the fourth lines are thus identical for the levered and unlevered firms, while taxes and free cash flows will show different values. The taxes of the levered firm are thus smaller by the product of the tax rate and interest on debt than the taxes of the firm financed solely by equity

$$\widetilde{Tax}_t^u - \widetilde{Tax}_t^l = \tau\,\widetilde{I}_t .$$

Financing by debt is thus favored in this model.

By Assumption 3.2 the free cash flows before taxes of the levered and unlevered firms are identical, only the tax payments are different,

$$\widetilde{FCF}_t^l = \widetilde{FCF}_t^u + \tau\,\widetilde{I}_t . \tag{3.9}$$

The firm financed by equity has lower free cash flows than the firm financed by debt, because interest may be deducted from the tax base. The following concerns the question as to the value of these tax advantages. A—if not the—central problem of the DCF theory is the establishment of the value of the tax advantages governed by credit conditions.

3.2.3 Financing Policies

No Default We are supposing at first that credit is not threatened by default and thus follow a widely held tradition within DCF literature,

$$\widetilde{I}_t = r_f\,\widetilde{D}_{t-1} . \tag{3.10}$$

This notion flagrantly contradicts the experience of banks with their borrowers. In reality financiers' claims are obviously under notable threat of default. In a later subsection we will show how default can be handled in our theory.

Components of Tax Advantages Now we make a first attempt at turning to the valuation of tax advantages of the firm financed by debt. The tax advantages are, as we just determined, attributed to the fact that interest on debt may be deducted in the firm's tax base. This comes to—in terms of the levered firm—a tax savings (also called tax shield) in the amount of

$$\tau r_f \widetilde{D}_{t-1} .$$

Whoever is involved professionally with valuation of firms as certified public accountant, investment banker or as business consultant, knows only too well that in practical terms both the tax rate and the interest rate are uncertain. Looking at the assumptions, we have, however, made sure that only the amounts of debt $\widetilde{D}_{t-1}$ can be uncertain. The interest rate of debt r_f as well as the tax rate τ are certain according to the requirements.

Value of Tax Advantages To value tax advantages appropriately, we need further information about the uncertainty to which they are exposed. It is true, we know—in accordance with the assumption—how high the tax rate and the interest rate will be. But we cannot, however, know without further assumptions regarding the financing policy at time $t = 0$, how high the debt of the firm to be valued will be at time $t > 0$.

We have no other options than to come to further assumptions regarding information about the firm's future debt policy. This is the only way in which we can come up with what amounts of debt $\widetilde{D}_{t-1}$ will be established in times $t > 0$, with what risk these amounts bear and how the resulting tax advantages are to be accordingly valued. Without any information of the levered firm the tax advantages cannot be properly valued.

The practically engaged evaluator may perplexedly note here that the valuation of the firm is bound to the assumptions pertinent to it. In so doing the firm value takes on an air of doing what one pleases of it, or—to put it more drastically—an element of manipulation. To that we must answer, every valuation is based on expectation about the future. Whoever does not forecast the turnover numbers, whoever does not know what the cost of materials will be, cannot value a firm. All of these and further assumptions come off as somewhat arbitrary. That also applies for the financing policy of the evaluator.

Different Financing Policies Now let us turn to different possible financing policies. We find that within this area of DCF literature, two concepts are regularly brought into play. Autonomous financing supposes that the amounts of debt are already fixed at the time of valuation. Financing based on value supposes, in contrast, that the debt ratios are fixed in the present.

We too will examine both financing policies. When debt ratios measured in market values are being dealt with, we will, however, to be more precise refer to it in the following as financing policy based on market values. Moreover, we will bring four further financing policies into the discussion. We will term these policy based on cash flows, policy based on dividends, policy based on book values and on cash flow-debt ratio. These six policies can be characterized in brief by the following:

1. With *autonomous financing methods*, the future amount of debt is deterministic.
2. With the *financing based on market values*, the evaluator sets the future debt ratios based on market values.
3. With the *financing based on book values*, the future debt ratios are not fixed to market values, but rather to book values.
4. With the *financing based on cash flows* the amount of debt is based on the firm's cash flows.
5. With the *financing based on dividends* the firm's amount of debt is managed so that a previously determined dividend can be distributed.
6. With the *financing based on dynamical leverage ratio* the evaluator sets the future cash flow-debt ratios.

We cannot and do not want to answer the question here as to which of these financing policies is particularly close to reality. Instead, we see our task as to compile all possibly conceivable financing policies, and to show how to go about valuing when these policies are met. The direction the specific firm goes in depends upon the credit agreements with the financiers as well as the goals and ideas of the managers.

Further, we will not discuss the question, which of the mentioned financing policies maximize the value of the levered company. Later on it will become apparent that with an extended leverage the value of the company increases. Hence, the owners of the company should select a leverage as high as possible if they act rationally. However, here the leverage policy will be considered as a term which is given exogenously. The owners will pursue a prespecified financing policy without racking one's brains if this policy will be the best option.

Assumption 3.3 (Given Debt Policy) *The debt policy of the firm (although probably uncertain) is already prescribed.*

To determine the values of firms under the different financing policies, we require an important equation. The statements of the fundamental theorem of asset pricing are valid for the levered as well as the unlevered firm,[16] particularly the valuation statements coming out of Theorem 2.2. We thus know that the value of the unlevered firm can be established with equation

$$\widetilde{V}_t^u = \frac{\mathrm{E}_Q\left[\widetilde{FCF}_{t+1}^u|\mathcal{F}_t\right]}{1+r_f} + \ldots + \frac{\mathrm{E}_Q\left[\widetilde{FCF}_T^u|\mathcal{F}_t\right]}{\left(1+r_f\right)^{T-t}} .$$

[16]See Sect. 2.3.4.

The validity of the fundamental theorem does not depend upon how the firm is financed. The value of the levered firm is thus given through the relation

$$\widetilde{V}_t^l = \frac{\mathrm{E}_Q\left[\widetilde{FCF}_{t+1}^l|\mathcal{F}_t\right]}{1+r_f} + \ldots + \frac{\mathrm{E}_Q\left[\widetilde{FCF}_T^l|\mathcal{F}_t\right]}{\left(1+r_f\right)^{T-t}}.$$

Using (3.9) we can immediately read from both valuation equations that the market value of the levered firm is different from the market value of the unlevered firm only in terms of the value of the tax advantages

$$\widetilde{V}_t^l = \widetilde{V}_t^u + \frac{\mathrm{E}_Q\left[\tau \widetilde{I}_{t+1}|\mathcal{F}_t\right]}{1+r_f} + \ldots + \frac{\mathrm{E}_Q\left[\tau \widetilde{I}_T|\mathcal{F}_t\right]}{\left(1+r_f\right)^{T-t}}.$$

With (3.10) and rule 2 (linearity) this yields

$$\widetilde{V}_t^l = \widetilde{V}_t^u + \frac{\tau r_f \,\mathrm{E}_Q\left[\widetilde{D}_t|\mathcal{F}_t\right]}{1+r_f} + \ldots + \frac{\tau r_f \,\mathrm{E}_Q\left[\widetilde{D}_{T-1}|\mathcal{F}_t\right]}{\left(1+r_f\right)^{T-t}}. \tag{3.11}$$

We will be able to use this equation for all financing policies. Fernández (2005) gives the same result in the following Presentation:[17]

$$\widetilde{V}_t^l = \widetilde{V}_t^u + \tau \widetilde{D}_t + \frac{\tau \,\mathrm{E}_Q\left[\widetilde{D}_{t+1} - \widetilde{D}_t|\mathcal{F}_t\right]}{1+r_f} + \ldots + \frac{\tau \,\mathrm{E}_Q\left[\widetilde{D}_T - \widetilde{D}_{T-1}|\mathcal{F}_t\right]}{(1+r_f)^{T-t}}. \tag{3.12}$$

3.2.4 Debt and Transversality (Again)

In the following we will focus on levered companies that accept loans which run forever. Anyone familiar with basic financial mathematics knows that the present value of a riskless loan equals the sum of discounted cash flows if the credit is temporary. So if credit is granted today in the amount of $\widetilde{D}_0$ and the borrower in later times pays both interest of $r_f \widetilde{D}_t$ and (possibly negative) redemptions of $\widetilde{D}_t - \widetilde{D}_{t+1}$, then

$$\widetilde{D}_0 = \sum_{t=0}^{T} \frac{(1+r_f)\widetilde{D}_t - \widetilde{D}_{t+1}}{(1+r_f)^t}$$

must hold if $\widetilde{D}_T = 0$ is assumed.

[17] See also Problem 4.

What will happen for $T \to \infty$? One can easily imagine that the loan is not repaid in full. But what does that mean for the above equation? Under what conditions can we state

$$\widetilde{D}_0 = \lim_{T\to\infty} \sum_{t=0}^{T} \frac{(1+r_f)\widetilde{D}_t - \widetilde{D}_{t+1}}{(1+r_f)^t}, \tag{3.13}$$

and under what conditions is this not permissible? Transversality, again, will give the answer. For this reason, we reassume this condition. However, we will concentrate on uncertainty from the beginning. It can immediately be seen that this is an assumption with regard to the infinite finance policy.

Assumption 3.4 (Debt Policy Satisfies Transversality) *The debt policy of the firm satisfies the transversality condition,*

$$\forall t \qquad \lim_{T\to\infty} \frac{\mathrm{E}_Q[\widetilde{D}_T|\mathcal{F}_t]}{(1+r_f)^{T-t}} = 0.$$

To fully understand this assumption, let us look at two (extreme in our eyes) examples of infinite financing policies. In the first case transversality will be violated, in the second one it will be fulfilled. Our readers must decide, whether the examples are intuitively clear.

First, assume that the payment obligations due to interest liabilities will be completely credit-financed. This boils down to the relation

$$\widetilde{D}_{t+1} = (1+r_f)\widetilde{D}_t,$$

and it is immediately clear that the transversality condition cannot be fulfilled: The creditor increases his loan from year to year and never gets a refund. Equation (3.13) can therefore never be satisfied for a positive $\widetilde{D}_0$. In finite time the credit might grow enormously, but would eventually be repaid.

The next example shows that Eq. (3.13) can be sustained with a financing policy that is only slightly different from the previous one. To this end, let us assume that an investor finances only half of the interest obligations by a credit. Again, the loan is increasing year by year. And it is also true that in finite time there is never a refunding. However, the new policy is now described by

$$\widetilde{D}_{t+1} = \left(1 + \frac{r_f}{2}\right)\widetilde{D}_t.$$

Anyone who believes that Eq. (3.13) is not fulfilled under this policy is wrong. This follows directly from

$$\begin{aligned}\lim_{T\to\infty}\frac{\mathrm{E}_Q[\widetilde{D}_T|\mathcal{F}_t]}{(1+r_f)^{T-t}} &= \lim_{T\to\infty}\frac{\left(1+\frac{r_f}{2}\right)^T}{(1+r_f)^{T-t}}\widetilde{D}_0\\ &= \lim_{T\to\infty}(1+r_f)^t\widetilde{D}_0\underbrace{\left(\frac{1+\frac{r_f}{2}}{1+r_f}\right)}_{<1}^T = 0.\end{aligned}$$

The difference between the two financing policies is quickly detected. For Eq. (3.13) to be satisfied, the lender must receive any payments from the debtor at any time. The compounding effect then ensures complete refunding of the loan. However, if the redemption payments go back to zero (as in the first example), the transversality condition is inevitably violated.

The issue raised here is only important for credit agreements with an infinite duration. Therefore, we will treat $T \to \infty$ only exceptionally, and will regularly restrict ourselves to contracts with finite duration.

3.2.5 Default

Authors who are involved in credit risks take care to thoroughly discuss default probabilities. Surprisingly, it is the same facts of the case that are regularly disregarded in the DCF literature. There is no doubt that it is necessary to pursue the question as to how a firm can be valued with the risk that it will not be able to meet all its credit obligations.

It will turn out that in the case of a levered firm default is becoming much more manifold.

There are legal stipulations that regulate under what conditions default for a levered company is given. We have already stressed that in most countries of the world there are several factors that can lead to bankruptcy. Lack of liquidity is such a factor everywhere. But there are also countries in which the managers are required to start bankruptcy proceedings when the firm's balance sheets read that the assets no longer cover the debts, or when the finance plans indicate the inability to pay in the near future.

Homogenous Expectations Up to now we have worked on the basis that debt and equity financiers are equally well informed. This condition is of particular importance with the threat of insolvency and can surely be seen critically. But there is no getting around conceding certain information about the firm to the debt financiers. No one loans out money without having beforehand checked up on the contract partner's business ideas, risks, and market chances in some detail. Yet asymmetric information as a rule is truer to reality than our condition of homogenous expectations. It, however, applies that whoever wants to deviate from this assumption, has to very precisely define the information which both sides either have or do not have access to.

Identical Cash Flows and Default Until now we have worked on the basis of some assumptions within the framework of our theory which should also remain valid in the case of default. We would in the following like to briefly discuss how we justify that.

We had thus continually assumed that gross cash flows from levered and unlevered firms are not different from each other. It should be stressed that until now levered firms not in danger of going into default have been dealt with. If we want to maintain the assumption, then it must be broadened to include the gross cash flows of the firm in danger of going into default and that not going into default being the same.

That is quite a far-reaching limitation. A firm can of course get into a situation due to financial difficulties which has consequences for its gross cash flows. Financial strains often cause suppliers as well as clients to reconsider continuing doing business with the firm affected. Some clients leave altogether or cancel long-term contracts; suppliers may deliver only on condition of prepayment. Managers who would remain faithful to the firm under more favorable circumstances look for other jobs, taking with them the important know-how required in such times and aggravating the crisis. All the financial consequences of a high leverage which we have pointed out here, are usually referred to in the literature as indirect costs of default. It can then be said that in our model we abstract the existence of such costs of default. But indirect costs of default are difficult to quantify. If you wanted to substitute with a more realistic premise and at the same time avoid having the new assumption remaining subject to change, then despite all difficulties, you would have to formulate a functional relation between gross cash flows and advanced leverage. A firm's gross cash flows have two components in a model of several periods: on the one hand their amount, and on the other their duration. Our assumption says that increasing leverage affects neither the amount nor the duration of the gross cash flows.

Let us now open up the question as to how great the amount is that the owners receive at time t. The starting point was the firm's identical gross cash flows before interest and tax $\widetilde{GCF}_t$. To arrive at the free cash flows from here, we have to deduct the firm's (internally financed) investments and taxes. It needs to be further clarified how these amounts differ from each other when dealing with, on the one hand, an unlevered firm and, on the other, a levered firm also in danger of going into default. Again, we only get further with the assumption that the investment and accruals of the firm in danger of going into default agrees with that of the firm not in danger of going into default. We can thus sum up our conditions in the following specification of Assumption 3.2.

Assumption 3.5 (Gross Cash Flows and Default) *The gross cash flows as well as the investment and accruals of the unlevered firm do not differ from those of the firm in danger of going into default.*

Bankruptcy Estate If the company does not file for bankruptcy, then the creditors' claims can be satisfied in full. Two parties are to be differentiated here, the state and the investor. The order in which the claims of the finance administration and the other creditors are satisfied does not matter as long as we are not dealing with going into default. The owners' claims will be settled last in any case. In the worst case the shareholders can end up with nothing. Since corporations do not have personal liability, we can disregard the owners having to make payments from their private pockets in very unfavorable situations.

As a rule the requisitioned property does not suffice in the case of bankruptcy to completely settle up with the state and the creditors. Thus it does matter which claims take priority. Is the state to be completely taken care of first? Or, are the other creditors to be paid off while the state has to stay? Answers are provided by the pertinent legal stipulations. We do not want to discuss that any further here, but solve the problem by introducing an appropriate assumption that is (more or less) satisfied in most industrial countries.

Assumption 3.6 (Prioritization of Debt) *The tax office's claims come before those of other creditors. The cash flows are always sufficient to at least pay off the tax debts in full.*

The tax office will therefore be given priority over the creditors when dealing with a firm in danger of going into default so that the tax claims can be satisfied in full. And the default is never so drastic in our concept that the state loses a share of its claims.

Notation The notation used so far is not sufficient for the deliberations to be put forth in the following. Let us again suppose that the firm took in a credit of $\widetilde{D}_t$ at time t. In the earlier section the variable $\widetilde{D}_t$ signified two different things, namely for one, the credit which the firm took in at time t, and, for the other, the amount, which apart from the interest it redeems at time $t + 1$.[18] In case of default, the amount, which the company amortizes at the time $t + 1$, will not coincide with the repayment sum to which it is legally obligated. $\widetilde{D}_t$ shall be the credit which has been raised at time t and $\widetilde{D}_{t+1}$ the corresponding amount a year later. Consequently, the difference between $\widetilde{D}_t$ and $\widetilde{D}_{t+1}$ accounts for the amount which the company needs to pay back to the creditor (or, if this amount is negative, has to be raised). In the following we will assume that the company pays back the amount $\widetilde{R}_{t+1}$ which can

[18] See Sect. 3.2.1.

be at the most as high as $\widetilde{D}_t - \widetilde{D}_{t+1}$, hence

$$\widetilde{R}_{t+1} \leq \widetilde{D}_t - \widetilde{D}_{t+1}.$$

If the repayment sum is smaller than the amount which the company owns its creditors, the term

$$\widetilde{D}_t - \widetilde{D}_{t+1} - \widetilde{R}_{t+1}$$

describes a remission of debts. We do not need a new symbol for the interest $\widetilde{I}_{t+1}$ resulting at time $t+1$.

Only looking at the relationship between the firm to be valued and its financiers in the case of default, it does not matter how the existing remainder of funds is distributed among the interest and principle repayment due. In terms of the tax office, however, it is different, since interest lowers the tax base, and the debt repayment, in contrast, does not.

We proceed on the basis that the tax office allows interest in the amount of $\widetilde{I}_{t+1}$ to be deducted from the tax base. On the other hand, the state in many countries insists that during bankruptcy the cancellation of debt be taxed in amount of $\widetilde{D}_t - \widetilde{D}_{t+1} - \widetilde{R}_{t+1}$. According to (3.8), the following applies for the taxes of the firm which is both levered and in danger of going into default at time t:

$$\widetilde{Tax}^l_{t+1} = \tau\left(\widetilde{GCF}_{t+1} - \widetilde{Accr}_{t+1} - \widetilde{I}_{t+1} + \widetilde{D}_t - \widetilde{D}_{t+1} - \widetilde{R}_{t+1}\right).$$

Since the unlevered firm's tax equation does not change and the gross cash flows as well as investments are identical, we now get

$$\begin{aligned}
\widetilde{FCF}^l_{t+1} &= \widetilde{GCF}_{t+1} - \widetilde{Inv}_{t+1} - \widetilde{Tax}^l_{t+1} \\
&= \widetilde{GCF}_{t+1} - \widetilde{Inv}_{t+1} - \widetilde{Tax}^u_{t+1} + \tau\left(\widetilde{I}_{t+1} - \widetilde{D}_t + \widetilde{D}_{t+1} + \widetilde{R}_{t+1}\right) \\
&= \widetilde{FCF}^u_{t+1} + \tau\left(\widetilde{I}_{t+1} - \widetilde{D}_t + \widetilde{D}_{t+1} + \widetilde{R}_{t+1}\right). \qquad (3.14)
\end{aligned}$$

The fundamental theorem of asset pricing now also applies to the levered firm in danger of going into default. We can thus establish the relation

$$\begin{aligned}
\widetilde{V}^l_t &= \sum_{s=t+1}^{T} \frac{\mathrm{E}_Q\left[\widetilde{FCF}^l_s|\mathcal{F}_t\right]}{(1+r_f)^{s-t}} \\
&= \widetilde{V}^u_t + \sum_{s=t+1}^{T} \frac{\tau\,\mathrm{E}_Q\left[\widetilde{I}_s - \widetilde{D}_{s-1} + \widetilde{D}_s + \widetilde{R}_s|\mathcal{F}_t\right]}{(1+r_f)^{s-t}}. \qquad (3.15)
\end{aligned}$$

Default Triggers Firstly, we want to examine whether a company that is over-indebted will be illiquid at a future point in time and, vice versa, whether a firm that becomes illiquid will have encountered over-indebtedness. We believe that the relationship between both triggers requires more attention than they are currently given in the literature.[19] Authors who address valuation problems seem to assume that it does not matter which insolvency trigger is used—a view we challenge although in Proposition 3.4 we have exactly shown that. While default has been intensively investigated in prior research, until now the relationship between these two triggers has not been subject to a detailed analysis. However, for investors and financiers (e.g., in context of insolvency risk forecast) it is important to understand, whether these triggers are substitutes to each other, or whether one trigger is stricter than the other in the sense that one default criterion is met earlier.

We analytically provide evidence that over-indebtedness always implies illiquidity although the converse is not true and that the relationship between both default triggers depends on the given financing policy. To this end, we must define what over-indebtedness and lack of liquidity shall be for levered firms. Whereas illiquidity focuses on cash flows, we will be using the term over-indebtedness if the assets of the firm are smaller in value than its debt. In the following, however, we consider only market values instead of, for example, book values in the case of over-indebtedness. The reason for our approach is obvious: by strictly using market values we are in a position to easily produce clear conceptual relationships and provide necessary and sufficient conditions for bankruptcies. That would be much more difficult, if not impossible, if we used book values or fair values. Hence, falling back on market values is in line with the simplification strategies that prevail in economics.

Definition 3.3 (Default) For a given financing policy, a levered firm will be *in danger of illiquidity at time t in state ω* if the cash flows in state $\omega \in \Omega$ do not suffice to fulfill the creditors' payment claims (interest and net redemption) at time t as contracted,

$$\widetilde{FCF}^l_t(\omega) - \big((1+r_f)\widetilde{D}_{t-1}(\omega) - \widetilde{D}_t(\omega)\big) < 0. \tag{3.16}$$

For a given financing policy $\overline{D}$, a levered firm will be *over-indebted at time t in state s* if the market value of debt exceeds the firm's market value,

$$\widetilde{V}^l_t(\omega) < \widetilde{D}_t(\omega). \tag{3.17}$$

Notice that both definitions refer to a future date t and the state ω from today's point of view. It can easily be seen that our definition covers also the unlevered firm.

[19]The following considerations are—in parts literally—taken from Kruschwitz et al. (2015).

Finally, we assess the consequences of bankruptcy. Consider a firm today with a given financing policy that is in danger of illiquidity at time t in state ω but not over-indebted. The management of the said firm will certainly be able to raise credit in order to ensure the continuance of the firm. If this new financing policy does not result in a lack of liquidity, the bankruptcy problem is solved. The situation could be interpreted as follows: the firm uses the new financing policy for refinancing. Illiquidity turns into a mere postponement of payments.

Yet what happens if the first financing policy in question leads to over-indebtedness at date t? Refinancing as in the previous paragraph is not possible since the "substance" of the firm, namely its expected future cash flows, does not suffice to satisfy the creditors' payment claims. Moreover, we assume that credit is only granted for a single period. Therefore, the creditors anticipate at date $t-1$ that the loan will not be repaid in full in t. Consequently, rational creditors will not agree to issue the necessary credit in time $t-1$ which again has an impact on the loan granted in $t-2$. As a result, we conclude that the creditors are able to detect later over-indebtedness already in $t=0$. Within our framework we thus conclude that over-indebted companies are unable to realize their initial financing strategy.

Valuation of Defaulting Firms The debt holders behave rationally. Therefore, the fundamental theorem of asset pricing is applicable for debt and we have for any time being if $\widetilde{R}_{s+1}$ is paid off in $s+1$

$$\widetilde{D}_s = \frac{\mathrm{E}_Q\left[\widetilde{I}_{s+1} + \widetilde{D}_{s+1} + \widetilde{R}_{s+1} | \mathcal{F}_s\right]}{1+r_f}. \tag{3.18}$$

Using rule 5 this gives us

$$r_f \widetilde{D}_s = \mathrm{E}_Q\left[\widetilde{I}_{s+1} + \widetilde{R}_{s+1} + \widetilde{D}_{s+1} - \widetilde{D}_s | \mathcal{F}_s\right]$$

and with rule 4 for all $s \geq t$ finally

$$r_f \,\mathrm{E}_Q\left[\widetilde{D}_s | \mathcal{F}_t\right] = \mathrm{E}_Q\left[\widetilde{I}_{s+1} - \widetilde{D}_s + \widetilde{D}_{s+1} + \widetilde{R}_{s+1} | \mathcal{F}_t\right]. \tag{3.19}$$

Entering in Eq. (3.15) results in

$$\widetilde{V}_t^l = \widetilde{V}_t^u + \sum_{s=t+1}^{T} \frac{\tau r_f \,\mathrm{E}_Q\left[\widetilde{D}_{s-1} | \mathcal{F}_t\right]}{\left(1+r_f\right)^{s-t}}.$$

This equation is not at all different from Eq. (3.11), through which we had precluded bankruptcy risks! That means that including the default risk has no impact whatsoever on the firm's value. If the financing policy concerns the credit amounts agreed upon, then we do not need to differentiate in the valuation equations between whether the bankruptcy risks are given or not. Just the possibility of default changes absolutely nothing in the valuation equations.

If this outcome is taken seriously, then it seems that even given the risk of bankruptcy, the value of firms can be successfully calculated with the DCF theory. It has of course to be examined if the conditions of the theory are still satisfied even when there are risks of default. And this is exactly where problems could come up: if the danger of going into default exists for the firm, it can happen that the creditors will not want to grant credit to the same extent they would if there was no risk of default. A financing policy which was agreed upon to the neglect of risks of default can no longer be maintained when considering these risks. But if the financing policies differ from each other with and without the inclusion of the risk of default, then the respective values of firms no longer correspond to each other either.

The message of this subsection can be summed up as follows: The problems of valuing firms when the risk of default exists do not lie in the failure of the DCF theory. On the contrary, this theory remains valid. The difficulties of taking the risks of default into consideration lie much more so in that the financing policies which are relevant for the firm must be formulated with more deliberation.

Over-Indebtedness Implies Danger of Illiquidity Another important implication of Eq. (3.19) concerns the relation of the two bankruptcy triggers.

Disregarding specific assumptions concerning the dynamics of the free cash flows, we can prove that over-indebtedness implies illiquidity. This result is immediately apparent. Just realize that debts represent the present value of cash outflows while assets represent the present value of cash inflows. Having said this, it must be that at some future point of time an outflow is greater than an inflow if debts exceed assets today.

This result is everything but trivial. To this end, consider an unlevered company whose market value contains information about its future cash flows. If we know that this market value is negative, this means that the owners of the company expect (at least in some states, not necessarily in all) that future cash flows are negative as well. That the same idea is true for levered firms is proven in the following theorem.

Theorem 3.5 (Over-Indebtedness Implies Danger of Illiquidity) *If a levered company is over-indebted at time t in some state, then there is a date $s \geq t$ and a state where the firm is in danger of illiquidity.*

Notice that illiquidity does not necessarily imply over-indebtedness.[20]

We prove the theorem by contradiction. To this end, we consider an over-indebted firm that will never be in danger of illiquidity. In this case the inequality

$$\widetilde{FCF}^l_s(\omega) - \left((1+r_f)\widetilde{D}_{s-1}(\omega) - \widetilde{D}_s(\omega)\right) \geq 0$$

[20]For details, we refer to Kruschwitz et al. (2015, p. 211f.).

applies for *all states* $\omega \in \Omega$ and times $s \geq t$. Multiplying the preceding inequality by the risk-neutral probabilities and summing up leads to

$$\mathrm{E}_Q\left[\widetilde{FCF}^l_s|\mathcal{F}_t\right] \geq \mathrm{E}_Q\left[(1+r_f)\widetilde{D}_{s-1} - \widetilde{D}_s|\mathcal{F}_t\right].$$

Dividing by $(1+r_f)^{s-t}$ and adding up over all t results in

$$\sum_{s=t+1}^{T} \frac{\mathrm{E}_Q\left[\widetilde{FCF}^l_s|\mathcal{F}_t\right]}{(1+r_f)^{s-t}} \geq \sum_{s=t+1}^{T} \frac{\mathrm{E}_Q\left[\left((1+r_f)\widetilde{D}_{s-1} - \widetilde{D}_s\right)|\mathcal{F}_t\right]}{(1+r_f)^{s-t}} \quad \text{and using (3.19)}$$

$$= \sum_{s=t+1}^{T} \frac{\mathrm{E}_Q\left[\widetilde{I}_s + \widetilde{R}_s|\mathcal{F}_t\right]}{(1+r_f)^{s-t}}.$$

Now, (3.18) implies that this sum is nothing more than $\widetilde{D}_t$ because if debt $\widetilde{D}_t$ is granted the debtor will get $\widetilde{I}_s + \widetilde{R}_s$ for all $s > t$ (see also Problem 1). Since the term on the left-hand side of the inequality is the firm value $\widetilde{V}^l_t$, we have a contradiction to over-indebtedness. This was to be shown. q.e.d.

Cost of Debt If debt were completely riskless, there would be no reason to negotiate an interest rate different from r_f with the creditor. Since we will later consider default it might be that in some (possibly very uncertain) states of the world the payments for interest and redemption lie below the riskless rate and therefore the firm demands a higher interest rate in the remaining states. Analogous to the cost of equity this requires a definition of cost of debt. Someone who invests $\widetilde{D}_t$ today is entitled to payments amounting to $\widetilde{D}_t + \widetilde{I}_{t+1}$ less remission of debts. Due to a remission of debts of $\widetilde{D}_t - \widetilde{D}_{t+1} - \widetilde{R}_{t+1}$, we obtain the following definition.

Definition 3.4 (Cost of Debt) The cost of debt $\widetilde{k}^D_t$ of a levered firm are conditional expected returns

$$\widetilde{k}^D_t := \frac{\mathrm{E}\left[\widetilde{D}_{t+1} + \widetilde{I}_{t+1} + \widetilde{R}_{t+1}|\mathcal{F}_t\right]}{\widetilde{D}_t} - 1.$$

However, unless there is the probability of default there is no reason whatsoever to assume that the cost of debt is different from the riskless rate

$$\widetilde{k}^D_t = r_f.$$

Notice that we do not require the cost of debt to be deterministic today. Although this will be a necessary requirement for different types of cost of capital later,[21] cost of debt will not be used itself to determine the value of firms and hence need not to be deterministic.

3.2.6 Example (Finite Case Continued)

Let us turn back to our finite example and suppose a tax rate of τ =50%. Now we will go into the question as to if a particular finance policy can lead to bankruptcy and, if possible, complete our model in a suitable way. To this end let us assume that the provisional (riskless) leverage policy takes the form

$$D_0 = 100, \quad D_1 = 100, \quad D_2 = 50 .$$

We want to evaluate the cash flow $\widetilde{FCF}_t^l$ of the levered firm with default risk.

In the case of no default the claims of the shareholders at time t amount to

$$\widetilde{FCF}_t^u(\omega) - \left(1 + (1-\tau)r_f\right) D_{t-1} + D_t .$$

In order to calculate these claims correctly we have to take our assumptions into consideration. First, the unlevered firm's gross cash flow must not be different from those of the levered firm (Assumption 3.2). Second, the unlevered firm's tax base must only be different from that of the levered firm by the paid interest and the cancelled debt as in (3.14).

Default Trigger (in Our Example) Default occurs when the creditors' payment claims cannot be satisfied in full. The exact meaning of this term is not entirely evident. In any case there exist different possibilities to specify them in the context of our model.

One of the possibilities to discuss default is if we deal with a situation in which the owners receive negative payments,

$$\widetilde{FCF}_t^u(\omega) - \left(1 + (1-\tau)r_f\right) D_{t-1} + D_t < 0.$$

In this case, we will talk about an interruption of payments. We have systematically compiled the corresponding amounts in Fig. 3.5 for all times t. The illustration shows that up through time $t = 2$, all creditors' claims can be satisfied. If we define default that way, bankruptcy is at issue at state $\omega = ddd$.

Of course, the owners would have the option to avoid default in such a situation by ceding a part of their assets. It stands to reason to define the default trigger in such a way that the assets of the owners are enclosed. Hence, default would only be

[21] See the subsections on TCF, FTE etc.

Fig. 3.5 Shareholder's claims if $D_0 = 100$, $D_1 = 100$, $D_2 = 50$, $\widetilde{k}^{D,nom} = r_f$ in the finite example

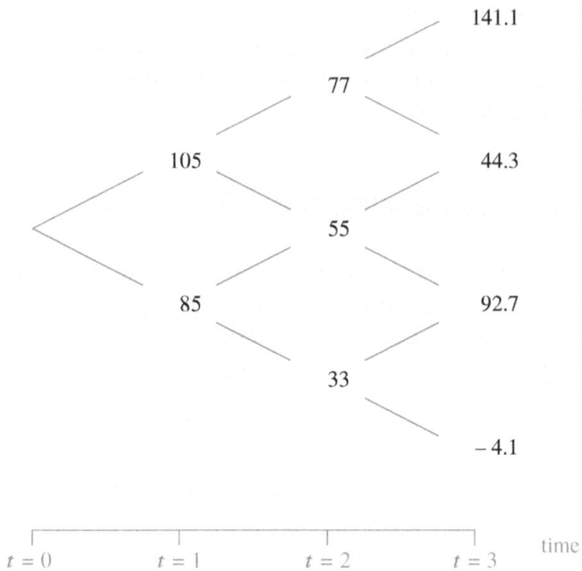

caused, if in a state ω

$$\widetilde{E}_t(\omega) + \widetilde{FCF}_t^u(\omega) - \left(1 + (1-\tau)r_f\right) D_{t-1} + D_t < 0$$

is obtained. Even if the shares of the shareholders will be assigned to the creditors the latter cannot be entirely satisfied. In contrast to the case studied before, in situations similar to those mentioned above we want to call this inability to pay.

If inability to pay exists in every state, we deal with a special case. This corresponds to Over-indebtedness. If the conditional expectation under Q is attained, the last inequality will be transferred to

$$\mathrm{E}_Q\left[\widetilde{V}_t + \widetilde{FCF}_t^l|\mathcal{F}_{t-1}\right] - \left(1 + r_f\right) D_{t-1} = \left(1 + r_f\right)\left(\widetilde{V}_{t-1} - D_{t-1}\right) < 0.$$

In this case the creditors can be sure that it will not be possible for the company to operate a credit in the amount of D_{t-1}. Consequently, in such a case they would be acting irrationally if they were to grant a credit of a dimension like that anyway.

Certainly, a default trigger can be defined in many ways. As we can show in our example, $t = 3$ will cause an interruption of payments as well as an inability to pay at the same time. But this does not include over-indebtedness. The terms and definitions do not necessarily have to coincide. Consequently, they can evoke different strategies of the investors and different legal consequences in particular.

Nominal Interest Rate If the creditors do not have to worry about default, then they will demand the riskless rate. That is not so, in contrast, when there is a danger of going bankrupt. Here the creditors run the risk that their interest and debt repayment demands would not be completely paid off in any state of the world that might occur. In order to get an adequate reward for this kind of risk they force the creditor to accept a nominal interest rate which is higher than the riskless rate. In the following the nominal rate will be designated by $\widetilde{k}_t^{D,nom}$. And we will have $\widetilde{k}_t^{D,nom} > r_f$ when there is a certain probability of bankruptcy. Regarding the calculation of the premium, we assume that the creditor knows the rule according to which the state takes priority and anticipates the repercussions of this rule. In the case of bankruptcy, the creditors retain the free cash flow to pay back debt granted. If, in contrast, there is no question of going into default, then besides the debt service, they receive the nominal interest agreed upon beforehand. Notice that we do not require our nominal rate of interest to be deterministic today.

We can maintain the resulting claims of the creditors,

$$\widetilde{R}_t(\omega) + \widetilde{I}_t(\omega) = \begin{cases} \min\left(\widetilde{FCF}_t^l(\omega) + \widetilde{E}_t(\omega), (1 + \widetilde{k}_{t-1}^{D,nom})D_{t-1}\right), & \text{default in } \omega, \\ \left(1 + \widetilde{k}_{t-1}^{D,nom}\right) D_{t-1}, & \text{else.} \end{cases} \tag{3.20}$$

At $t = 0, 1$ and in the states $\omega = uu$ and $\omega = ud, du$ bankruptcy (in terms of interruption of payments or inability to pay) cannot occur. Hence, in these states the financiers will agree on a nominal rate of $\widetilde{k}_2^{D,nom}(\omega) = r_f$. Using (3.9) it is now easy to determine the levered cash flows $\widetilde{FCF}^l$ for all states except ddd and ddu.

State $\omega = dd$ is different. If the next movement is down (and only if it is down), bankruptcy enters in. Hence, the creditors will negotiate a different nominal rate $\widetilde{k}_2^{D,nom}(dd) > r_f$. We assumed that the state's claims take priority over the creditors' claims and that the firm's cash flow is sufficient in any case to pay the taxes due. With this in aim, let us concentrate on the situation in which the creditors' claims cannot be paid off in full. In this situation from Eqs. (3.20) and (3.14) the following is valid (notice that $\widetilde{E}_3 = 0$):

$$\begin{aligned} \widetilde{R}_3(ddd) + \widetilde{I}_3(ddd) &= \widetilde{FCF}_3^l(ddd) + \widetilde{E}_3 = \\ &= \widetilde{FCF}_3^u(ddd) + \tau(\widetilde{I}_3(ddd) + \widetilde{R}_3(ddd) + D_3 - D_2) + \widetilde{E}_3 \end{aligned}$$

and from that

$$\begin{aligned} \widetilde{FCF}_3^l(ddd) = \widetilde{R}_3(ddd) + \widetilde{I}_3(ddd) &= \frac{1}{1-\tau}\left(\widetilde{FCF}_3^u(ddd) - \tau D_2\right) \\ &= \frac{1}{1-0.5}(48.4 - 0.5 \cdot 50) \\ &= 46.8\,. \end{aligned}$$

It remains to evaluate the nominal rate $\widetilde{k}_2^{D,nom}$ to determine the cash flow $\widetilde{FCF}_3^l(ddu)$. The financiers will only be ready to grant credit if the market price of their capital lending just corresponds to the credit volumes D_2. Due to Eq. (3.19) and $D_3 = 0$, then the following must also apply,

$$D_2 = \frac{\mathrm{E}_Q\left[\widetilde{R}_3 + \widetilde{I}_3|\mathcal{F}_2\right]}{1+r_f}. \tag{3.21}$$

Using the conditional Q-probabilities from Fig. 3.1 the above Eq. (3.21) gives

$$D_2 = \frac{\left(1+\widetilde{k}_2^{D,nom}(dd)\right) D_2\, Q_3(u|dd) + \frac{\widetilde{FCF}_3^u(ddd)-\tau D_2}{1-\tau}\, Q_3(d|dd)}{1+r_f}$$

$$1.1 \cdot 50 \approx \left(1+\widetilde{k}_2^{D,nom}(dd)\right) \cdot 50 \cdot 0.4167 + \frac{48.4 - 0.5 \cdot 50}{1-0.5}\, 0.5833$$

with the solution

$$\widetilde{k}_2^{D,nom}(dd) \approx 32.962\,\%\,.$$

Hence,

$$\begin{aligned}\widetilde{FCF}_3^l(ddu) &= \widetilde{FCF}_3^u(ddu) + \tau\, \widetilde{k}_2^{D,nom}(dd)\, D_2 \\ &\approx 145.2 + 0.5 \cdot 0.32962 \cdot 50 \approx 153.44\,.\end{aligned}$$

We run into another problem here, which, luckily, does not have any further repercussions in our example. However, much higher the agreed upon nominal rate is that much more likely it is that an inability to pay will be set off in the states, which up until now have not been affected by bankruptcy. Yet in our example, a nominal rate of 32.96% does not result in additional default situations.

Finally we have completed the evaluation of all levered cash flows. The summarized results can be found in Fig. 3.6.

3.2.7 Problems

1. Show that the recursion (3.19) implies

$$\widetilde{D}_t = \sum_{s=t+1}^{T} \frac{\mathrm{E}_Q\left[\widetilde{I}_s + \widetilde{R}_s|\mathcal{F}_t\right]}{(1+r_f)^{s-t}}\,.$$

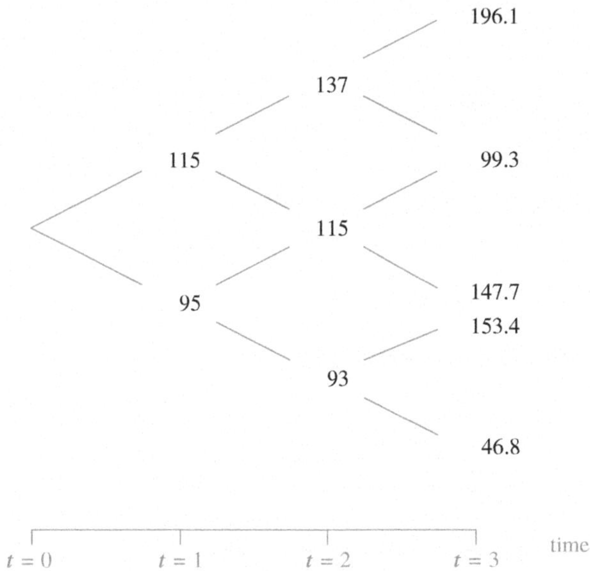

Fig. 3.6 Levered cash flows $\widetilde{FCF}^l$ with default in the finite example

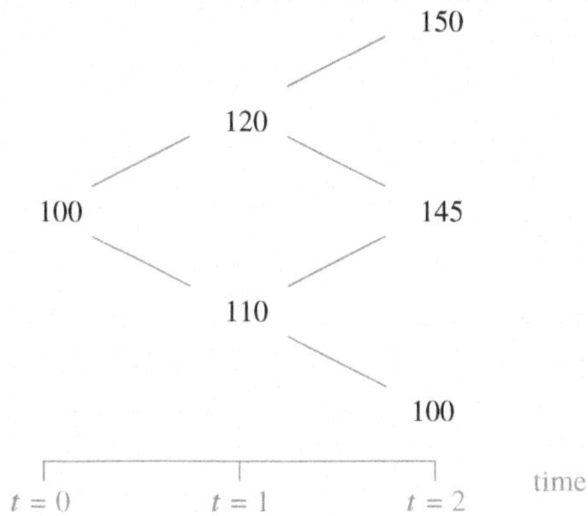

Fig. 3.7 Debt $\widetilde{D}_t$ of Problem 2

2. A levered firm lives until $T = 3$. Assume that the conditional Q-probability of the up-movement is 0.25 and the riskless rate is 10%, the tax rate is 50%. Evaluate the tax shield $\widetilde{V}_0^l - \widetilde{V}_0^u$ if the debt schedule (without default) is as in Fig. 3.7.
3. Prove that the tax shield $\widetilde{V}_t^l - \widetilde{V}_t^u$ satisfies

$$\widetilde{V}_t^l - \widetilde{V}_t^u = \frac{\mathrm{E}_Q\left[\widetilde{V}_{t+1}^l - \widetilde{V}_{t+1}^u | \mathcal{F}_t\right]}{1+r_f} + \frac{\tau r_f \widetilde{D}_t}{1+r_f} .$$

4. Prove that from (3.11) it follows that

$$\widetilde{V}_t^l = \widetilde{V}_t^u + \tau \widetilde{D}_t + \sum_{s=t+1}^{T} \frac{\tau \, \mathrm{E}_Q\left[\widetilde{D}_s - \widetilde{D}_{s-1} | \mathcal{F}_t\right]}{(1+r_f)^{s-t}} .$$

This is the main result in Fernández (2005).

3.3 Autonomous Financing

3.3.1 Adjusted Present Value (APV)

When all future amounts of debt are already determined at valuation time $t = 0$, we are speaking of autonomous financing. In this case, the firm is following a completely fixed redemption plan. We are not really interested in whether or not autonomous financing is dealing with a realistic assumption. We, however, suppose that autonomous financing is pretty close to reality.

> **Definition 3.5 (Autonomous Financing)** A firm is autonomously financed exactly then when its future amount of debt $\widetilde{D}_t$ is already a certain quantity today.

Under this assumption, the tax advantages are also certain and can be discounted with the riskless rate. These leads straight to the so-called APV formula. The abbreviation stands for adjusted present value.

Theorem 3.6 (APV Formula) *In the case of autonomous financing, the following equation is valid for the market value of the levered firm at any time:*

$$\widetilde{V}_t^l = \widetilde{V}_t^u + \sum_{s=t+1}^{T} \frac{\tau r_f D_{s-1}}{\left(1+r_f\right)^{s-t}} .$$

This theorem can be proven as in the following. We work from the base of Eq. (3.11) and make use of the fact that our firm is following a fixed redemption policy. If the $\widetilde{D}_t$ are, however, no longer random variables, then the last equation is simplified on the basis of rule 3 to

$$\widetilde{V}_t^l = \widetilde{V}_t^u + \frac{\tau r_f D_t}{1+r_f} + \ldots + \frac{\tau r_f D_{T-1}}{\left(1+r_f\right)^{T-t}} .$$

And that is how our theorem is proven.

Notice that our equation also holds for a firm with debt threatened by default! The value of the firm in danger of bankruptcy exactly corresponds to the value above, as long as the granted debt is certain. Although it can come to bankruptcy, the value of firms continues to be established by discounting the tax advantages from granted debt with the riskless interest rate and not the cost of debt or any other discount rate! What at first glance appears an unexpected result comes up because the creditors anticipate the threat of bankruptcy and therefore require interest payments, which perfectly compensate a possible loss of value due to bankruptcy.

Long-Term and Constant Amount of Debt Finally, we want to look at the case where the amount of debt always remains the same. We then require that at time t the current debt will not change through redemption measures or further loans. In this case the last valuation formula can be simplified to an equation, which is named after those who discovered it.

Theorem 3.7 (Modigliani–Miller Formula) *If the firm goes on forever, the conditions of Theorem 3.6 are met and debt remains constant, then the following is valid for the market value of the levered firm*

$$\widetilde{V}_t^l = \widetilde{V}_t^u + \tau D_t .$$

To prove the theorem we convert the right summands in Theorem 3.6 with help of the geometric annuity. If debt remains constant we get

$$\begin{aligned}\widetilde{V}_t^l &= \widetilde{V}_t^u + \tau r_f D_t \sum_{s=t+1}^{\infty} \frac{1}{(1+r_f)^{s-t}} \\ &= \widetilde{V}_t^u + \tau r_f D_t \frac{1}{r_f} .\end{aligned}$$

And that is what we wanted to show.[22] q.e.d.

We get a somewhat altered representation, if we concentrate on time $t = 0$ while supposing that the expected cash flows remain constant at that time. The amount of debt D_0 as the product of the debt ratio l_0 and market value of the levered firm can be written,

$$\begin{aligned}V_0^l &= V_0^u + \tau\, l_0\, V_0^l \\ (1 - \tau\, l_0) V_0^l &= V_0^u .\end{aligned}$$

If we use the assumption that the expected free cash flows remain the same in time, then we can calculate the market value of the unlevered firm as cash value of a

[22]Notice that transversality for debt is trivially satisfied in this case since $\widetilde{D}_t$ is constant.

perpetual return, from which

$$(1 - \tau\, l_0)\, V_0^l = \frac{\mathrm{E}\left[\widetilde{FCF}^u\right]}{k^{E,u}}$$

and

$$V_0^l = \frac{\mathrm{E}\left[\widetilde{FCF}^u\right]}{(1 - \tau\, l_0)k^{E,u}}$$

follow. The last equation is also called Modigliani–Miller adjustment. The valuation equation proven in this chapter solves the problem as to how the market value is to be determined in full. We will come back to this equation once more in relation to the Miles–Ezzell adjustment.[23]

Over-indebtedness and Illiquidity with Autonomous Financing In the case of autonomous financing both default triggers can be precisely characterized. This is the main result of our next proposition where we assumed constant debt for simplicity.

Theorem 3.8 (Autonomous Financing) *A levered firm with an infinite life span whose amount of debt always remains the same is over-indebted in time t in state ω if and only if for its unlevered cash flows*

$$\widetilde{FCF}_t^u(\omega) < \frac{(1 - \tau)(k^{E,u} - g)}{1 + g}\, \widetilde{D}.$$

If the condition

$$\widetilde{FCF}_t^u(\omega) < r_f(1 - \tau)\, \widetilde{D}$$

is satisfied, the levered firm is in danger of illiquidity at date t in state ω.

Specifically, illiquidity (in state ω) implies over-indebtedness at time t (in the same state ω) if $g < \frac{k^{E,u} - r_f}{1 + r_f}$.

Notice that the right-hand side of both inequalities is constant. If the cash flows of an unlevered company fall below this threshold, over-indebtedness occurs. The second inequality offers a more intuitive economic interpretation. If the cash flows go below the required interest payments after taxes, the firm is in danger of illiquidity.

The proof of the theorem is straightforward. The company is in danger of over-indebtedness if $\widetilde{V}_t^l(\omega) < \widetilde{D}$ holds. For the financing policy considered here,

---

[23] See Sect. 3.4.4.

$\widetilde{V}_t^l(\omega) = \widetilde{V}_t^u(\omega) + \tau \widetilde{D}$ is valid. By plugging in, we see that

$$D > \frac{1}{1-\tau} \widetilde{V}_t^u(\omega)$$

is true. Using Theorem 3.2 and solving for $\widetilde{FCF}_t^u(\omega)$ proves the proposition.

In order to prove the second statement we start with the fact that (due to constant debt) the firm is in danger of illiquidity if $\widetilde{FCF}_t^l(\omega) < r_f \widetilde{D}$ holds. Making use of the relationship between the free cash flows of a levered and those of an unlevered firm (3.10) and employing constant debt we get

$$\widetilde{FCF}_t^u(\omega) + \tau r_f \widetilde{D} < r_f \widetilde{D}$$

which proves the second statement. q.e.d.

3.3.2 Example (Continued)

The Finite Case Without Default Here debt will be riskless, hence $\widetilde{k}_t^D = r_f$. If we suppose a future development of the amount of debt of

$$D_0 = 100, \quad D_1 = 100, \quad D_2 = 50\ ,$$

the value of the levered firm at time $t = 0$ is gotten with

$$\begin{aligned} V_0^l &= V_0^u + \frac{\tau r_f D_0}{1+r_f} + \frac{\tau r_f D_1}{(1+r_f)^2} + \frac{\tau r_f D_2}{(1+r_f)^3} \\ &\approx 229.75 + \frac{0.5 \cdot 0.1 \cdot 100}{1.1} + \frac{0.5 \cdot 0.1 \cdot 100}{1.1^2} + \frac{0.5 \cdot 0.1 \cdot 50}{1.1^3} \approx 240.30\ . \end{aligned}$$

The value of the levered firm is not essentially different from the value of the unlevered firm. That has to do with the fact that the firm in our example only has a lifetime of three years.

We deduced the market value of the levered firm at time $t = 1$ in an analogous way,

$$\begin{aligned} \widetilde{V}_1^l &= \widetilde{V}_1^u + \frac{\tau r_f D_1}{1+r_f} + \frac{\tau r_f D_2}{(1+r_f)^2} \\ &= \widetilde{V}_1^u + \frac{0.5 \cdot 0.1 \cdot 100}{1.1} + \frac{0.5 \cdot 0.1 \cdot 50}{1.1^2} \\ &\approx \begin{cases} 199.88, & \text{if the development in } t = 1 \text{ is up,} \\ 164.74, & \text{if the development in } t = 1 \text{ is down.} \end{cases} \end{aligned}$$

Finally, we want to determine another additional outcome of our example. The levered firm's debt ratio in regard to time $t = 1$ is an uncertain quantity. The following is valid:

$$\widetilde{l}_1 \approx \begin{cases} \frac{100}{199.88} = 50.03\%, & \text{if the development in } t = 1 \text{ is up,} \\ \frac{100}{164.74} = 60.70\%, & \text{if the development in } t = 1 \text{ is down.} \end{cases}$$

If the firm is following an autonomous financing policy, it cannot be supposed that the debt ratio is certain. That is much more characteristic of financing based on market values.

Valuation in the Finite Case with Default Risk It is not at all complicated to value the firm threatened with going into default in our example: we can use the APV formula. Therefore the value of the firm in danger of bankruptcy is calculated in our example by means of the Theorem 3.6 and exactly corresponds to the value above

$$V_0^l \approx 240.30\,.$$

Another way of obtaining this value of the firm would be to use the levered cash flows from Fig. 3.6, determine the expectations under Q and discount them with the riskless rate. This must yield just the same value.[24]

An additional result, which, however, is not required for the valuation of the firm, is that for an amount of credit of $D_2 = 50$, we get at $\omega = dd$ a cost of debt of

$$\begin{aligned} \widetilde{k}_2^D(dd) &= \frac{\left(1 + \widetilde{k}_2^{D,nom}(dd)\right) D_2\, P_3(u|dd) + \frac{1}{1-\tau}\left(\widetilde{FCF}_3^u(ddd) - \tau D_2\right) P_3(d|dd)}{D_2} - 1 \\ &\approx \frac{(1 + 0.32962)\cdot 50 \cdot 0.5 + \frac{1}{1-0.5}\cdot(48.4 - 0.5\cdot 50)\cdot 0.5}{50} - 1 \\ &\approx 13.281\%. \end{aligned}$$

If the considerations employed above in relation to the nominal interest rates and their resultant cost of debt rates are systematically used again for other values of D_2, then for the interval $D_2 \leq 70$, the relation depicted in Fig. 3.8 is gotten (see the Problem 5 below).

The Infinite Case Let the tax rate be $\tau = 50\%$. The levered firm maintains a debt schedule such that the amount of debt remains constant, $D_t = 100$. Debt is not threatened by default. As already indicated in the Modigliani–Miller formula the

[24] See Problem 4.

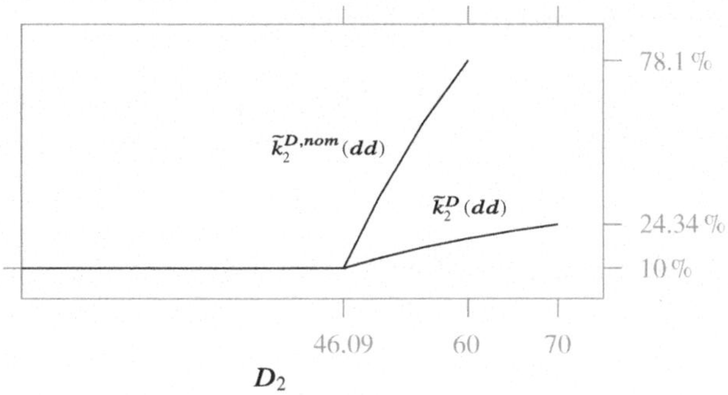

Fig. 3.8 Cost of debt and nominal interest rate with increasing leverage

value of the levered firm is given by

$$\begin{aligned} V_0^l &= V_0^u + \sum_{t=0}^{\infty} \frac{\tau r_f D_t}{\left(1+r_f\right)^{t+1}} \\ &= V_0^u + \tau D_0 \\ &= 500 + 0.5 \cdot 100 = 550\,. \end{aligned}$$

3.3.3 Problems

1. Let debt be riskless. Assume that the cash flows of the unlevered firm are weak auto-regressive. What assumptions on the debt schedule are necessary such that the cash flows of the levered firm $\widetilde{FCF}_t^l$ are weak auto-regressive as well?
2. Show that in the infinite example with constant (riskless) debt for all t

$$\widetilde{V}_t^l = \frac{\widetilde{FCF}_t^u}{k^{E,u}} + \tau D_t\,.$$

3. Show in the infinite example with constant (riskless) debt that the dividend-price ratio of the levered firm is a random variable (i.e., not deterministic) if $r_f \neq k^{E,u}$.
4. Consider the finite example with default. Evaluate the Q-expected cash flows (see Fig. 3.6) and verify that the firm has indeed a value of 240.30.
5. Consider the finite example with default. Evaluate the cost of debt $\widetilde{k}_2^D$ as a function of debt $D_2 \leq 70$.

3.4 Financing Based on Market Values

Let us turn our attention now to a further financing policy. In the following we will suppose that the managers of the firm to be valued are following a policy based on market values.

Definition 3.6 (Financing Based on Market Values) A firm's financing is based on market values exactly then when its debt ratios $\widetilde{l}_t$ are today already certain quantities.

A characterization of this financing in another context was that the firm's leverage "breathes" with the equity's market value. If the equity's market value changes, then the amount of debt has to be adjusted.

Uncertain Tax Advantages If a firm's debt ratios and not its amount of debt are available, then autonomous financing is no longer the case. To illustrate the consequences, we suppose that management is aiming towards coming up with a debt ratio of 50:100, for instance, at a future time $t > 0$.[25] If we solve the debt ratio's definition equation (3.5) according to $\widetilde{D}_t$, then with a deterministic ratio we get

$$l_t \widetilde{V}_t = \widetilde{D}_t .$$

That means: If the value $\widetilde{V}_t$ is an uncertain quantity from today's perspective, then the amount of debt relevant at this time is also stochastic, because the multiplication of a random variable by a real number results again in a random variable. Half of an uncertain quantity is of course also uncertain. In order to fully understand the relations, look at Fig. 3.9. With financing based on market values, the evaluator cannot say with certainty at time $t = 0$ how big the amount of debt will turn out to be at time t, since the value $\widetilde{V}_t$ is still uncertain and the amount of debt is firmly linked with this through the ratio. If this uncertainty is resolved—just a second after time t—then the interest payments to be rendered at time $t + 1$ are, in contrast, certain (if we neglect default for the moment). The same goes for the resulting tax savings $\tau \widetilde{I}_{t+1}$ at time $t + 1$. The tax savings is thus to be discounted with the riskless rate from time $t+1$ to time t. But the discounting of t to 0 may not be carried out with r_f. It is uncertain from today's perspective as to how much tax the firm proportionately financed by debt will save. Even with no default the discounting from t to 0 cannot be done with r_f. Today we cannot know how large the tax advantages from debt are.

[25] We do not want to further pursue where management is getting this target quantity from.

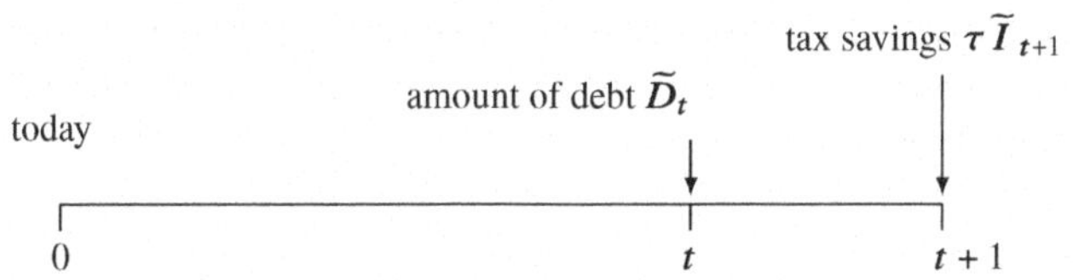

Fig. 3.9 Time structure of financing based on market values

Miles and Ezzell (1980) have examined this case in detail and have determined that the APV equation of Theorem 3.6 is no longer suitable. The tax savings per terms of credit are uncertain and uncertain tax savings may not be discounted with the riskless rate.[26]

Three Calculation Procedures In the case of such a leverage policy, there are three different calculation procedures, which all lead to the same value of the firm. This value must differ from the value that would be calculated with the APV equation, since it is not based on an autonomous financing policy.

Which of the three calculations should be used by the evaluator depends upon, among other things, the state of information that she has on hand. We point out here that the content of the three equations which we have to prove is independent of financing based on market values: a policy based on market values is not absolutely necessary in all cases. Somewhat weaker conditions are instead enough: What is always important is that particular cost of capital are deterministic. To make this relation—which does at first glance seem complicated—understandable, we will first present the three formulations as generally as possible. At the end we will then show how they interrelate. It is not until this second step that the assumption of financing based on market values (and the fact that free cash flows of the unlevered firm are weak auto-regressive) will be made use of.

3.4.1 Flow to Equity (FTE)

In this section we will work with the assumption that the levered firm's cost of equity is deterministic. In order to do so we must define the cost of equity. It is recommended to start off with determining the refluxes, which the equity financiers of the levered firm are entitled to. The starting quantities are the free cash flows of the indebted firm $\widetilde{FCF}^l_{t+1}$.

We have to deduct the payments to the creditors. These are entitled to interest as well as debt repayments at time $t + 1$. The interest claims amount to $\widetilde{I}_{t+1}$. We can

[26]"Even though the firm might issue riskless debt, if financing policy is targeted to realized market values, the amount of debt outstanding in future periods is not known with certainty (unless the investment is riskless) ..." Miles and Ezzell (1980, p. 721).

evaluate the debt service as the difference between the paying back of former debt and the current value of debt, thus as $\widetilde{R}_{t+1}$. Altogether, the creditors are entitled payments in the amount of

$$\widetilde{I}_{t+1} + \widetilde{R}_{t+1}.$$

If this is deducted from the starting amount, there then remains a residual amount for the owners (value of equity plus a dividend) of

$$\widetilde{E}_{t+1} + \widetilde{Div}_{t+1} := \widetilde{E}_{t+1} + \widetilde{FCF}^l_{t+1} - \widetilde{I}_{t+1} - \widetilde{R}_{t+1}. \tag{3.22}$$

This makes it clear as to how the definition of the cost of equity should read.

Definition 3.7 (Cost of Equity of the Levered firm) The cost of equity $\widetilde{k}_t^{E,l}$ of a levered firm are conditional expected returns

$$\widetilde{k}_t^{E,l} := \frac{\mathrm{E}\left[\widetilde{E}_{t+1} + \widetilde{FCF}^l_{t+1} - \widetilde{I}_{t+1} - \widetilde{R}_{t+1} | \mathcal{F}_t\right]}{\widetilde{E}_t} - 1.$$

The index E with the cost of capital indicates that the cost of equity is being dealt with.

We now require that this cost of equity is deterministic. If we were to carry this assumption over to an actual firm listed on the exchange, it would entail being able to determine a firm's future (conditional) expected returns on shares. We are fully aware that this condition is very rough. But it would be underhanded if we did not lay bare the implications of the assumptions, which form the basis of the various theories on discounted cash flow.

The valuation equation, which we now get is termed flow to equity (FTE), or also equity approach, in the literature. The reason flow to equity is spoken of is that the entire cash flows after taxes are not discounted, but rather those cash flows after taxes which the firm's owners are entitled to.

Theorem 3.9 (Flow to Equity) *If the cost of equity of the levered firm $k_t^{E,l}$ are deterministic, then the value of equity at time t is*

$$\widetilde{E}_t = \sum_{s=t+1}^{T} \frac{\mathrm{E}\left[\widetilde{FCF}^l_s - \widetilde{I}_s - \widetilde{R}_s | \mathcal{F}_t\right]}{\left(1 + k_t^{E,l}\right) \dots \left(1 + k_{s-1}^{E,l}\right)}.$$

We have already used the method of proof required.[27] We can thus spare our readers it here.

3.4.2 Total Cash Flow (TCF)

If it is supposed that instead of the levered firm's cost of equity the firm's average cost of capital is deterministic, then it is the TCF approach and not the FTE approach which is being dealt with.

First the cost of capital which is now relevant has to be defined again. Which payments do the financiers of the levered firm receive? The answer is easily given. It is of course the free cash flows of the levered firm $\widetilde{FCF}_t^l$ that are the subject here. The capital employment of both groups of financiers is $\widetilde{E}_t + \widetilde{D}_t = \widetilde{V}_t^l$, so that the definition of the cost of capital for the case we now have to look at is absolutely clear.

Definition 3.8 (Weighted Average Cost of Capital—Type 1) The weighted average cost of capital $\widetilde{k}_t^{\varnothing}$ of a levered firm are the conditional expected returns

$$\widetilde{k}_t^{\varnothing} := \frac{\mathrm{E}\left[\widetilde{V}_{t+1}^l + \widetilde{FCF}_{t+1}^l | \mathcal{F}_t\right]}{\widetilde{V}_t^l} - 1.$$

How close to reality is the assumption of deterministic weighted average cost of capital? If we take a firm listed on the stock exchange for instance, then this condition calls for a knowledge of the entire future returns of the firm. A knowledge is needed thus not of the shares, or the (conditional) expectation of the returns on debt, but rather of the weighted average of both random quantities. A totally different assumption is being dealt with here than that condition on which the FTE formulation is based. We will be able to find out somewhat later if and in how far both conditions are compatible.

If we want to know, which value the levered firm has at time t, we can find the answer analogous to Theorem 2.1. The case being looked at here is termed total cash flow formulation (TCF), because the entire expected cash flows after taxes are discounted with the weighted average cost of capital.

[27] See Theorem 2.1.

Theorem 3.10 (Total Cash Flow) *If the weighted average cost of capital $k_t^{\varnothing}$ are deterministic, then the value of the firm at time t comes to*

$$\widetilde{V}_t^l = \sum_{s=t+1}^{T} \frac{\mathrm{E}\left[\widetilde{FCF}_s^l | \mathcal{F}_t\right]}{\left(1+k_t^{\varnothing}\right)\dots\left(1+k_{s-1}^{\varnothing}\right)}.$$

A formal proof could be carried out again just as in Sect. 2.3.3, which is why we forgo with presenting it here again.

What can we say about the weighted average cost of capital (of type 1) and the cost of equity of a levered firm? Can we, for instance, ascertain that deterministic cost of equity also results from deterministic average cost of capital? Are then the FTE and TCF formulations compatible with each other? Or do both assumptions mutually exclude each other? Answers to all these questions are gotten by the so-called textbook formula.

Theorem 3.11 (TCF Textbook Formula) *For the type 1 weighted average cost of capital of the firm, the following relation is always valid:*

$$\widetilde{k}_t^{\varnothing} = \widetilde{k}_t^{E,l}\left(1-\widetilde{l}_t\right) + \widetilde{k}_t^D \widetilde{l}_t.$$

It is just now that it becomes really clear why weighted average cost of capital is spoken of in relation with the TCF formulation. The levered firm's cost of equity is weighted with the equity ratio, and the cost of debt with the debt ratio.

To prove the theorem, we use the definition of the levered firm's cost of equity. And after a few simplifications, we get

$$\left(1+\widetilde{k}_t^{E,l}\right)\widetilde{E}_t = \mathrm{E}\left[\widetilde{E}_{t+1} + \widetilde{FCF}_{t+1}^l - \widetilde{I}_{t+1} - \widetilde{R}_{t+1} | \mathcal{F}_t\right].$$

Since the firm's total value corresponds to the sum of equity and debt, you can apply according to rule 5 and under use of the Definitions 3.4, 3.7, and 3.8, the following:

$$\left(1+\widetilde{k}_t^{E,l}\right)\widetilde{E}_t + \left(1+\widetilde{k}_t^{D}\right)\widetilde{D}_t = \mathrm{E}\left[\widetilde{V}_{t+1}^l + \widetilde{FCF}_{t+1}^l | \mathcal{F}_t\right]$$
$$\widetilde{V}_t^l + \widetilde{k}_t^{E,l}\widetilde{E}_t + \widetilde{k}_t^D \widetilde{D}_t = \left(1+\widetilde{k}_t^{\varnothing}\right)\widetilde{V}_t^l.$$

After dividing by the firm's market value, you come up with

$$1 + \widetilde{k}_t^{E,l}\frac{\widetilde{E}_t}{\widetilde{V}_t^l} + \widetilde{k}_t^D \frac{\widetilde{D}_t}{\widetilde{V}_t^l} = \widetilde{k}_t^{\varnothing} + 1.$$

Such is the assertion. q.e.d.

The textbook formula as it appears in Theorem 3.11 is remarkable in several aspects. To begin with, it is striking that it is obviously valid regardless of whether the relevant variables are understood as random variables or as deterministic quantities. Neither the weighted average cost of capital (type 1) nor the cost of equity of the levered firm (both a prerequisite of the FTE and the TCF approach) need to be deterministic in order to prove the textbook formula. A closer look at the textbook formula allows us to make the following determinations:

1. If it is assumed that the levered firm's weighted average cost of capital (type 1) as well as cost of equity and debt are certain, then the debt ratios must also be certain.

   That is a big limitation, which cannot simply be accepted. But if we are working on the basis of certain debt ratios, then the textbook formula shows how the different cost of capital involved can be converted into each other. TCF and FTE may alternatively be used and inevitably lead to the same result.
2. If, on the other hand, in the case of no default the future debt ratios are seen as uncertain, either the weighted average cost of capital (type 1), or the cost of equity of the levered firm have to be uncertain.

   If the weighted average cost of capital (type 1) is deterministic, then the TCF concept has to be used; but if, on the other hand, the cost of equity is certain, then the FTE formulation has to be put into use, since uncertain cost of capital simply cannot be used to discount with. It does not make sense to pose the question here as to whether TCF and FTE methods lead to the same result. The textbook formula has no practical value in the case of uncertain debt ratios.

What further stands out with the textbook formula as it appears in Theorem 3.11 is that it is different from the usual textbook formula as it is given in relation to the weighted cost of capital (WACC) concept. In the former, the cost of debt cannot be reduced to the firm's profit tax rate. We now want to discuss the question as to whether this cost of capital that is found in the literature also makes economic sense or whether it puts forth totally useless quantities.

3.4.3 Weighted Average Cost of Capital (WACC)

Look at the Definition 3.8 of the weighted average cost of capital. We now want to alter a very insignificant detail of this definition and call the resulting quantities $WACC$ (weighted average cost of capital). The unlevered firm's free cash flows take the place of the levered firm's free cash flows.

Definition 3.9 (Weighted Average Cost of Capital—Type 2) The cost of capital $\widetilde{WACC}$ of a levered firm are the expected returns

$$\widetilde{WACC}_t := \frac{\mathrm{E}\left[\widetilde{V}^l_{t+1} + \widetilde{FCF}^u_{t+1}|\mathcal{F}_t\right]}{\widetilde{V}^l_t} - 1.$$

If these cost of capital is deterministic, we can again prove the existence of a valuation equation analogous to our previous approach. Beforehand, however, we want to discuss the question as to how realistic the assumption is that such cost of capital is observed on the market.

Whoever wants to establish the cost of capital in the sense of Definition 3.9, would have to look at a firm, which is on the one hand levered $\left(\widetilde{V}^l_t\right)$, and on the other pays free cash flows in an amount as if it were not levered, $\widetilde{FCF}^u_t$. It is clear that apples and oranges are being mixed here, and thus we may assume that no one can a priori know such cost of capital. We think that every other assertion would be senseless.

If we just momentarily free ourselves from this observation and the shackles it would enchain us in, then we could still formulate a valuation equation on the basis of this—albeit somewhat odd – definition of cost of capital. It would read as follows:

Theorem 3.12 (Weighted Average Cost of Capital) *If the levered firm's cost of capital $WACC_t$ are deterministic, then the value at time t of the firm financed by debt comes to*

$$\widetilde{V}^l_t = \sum_{s=t+1}^{T} \frac{\mathrm{E}\left[\widetilde{FCF}^u_s|\mathcal{F}_t\right]}{(1+WACC_t)\dots(1+WACC_{s-1})}.$$

The proof shows a clear course.

Critical readers will ask why we waste so much time on a cost of capital definition about which we have said that it makes no economic sense. The reason lies in the fact that this cost of capital definition—the direct interpretation of which makes no sense—will prove itself to be extremely useful in the following.

Theorem 3.13 (WACC Textbook Formula) *For the firm's type 2 weighted average cost of capital, the following relation is always valid:*

$$\widetilde{WACC}_t = \widetilde{k}^{E,l}_t \left(1 - \widetilde{l}_t\right) + \widetilde{k}^D_t (1-\tau)\widetilde{l}_t.$$

The WACC textbook formula is different from the TCF textbook formula only in that the interest on debt is reduced by the tax rate. That corresponds to the usual textbook formula given in the literature. Then the weighted average cost of capital results in that the cost of equity of the levered firm $\widetilde{k}^{E,l}_t$ is weighted with the equity ratio and the cost of debt—reduced by the firm's income tax rate—with the debt ratio. Our calculation proves that this relation is valid independent of whether cost of equity and the debt ratio are certain or uncertain.

In order to prove the theorem we give the Definition 3.9 of the firm's cost of equity using (3.14) in the form

$$\left(1+\widetilde{WACC}_t\right)\widetilde{V}_t^l = \mathrm{E}\left[\widetilde{E}_{t+1}+\widetilde{D}_{t+1}+\widetilde{FCF}^l_{t+1}-\tau\left(\widetilde{I}_{t+1}+\widetilde{R}_{t+1}+\widetilde{D}_{t+1}-\widetilde{D}_t\right)|\mathcal{F}_t\right].$$

From taking advantage of Definitions 3.4 and 3.7 we get

$$\begin{aligned}\left(1+\widetilde{WACC}_t\right)\widetilde{V}_t^l &= \mathrm{E}\Big[\widetilde{E}_{t+1}+\widetilde{FCF}^l_{t+1}-\widetilde{I}_{t+1}-\widetilde{R}_{t+1}+ \\ &\qquad +(1-\tau)\left(\widetilde{D}_{t+1}+\widetilde{I}_{t+1}+\widetilde{R}_{t+1}\right)-\tau\widetilde{D}_t|\mathcal{F}_t\Big] \\ &= \left(1+k_t^{E,l}\right)\widetilde{E}_t+\left(\left(1+\widetilde{k}_t^D\right)(1-\tau)+\tau\right)\widetilde{D}_t.\end{aligned}$$

Divided by $\widetilde{V}_t^l$ and observing Definition 3.5, we finally get to the following representation:

$$\widetilde{WACC}_t = \widetilde{k}_t^{E,l}\left(1-\widetilde{l}_t\right)+\widetilde{k}_t^D(1-\tau)\widetilde{l}_t.$$

And that is what we wanted to show. q.e.d.

This textbook formula also allows for the following conclusions.

1. If it is assumed that the weighted average cost of capital as well as the cost of equity and debt of the levered firm are certain today, then the debt ratios must be certain. We are then dealing with a financing policy based on market values. FTE and WACC result in identical values of the firm in this case.
2. If the future debt ratios are, however, assumed to be uncertain, then in the case of no default either the weighted average cost of capital, or the cost of equity of the levered firm have to be uncertain. Thus one of the two theorem's formulations cannot be used to calculate with.

We want to summarize our statements made up to now on financing based on market values in Fig. 3.10. The illustration makes clear that the three procedures FTE, TCF, and WACC result in an identical value of the firm exactly then when the debt ratio is deterministic. In all other cases, only one of the three procedures can be used at most.

The attentive reader will notice that in all statements in this and the former section we have not made use of our assumption that the cash flows are weak autoregressive. We now turn to the adjustment formulas where this assumption will be necessary.

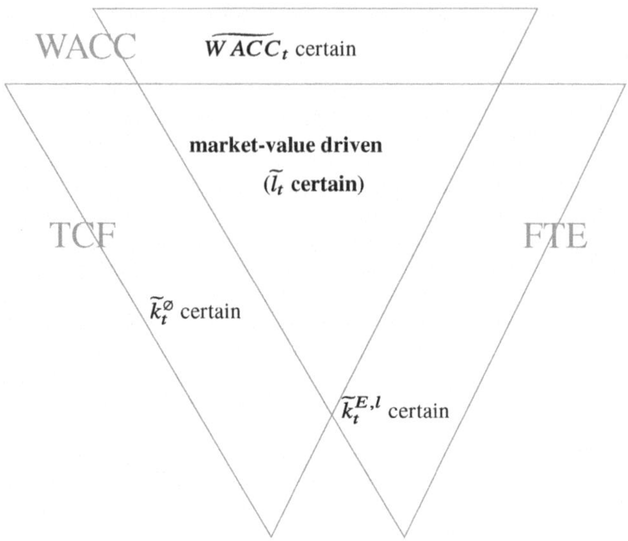

Fig. 3.10 DCF theory for financing based on market value

3.4.4 Miles–Ezzell- and Modigliani–Miller Adjustments

In the previous sections we got three different valuation equations for a levered firm with financing based on market values: FTE, TCF, and WACC formulas. We could clearly work out that these valuation equations can always typically be used when either the levered firm's cost of equity or the weighted average cost of capital (from type 1 or 2) is deterministic. We could make connections between the different cost of capital relevant for the three formulations with the so-called textbook formulas. Financing policy based on value stands out in that the debt ratios are deterministic. Our analysis of the textbook formulas established that with this type of financing policy, deterministic cost of capital of the two remaining valuation formulations logically results from deterministic cost of capital of a valuation formulation.

Until now, however, the relationship these three cost of capital demonstrate to the cost of capital of an unlevered firm has remained a secret. And exactly that is the subject of our subsequent considerations. If we require that the levered firm follows a financing policy based on market values, and if in addition we assume that the cost of equity of the unlevered firm are deterministic, then two questions arise:

1. Under these conditions, are the requirements of Theorems 3.9 and 3.12 met? Are the levered firm's cost of equity and the weighted average cost of capital then also deterministic?
2. Can we calculate the levered firm's cost of capital from the unlevered firm's cost of capital?

Adjustment According to Miles and Ezzell The answer to both questions is given by the so-called adjustment formula from Miles and Ezzell (1980).

Theorem 3.14 (Miles–Ezzell Adjustment Formula) *Financing based on market values is under consideration. The cash flows of the unlevered firm are weak autoregressive. If the unlevered firm's cost of capital or the WACC of the levered firm are deterministic, the following relation is valid:*

$$1 + WACC_t = \left(1 + k_t^{E,u}\right)\left(1 - \frac{\tau r_f}{1 + r_f} l_t\right),$$

in which all quantities in the equation are deterministic.

We prove this theorem as follows. According to the fundamental theorem and using Eq. (3.14), the following is valid for the market value: of the levered firm

$$\widetilde{V}_t^l = \frac{\mathrm{E}_Q\left[\widetilde{V}_{t+1}^l + \widetilde{FCF}_{t+1}^u + \tau\left(\widetilde{I}_{t+1} + \widetilde{R}_{t+1} + \widetilde{D}_{t+1} - \widetilde{D}_t\right) | \mathcal{F}_t\right]}{1 + r_f}.$$

Since the market value of the firm at time t is already known, the following results from rules 2 and 5 and Eq. (3.19):

$$\widetilde{V}_t^l = \frac{\mathrm{E}_Q\left[\widetilde{V}_{t+1}^l + \widetilde{FCF}_{t+1}^u | \mathcal{F}_t\right]}{1 + r_f} + \frac{\tau r_f}{1 + r_f} \widetilde{D}_t.$$

Using the debt ratio, this can be rewritten in the form

$$\left(1 - \frac{\tau r_f}{1 + r_f} l_t\right) \widetilde{V}_t^l = \frac{\mathrm{E}_Q\left[\widetilde{V}_{t+1}^l + \widetilde{FCF}_{t+1}^u | \mathcal{F}_t\right]}{1 + r_f}$$

or

$$\widetilde{V}_t^l = \frac{\mathrm{E}_Q\left[\widetilde{V}_{t+1}^l + \widetilde{FCF}_{t+1}^u | \mathcal{F}_t\right]}{\left(1 - \frac{\tau r_f}{1+r_f} l_t\right)(1 + r_f)}.$$

We are then looking at a type of recursive relationship from which we have already gotten a valuation equation several times.[28] Following this direction, we get this

[28]See, for example, our proof of the Theorem 2.1 in Sect. 2.3.3.

relation for the value of the levered firm

$$\widetilde{V}_t^l = \sum_{s=t+1}^{T} \frac{\mathrm{E}_Q\left[\widetilde{FCF}_s^u|\mathcal{F}_t\right]}{\left(1-\frac{\tau r_f}{1+r_f}l_{s-1}\right)\dots\left(1-\frac{\tau r_f}{1+r_f}l_t\right)\left(1+r_f\right)^{s-t}}.$$

Now we will only get further by falling back upon the Assumption 3.1 and the Theorem 3.3 supported by it.[29] If we use this theorem, we get

$$\widetilde{V}_t^l = \sum_{s=t+1}^{T} \frac{\mathrm{E}\left[\widetilde{FCF}_s^u|\mathcal{F}_t\right]}{\left(1-\frac{\tau r_f}{1+r_f}l_t\right)\left(1+k_t^{E,u}\right)\dots\left(1-\frac{\tau r_f}{1+r_f}l_{s-1}\right)\left(1+k_{s-1}^{E,u}\right)}.$$

From that now results the recursive relation

$$\widetilde{V}_t^l = \frac{\mathrm{E}\left[\widetilde{V}_{t+1}^l + \widetilde{FCF}_{t+1}^u|\mathcal{F}_t\right]}{\left(1-\frac{\tau r_f}{1+r_f}l_t\right)\left(1+k_t^{E,u}\right)}$$

or

$$\left(1-\frac{\tau r_f}{1+r_f}l_t\right)\left(1+k_t^{E,u}\right) = \frac{\mathrm{E}\left[\widetilde{V}_{t+1}^l + \widetilde{FCF}_{t+1}^u|\mathcal{F}_t\right]}{\widetilde{V}_t^l}.$$

A comparison with the Definition 3.9 shows that we have proven the claim. q.e.d.

If the equation from Theorem 3.14 is linked up with the textbook formula from Theorem 3.13, the meaning of the outcome becomes much clearer. Putting the textbook formula into the equation of Theorem 3.14 and slightly reworking it results in

$$k_t^{E,l} = k_t^{E,u} + L_t\left(k_t^{E,u} - k_t^D + \tau\left(k_t^D - \frac{1+k_t^{E,u}}{1+r_f}r_f\right)\right), \tag{3.23}$$

in which L_t represents the debt-equity ratio in the sense of Eq. (3.6). The cost of capital of the levered firm can be determined with this formula, if the cost of capital of the unlevered firm, the cost of debt, the income tax rate as well as the aspired leverage ratio and the riskless interest rate are known. If the above equation is solved according to $k_t^{E,u}$, the leverage ratio, and income tax rate are known, it calls for converting the cost of capital of a levered firm into the cost of capital of the unlevered firm. The condition is that the levered firm follows a financing policy based on market values.

[29]See Sect. 3.1.2.

The reader may want to take the time and take another look at Eq. (3.23). It is different in two not so unimportant details which are found in the original theorem from Miles and Ezzell (1980). We want to mention these differences with absolute clarity as the work from Miles and Ezzell has firmly established itself in today's textbook literature. With their formula there is no time index for the leverage ratio and also no time index for the cost of capital. In the current literature then, the adjustment formula does not run as it does in our Theorem 3.14, but rather

$$1 + WACC = \left(1 + k^{E,u}\right)\left(1 - \frac{\tau r_f}{1 + r_f} l\right). \tag{3.24}$$

Miles and Ezzell derived their result under the limitation of the assumption that the cost of capital and the debt ratio are constant in time. As a rule, this limitation is clearly pointed out in the textbook literature. The outcome that we have shown thus has much fewer restrictions than the original result from Miles and Ezzell.

Second, our adjustment formula also holds in case of a firm in danger of default. Even though the firm can go bankrupt, still not the cost of debt or any other discount factor but the riskless interest rate is found in Theorem 3.14. This is a surprising, but an inescapable consequence of our assumptions, that not only the owners, but also the creditors anticipate the threat of bankruptcy.

Problematic Adjustment According to Modigliani and Miller In the discussion of autonomous financing, we had mentioned that besides the Miles–Ezzell adjustment, there is yet another adjustment formula. It is termed Modigliani–Miller adjustment, originates from Theorem 3.7 and takes the form

$$WACC = k^{E,u}(1 - \tau l_0). \tag{3.25}$$

In practice, this adjustment formula is very popular, supposedly because it looks much more simple than the Miles–Ezzell equation (3.24). If you follow the relevant literature, then you get Eq. (3.25) from the conditions of Theorem 3.7 and particularly from the assumption of autonomous financing. Such a firm then cannot be financed based on market values. We will now present a surprising outcome.

Theorem 3.15 (Contradiction of the Modigliani–Miller Adjustment) *The cash flows of the unlevered firm are weak auto-regressive. If the weighted average cost of capital of type 2 ($WACC$) and the unlevered firm's cost of equity ($k^{E,u}$) are deterministic, then the firm is financed based on market values.*

First off we will prove the theorem and end up trying to recognize its significance. To prove the theorem we turn to the Theorems 3.1, 3.7, and 3.12 and use the fact that cash flows are weak auto-regressive. The following then applies:

$$\underbrace{\left(1-\tau\widetilde{l}_t\right)\sum_{s=t+1}^{T}\frac{(1+g_t)\dots(1+g_{s-1})\widetilde{FCF}_t^u}{(1+WACC_t)\dots(1+WACC_{s-1})}}_{=\widetilde{V}_t^l} =$$

$$= \underbrace{\sum_{s=t+1}^{T}\frac{(1+g_t)\dots(1+g_{s-1})\widetilde{FCF}_t^u}{\left(1+k_t^{E,u}\right)\dots\left(1+k_{s-1}^{E,u}\right)}}_{=\widetilde{V}_t^u}.$$

If we shorten $\widetilde{FCF}_t^u$, there remains

$$\left(1-\tau\widetilde{l}_t\right)\sum_{s=t+1}^{T}\frac{(1+g_t)\dots(1+g_{s-1})}{(1+WACC_t)\dots(1+WACC_{s-1})} =$$

$$= \sum_{s=t+1}^{T}\frac{(1+g_t)\dots(1+g_{s-1})}{\left(1+k_t^{E,u}\right)\dots\left(1+k_{s-1}^{E,u}\right)}.$$

Besides the debt ratio $\widetilde{l}_t$ we only find deterministic quantities. It is no problem to convert them according to $\widetilde{l}_t$. But then $\widetilde{l}_t$ has to be a deterministic quantity itself. That is what we wanted to show. q.e.d.

Of what significance is our assertion now? A Modigliani–Miller adjustment formulated as in Eq. (3.25) requires that the weighted average cost of capital as well as the equity of the unlevered firm are deterministic. The equation does not make sense under other conditions. Under this condition—we have just proven this—the case of financing based on market values is now indeed conceivable. And here is where the anomaly lies: the condition of the Modigliani–Miller model was, namely, autonomous financing with constant debt. Since a firm cannot be financed autonomously as well as based on market values, we have a contradiction. We do not object that there will be real numbers WACC that (in the case of autonomous financing) lead to the correct value of the levered firm. These numbers are appropriate discount rates given the above setup—but they cannot be interpreted as cost of capital as in Definition 3.9. This again highlights that cost of capital and discount rates cover different economic items.

Can we go a step further and claim to have refuted the theory of Modigliani and Miller? Have we perhaps detected an error in the argumentation of both authors? In answering this question, we have to carefully separate two aspects from each other. In this book we take the point of view that cost of capital are expected returns. For us that is the nucleus of a theory of valuation of firms. If this line of thought is followed, then the ideas of Modigliani and Miller simply do not hold up. Whoever interprets $WACC$ as expected returns, cannot simultaneously suppose a deterministic debt ratio and the Modigliani–Miller model (a constant amount of debt), without getting caught in a contradiction. To come at it from a totally different angle, we can ask if Modigliani and Miller had even understood $WACC$ as cost of capital and been aware of the contradiction. The answer here is unambiguous. For both authors—as, moreover, also for Miles and Ezzell—the weighted cost of capital $WACC$ was always only a quantity, which when used as a discount rate leads to the correct outcome; that is, the correct value of the firm.[30] Not one of these authors thought of an interpretation of these quantities as expected returns. This is why we are far away from blaming Modigliani and Miller for making an error.

3.4.5 Over-Indebtedness and Illiquidity with Financing Based on Market Values

We now turn to the case of financing based on market values. Here, the case of over-indebtedness will never occur. Illiquidity is possible and a sufficient condition can be precisely formulated.

Theorem 3.16 (Over-Indebtedness and Debt Ratio) *A levered firm with an infinite life span whose debt ratio l always remains the same is never over-indebted.*

If the condition

$$\frac{\widetilde{FCF}^u_t(\omega)}{\widetilde{FCF}^u_{t-1}(\omega)} < \frac{(1+r_f(1-\tau))(1+g)}{1+\frac{k^{E,u}-g}{l}-\frac{1+k^{E,u}}{1+r_f}r_f\tau+g}$$

is satisfied, then the firm is in danger of illiquidity at date t in state ω.

Again, the implications of this proposition can be illustrated by means of a binomial tree with only the case of illiquidity being of interest. The second part of the theorem requires that the growth factor for the down-movement (the left-hand side of the inequality) must not fall below a specific threshold.

The first statement of the theorem can easily be proven because for $l \leq 1$ we obtain $l\ \widetilde{V}^l_t(s) \leq \widetilde{V}^l_t(s)$ and thus $\widetilde{D}_t(s) \leq \widetilde{V}^l_t(s)$. The proof of the second statement is more sophisticated. Let us assume that the firm always remains liquid. In this case

$$\widetilde{FCF}^l_t(\omega) \geq (1+r_f)\widetilde{D}_{t-1}(\omega) - \widetilde{D}_t(\omega).$$

[30] That $(1-\tau l_0)k^{E,u}$ has this character was shown for the case of constant expected free cash flows in Sect. 3.3.1.

To refer to the unlevered firm's cash flows, we make use of Eq. (3.10) and obtain

$$\begin{aligned}\widetilde{FCF}_t^u(\omega) + \tau r_f \widetilde{D}_{t-1}(\omega) &\geq (1 + r_f)\widetilde{D}_{t-1}(\omega) - \widetilde{D}_t(\omega) \\ \widetilde{FCF}_t^u(\omega) &\geq (1 + r_f(1-\tau))\widetilde{D}_{t-1}(\omega) - \widetilde{D}_t(\omega) \\ \widetilde{FCF}_t^u(\omega) &\geq (1 + r_f(1-\tau)) l \widetilde{V}_{t-1}^l(\omega) - l\widetilde{V}_t^l(\omega).\end{aligned}$$

In the case of an eternally active firm with constant cost of capital, the firm value can be calculated by dividing the expected free cash flow by the cost of capital less the constant growth rate. For financing based on market values $\widetilde{V}_t^l(\omega) = \frac{(1+g)\widetilde{FCF}_t^u(\omega)}{WACC-g}$ suits. Therefore, we obtain a total of

$$\begin{aligned}\widetilde{FCF}_t^u(\omega) &\geq (1 + r_f(1-\tau)) l \frac{(1+g)\widetilde{FCF}_{t-1}^u(\omega)}{WACC - g} - l \frac{(1+g)\widetilde{FCF}_t^u(s)}{WACC - g} \\ \left(1 + \frac{l(1+g)}{WACC - g}\right)\widetilde{FCF}_t^u(\omega) &\geq (1 + r_f(1-\tau)) l \frac{(1+g)\widetilde{FCF}_{t-1}^u(\omega)}{WACC - g}\end{aligned}$$

which proves the assertion. q.e.d.

3.4.6 Example (Continued)

The Finite Case Without Default In our example the firm will be financed based on market values. In this case all three approaches FTE, TCF, and WACC will yield the same value of the firm. Since the leverage ratios are given, we concentrate on the WACC approach.

Now we suppose in contrast to the autonomous financing that the following capital structures are realized at future times:

$$l_0 = 50\%\,, \quad l_1 = 20\%\,, \quad l_2 = 0\%\,.$$

The weighted average cost of capital results from the Miles–Ezzell equation with

$$\begin{aligned}WACC_0 &= \left(1 + k^{E,u}\right)\left(1 - \frac{\tau r_f}{1 + r_f} l_0\right) - 1 \\ &= (1 + 0.2)\left(1 - \frac{0.5 \cdot 0.1}{1 + 0.1} \cdot 0.5\right) - 1 \approx 17.27\%\,, \\ WACC_1 &\approx 18.91\%, \\ WACC_2 &= 20\%.\end{aligned}$$

With that the value of the firm amounts to

$$V_0^l = \frac{\mathrm{E}\left[\widetilde{FCF}_1^u\right]}{1+WACC_0} + \frac{\mathrm{E}\left[\widetilde{FCF}_2^u\right]}{(1+WACC_0)(1+WACC_1)} + \\ + \frac{\mathrm{E}\left[\widetilde{FCF}_3^u\right]}{(1+WACC_0)(1+WACC_1)(1+WACC_2)}$$

$$\approx \frac{100}{1.1727} + \frac{110}{1.1727 \cdot 1.1891} + \frac{121}{1.1727 \cdot 1.1891 \cdot 1.20} \approx 236.46\,.$$

Financing based on market values obviously leads to a totally different value of the firm than autonomous financing.

When considering default we need the value of the company at time $t = 1$. Here we get

$$\widetilde{V}_1^l = \frac{\mathrm{E}\left[\widetilde{FCF}_2^u|\mathcal{F}_1\right]}{1+WACC_1} + \frac{\mathrm{E}\left[\widetilde{FCF}_3^u|\mathcal{F}_1\right]}{(1+WACC_1)(1+WACC_2)}$$

$$\approx \begin{cases} \frac{121}{1.1891} + \frac{133.1}{1.1891 \cdot 1.20} \approx 195.04, & \text{if up;} \\ \frac{99}{1.1891} + \frac{108.9}{1.1891 \cdot 1.20} \approx 159.58, & \text{if down.} \end{cases}$$

Due to the financing policy based on market values, the payments for the creditors shown in Fig. 3.11 will be yielded in the future. Please observe that $l_2 = 0$ applies.[31]

The Finite Case with Default Now we will go into the question as to if a finance based on market values can lead to bankruptcy and, if possible, complete our model in a suitable way. To this end we remind our reader that the provisional leverage policy is assumed to take the form

$$l_0 = 50\%\,, \quad l_1 = 20\%\,, \quad l_2 = 0\%\,.$$

We want to evaluate the free cash flows $\widetilde{FCF}_t^l$ of the levered firm with default risk. Default enters in if

$$\widetilde{FCF}_t^l - \left(1 + r_f\right) l_{t-1}\, \widetilde{V}_{t-1}^l + l_t\, \widetilde{V}_t^l < 0$$

is given. Again, we have systematically compiled the corresponding amounts in Fig. 3.12. The figure shows that at time $t = 1$ a problem comes up, the case of bankruptcy is at issue.

[31] Notice that with this financing policy the binomial model is not (fully) recombining: even with a nominal interest rate of 10% the states ud and du do not yield the same cash flows to the debt holder. This is so because the debt and hence the tax shields are different: $\widetilde{D}_2(ud) = l_1 \widetilde{V}_1^l(u) \neq l_1 \widetilde{V}_1^l(d) = \widetilde{D}_2(du)$. The same does not apply at $t = 3$ because $l_2 = 0$.

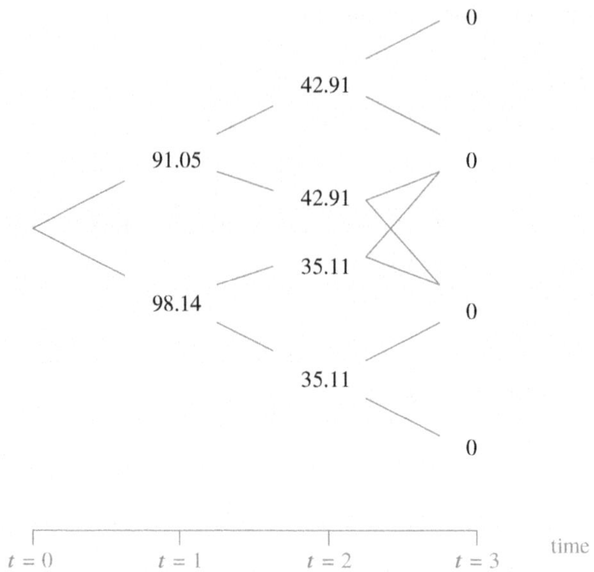

Fig. 3.11 Debtor's claims if $l_0 = 50\%$, $l_1 = 20\%$, $l_2 = 0\%$

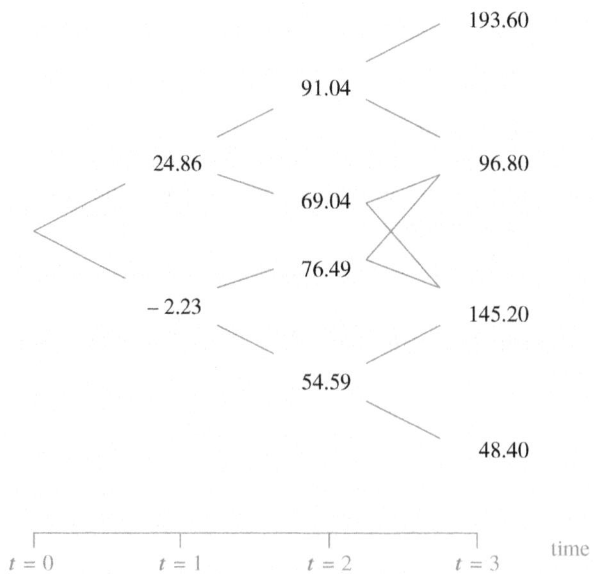

Fig. 3.12 Shareholder's claims without default if $l_0 = 50\%$, $l_1 = 20\%$, $l_2 = 0\%$

This generates an interruption of payments but does not cause an inability to pay. Therefore, in contrast to the situation in Sect. 3.2.6, the shareholders can avert a default. It is quite obvious that in $t = 1$ the credit D_0 as well as the owing interests $r_f D_0$ cannot be paid completely. A possible solution would be an extension for payment. Assuming that the creditors accept an extension for capital deficit of 2.23 until $t = 2$, a default would be prevented. But such a step disagrees with our assumptions: We assumed that the investors pursue an exogenous leverage policy even if it is not optimal. In our case, it is the described extension for credit which disagrees with the assumption. This example shows exactly the limitations of our model. If (and only if) the leverage policy is given, the default risk has no influence at all on the value of the company.

As a matter of course, in a situation such as shown in Fig. 3.12, the owners of the company will certainly demand a financing policy which is different from the one originally planned. It is obvious that a different financing policy leads to another company value. But we will not care about the question which financing policy would be the most reasonable. Even though the originally agreed financing policy could be evaluated, we state that this policy is economically illogical. Therefore, we will cease the discussion of our example.

The Infinite Case Let us turn to the infinite case. We assume that the leverage ratio $l = 50\%$ remains constant. If we use the Miles–Ezzell adjustment (Theorem 3.14), the weighted average cost of capital are

$$WACC = (1 + k^{E,u}) \left(1 - \frac{\tau r_f}{1 + r_f} l\right) - 1 \approx 17.273\%$$

and from Theorem 3.12 we get

$$\begin{aligned} V_0^l &= \sum_{t=1}^{\infty} \frac{\mathrm{E}\left[\widetilde{FCF}_t^u | \mathcal{F}_0\right]}{(1 + WACC)^t} \\ &= \sum_{t=1}^{\infty} \frac{FCF_0^u}{(1 + WACC)^t} = \frac{FCF_0^u}{WACC} \\ &\approx \frac{100}{0.17273} \approx 578.947\,. \end{aligned}$$

This is the value of the levered firm at $t = 0$.

3.4.7 Problems

1. Consider a company having (unlevered) cash flows as in Fig. 2.2. The tax rate is 50% and the riskless interest rate 10%. Assume further that $WACC = 18\%$, but nothing is known about the cost of equity $k^{E,u}$. We do not require that the company maintains a deterministic leverage ratio $\widetilde{l}$ and will show with this problem that the other DCF methods of this chapter are not applicable.
   (a) Evaluate the value of the firm using the WACC method for $t = 0, 1$.
   (b) Convince yourself that no assumptions are made yet about the expected future amount of debt since we do not require a deterministic leverage ratio. Instead, for $t = 0, 1$ we will assume the following debt: schedule

$$D_0 = 50, \quad \widetilde{D}_1 = \begin{cases} 60 & \text{if up,} \\ 40 & \text{if down.} \end{cases}$$

   Determine the leverage ratio at $t = 1$ and show that the firm is not financed based on market values.
   (c) Evaluate the weighted cost of capital (type 1) at $t = 1$ as well as the cost of equity of the levered firm and show that they both are random variables.
2. Show that for $k^{E,u} > r_f$ the Miles–Ezzell-WACC from (3.24) is always larger than $k^{E,u}(1 - \tau l_0)$ if $l_0 = l$ is the leverage ratio of the firm.
3. Verify that in the infinite example

$$\widetilde{V}_t^l = \frac{\widetilde{V}_t^u}{1 - \frac{1+k^{E,u}}{1+r_f}\frac{r_f}{k^{E,u}}\tau l}.$$

   (This is the main result of Miles and Ezzell (1985).)
4. Cost of capital are often evaluated using the capital asset pricing model (CAPM). Due to the CAPM any cost of capital k are given by

$$k_t = r_f + \left(\mathrm{E}\left[r_M\right] - r_f\right)\beta_t,$$

   where r_M is the return on the market portfolio and β_t the so-called beta factor. Let β_t^{WACC} be the beta factor of $WACC_t$ and $\beta_t^{E,u}$ of $k_t^{E,u}$. Write down a beta form of the Miles–Ezzell formula.

3.5 Financing Based on Book Values

Until now, we have debated two forms of financing policy, which are often discussed in the literature. With autonomous financing the taking out and redemption of debt followed a static, pre-given plan, which did not take any kind of random developments into consideration. With financing based on market values in contrast, the risk of debt was linked to the random development of the equity's market value by a given relation. For firms listed on the exchange that means that with climbing share prices, loans are to be taken out, and that with falling prices, debts are to be redeemed. We have stressed again and again that we want to lay back on making claims about which of the different financing policies is particularly realistic. If we bring another financing policy into play in the following, it is because we have the impression that it most probably plays an important role in business practice. If the managers of a firm announce that they are planning on lowering or raising the leverage ratio, then they are usually not measuring the leverage ratio in market values, but in book values. Both value formulations widely diverge from each other. That motivates us to analyze a third financing policy in the following section. Just as financing based on market values, this is based on debt ratios; this time, however, as book values.

3.5.1 Assumptions

With debt and equity as book values, those amounts are in question with which the debts or—according to case—equity are reported in the balance books of the firm to be valued. The first assumption consists in there being no difference between market value and book value of the debt. The credit amounts given in the balance sheets of the firm to be valued correspond to their market prices. Furthermore, we will assume that there is no danger of default.

Assumption 3.7 (Book Value of Debt) *The firm will not default*

$$\widetilde{R}_{t+1} = \widetilde{D}_t - \widetilde{D}_{t+1} \quad \textit{and} \quad \widetilde{I}_{t+1} = r_f \widetilde{D}_t .$$

Furthermore, the debt's market value continuously corresponds to its book value,

$$\underline{\widetilde{D}}_t = \widetilde{D}_t .$$

It is different with equity. If you are working from an initial quantity of $\underline{\widetilde{E}}_t$ and inquire about the book value of the equity at time $t+1$, then you have to look at those quantities, which can change it. There are three:

1. Equity grows, if the owners subscribe additional equity within the framework of an increase of capital. The amount of the increase in capital between the times t and s is designated by $\underline{\widetilde{e}}^{I}_{t,s}$.[32]

[32]It is possible that the amount of increase in capital turns out to be different between the unlevered and levered companies. At first glance, this sounds paradoxical, because if both increases in capital diverge there should be a statement about the appropriation of the additional funds. Nevertheless, it can be proven that such conditions are not necessary due to our assumptions regarding the policies of investment and distribution. The explanation is simple: We have mentioned nothing about the asset side on the balance sheet in our model.

2. Equity grows further if the managers retain earnings. The levered firm's earnings after taxes at time $t+1$ amount to $\left(\widetilde{EBIT}_{t+1} - \widetilde{I}_{t+1}\right)(1-\tau)$.
3. Equity decreases if the firm pays dividends to the owners. In relation to the FTE approach and using Eq. (3.14), we made clear that payments in the amount of

$$\widetilde{FCF}^u_{t+1} + \tau \widetilde{I}_{t+1} - \left(\widetilde{I}_{t+1} + \widetilde{D}_t - \widetilde{D}_{t+1}\right)$$

are being dealt with.[33]

For the book value of the equity at time $t+1$, we get a total of

$$\begin{aligned}\underline{\widetilde{E}}^l_{t+1} &= \underline{\widetilde{E}}^l_t + \underline{\widetilde{e}}^l_{t,t+1} + \left(\widetilde{EBIT}_{t+1} - \widetilde{I}_{t+1}\right)(1-\tau) \\ &\quad - \left(\widetilde{FCF}^u_{t+1} + \tau \widetilde{I}_{t+1} - \left(\widetilde{I}_{t+1} + \widetilde{D}_t - \widetilde{D}_{t+1}\right)\right) \\ &= \underline{\widetilde{E}}^l_t + \underline{\widetilde{e}}^l_{t,t+1} + \widetilde{EBIT}_{t+1}(1-\tau) - \widetilde{FCF}^u_{t+1} + \underline{\widetilde{D}}_t - \underline{\widetilde{D}}_{t+1}.\end{aligned}$$

This gives nothing more than the clean surplus relation.

Assumption 3.8 (Clean Surplus Relation) *The book value of a levered firm results from*

$$\underline{\widetilde{E}}^l_{t+1} = \underline{\widetilde{E}}^l_t + \underline{\widetilde{e}}^l_{t,t+1} + \widetilde{EBIT}_{t+1}(1-\tau) - \widetilde{FCF}^u_{t+1} + \underline{\widetilde{D}}_t - \underline{\widetilde{D}}_{t+1}.$$

Since $\underline{\widetilde{V}}_t = \underline{\widetilde{E}}^l_t + \underline{\widetilde{D}}_t$, the book value of the firm's value then obeys the following equation.

Theorem 3.17 (Operating Assets Relation) *The book value of a levered firm results from*

$$\underline{\widetilde{V}}^l_{t+1} = \underline{\widetilde{V}}^l_t + \underline{\widetilde{e}}^l_{t,t+1} + \widetilde{EBIT}_{t+1}(1-\tau) - \widetilde{FCF}^u_{t+1}.$$

Furthermore, the book values of the levered and the unlevered firm differ only if there are different changes in subscribed capital.

Due to the fact that the earnings before interest and taxes as well as the free cash flows of the unlevered firm are random variables, the book value of the firm must be stochastic as well.

The financing policy to be looked at in this section is now characterized by the following definition.

[33] See Sect. 3.4.1.

Definition 3.10 (Financing Based on Book Values) A firm is financed based on book values if the debt ratios to book values $\underline{\widetilde{l}}_t$ are deterministic.

How is a firm's market value to be determined if we suppose a financing policy based on book values? In order to get any further, we have to characterize such a firm more in detail. In doing so we want to differentiate three cases that deal with the investment policy of the firm.

In two of them we have to work with assumptions which combine the volume of investment functionally with other economic ratios of the company. This might surprise the attentive reader due to the principle we assumed earlier. This stated that investments will be carried out only if their net present value is positive. If we adhere to this principle, it is not at all apparent that the volume of investment will be directly linked to specific characteristics like the cash flow or depreciation in a certain way.[34] But admittedly, we are not able to develop valuation equations without such relationships.

1. The firm could carry out a policy of full distribution. In this case the owners annually receive a dividend in amount of the net profit after taxes.
2. The firm could dispense with the policy of full distribution, but carry out an investment policy, which is heavily linked to accruals. In this case the firm would limit itself to undertaking replacement investments.
3. The firm could not link its investments to the accruals but instead to the cash flows. If the cash flows grow, a lot is invested; with low cash flow, in contrast, the investments are returned.

We can give valuation formulas for each of these cases. Each of these valuation equations does indeed require that the changes in the subscribed capital are deterministic. Thus

Assumption 3.9 (Subscribed Capital) *The changes in subscribed capital* $\underline{\widetilde{e}}^{\,l}_{t,t+1}$ *are deterministic for all* $t \geq 0$.

Investment and Accruals In the following we will examine three different investment or distribution policies, as the case may be. Although to do so, we need to more precisely define our notion of investment expenses within the framework of our model. For that we look at Fig. 3.4. This presents a relation between the free cash flow, the gross cash flow as well as the investments. Therefore, using (3.8) the

[34]There are plenty of research studies about the question of whether the volume of investment is linked to the cash flow of the company, for example. We refer to Fazzari et al. (1987) who show that with market imperfections some firms are constrained in their ability to raise funds externally, hence fluctuations in cash flows account for economically important movements in investment.

following relation is valid for the unlevered firm:

$$\widetilde{FCF}^{u}_{t+1} = \widetilde{GCF}_{t+1} - \tau \widetilde{EBIT}_{t+1} - \widetilde{Inv}_{t+1}. \tag{3.26}$$

We must also more precisely define the relation between the gross cash flows and accruals in the firm. For that we again take a look at the figure and infer the relation

$$\widetilde{GCF}_{t+1} = \widetilde{EBIT}_{t+1} + \widetilde{Accr}_{t+1}$$

with which the above equation can be simplified to

$$\widetilde{EBIT}_{t+1}(1-\tau) - \widetilde{FCF}^{u}_{t+1} = \widetilde{Inv}_{t+1} - \widetilde{Accr}_{t+1}. \tag{3.27}$$

Let us next turn to the full distribution policy.

3.5.2 Full Distribution Policy

It is doubtful whether there are really firms, which continuously distribute their earnings fully. Those persons based on the tradition of Anglo-Saxon financing theory would even regard such a dividend policy as rather foolish. If you believe, namely that the managers should go ahead with all investment projects, which have a positive NPV, then only those funds would be distributed which have no chance of turning over a profit within the firm. If the firm resolutely adheres to this idea, then the dividend policy is a plain residuum. And then too of course if the managers do not retain earnings on principle, we can hardly be speaking of far-reaching ideas being made on the managerial level regarding a sensible dividend policy. But if we still discuss this case further on, it is because it has a long tradition in Germany within the practice of valuation of firms.[35]

The profit after interest and taxes that the levered firm attains amounts to

$$\left(\widetilde{EBIT}_{t+1} - \widetilde{I}_{t+1}\right)(1-\tau).$$

When we were previously discussing the FTE formulation, we already made it clear that the owners of the levered firm annually receive distributions in the amount of (see (3.22))

$$\widetilde{Div}_{t+1} = \widetilde{FCF}^{u}_{t+1} + \tau \widetilde{I}_{t+1} - \left(\widetilde{D}_t + \widetilde{I}_{t+1} - \widetilde{D}_{t+1}\right).$$

In the case of full distribution of the profit made, both amounts must be identical. This leads us to the following definition.

[35] See, for example, Institut der Wirtschaftsprüfer in Deutschland (2013).

Definition 3.11 (Full Distribution) The levered firm for which

$$\left(\widetilde{EBIT}_{t+1} - \widetilde{I}_{t+1}\right)(1-\tau) = \widetilde{Div}_{t+1}$$

is valid each time $t \geq 0$, is following a policy of full distribution.

This can be rearranged to

$$\widetilde{FCF}^u_{t+1} = \widetilde{EBIT}_{t+1}(1-\tau) + \underline{\widetilde{D}}_t - \underline{\widetilde{D}}_{t+1}\,.$$

Let us make use again of the considerations of the previous section, particularly in relation to gross and free cash flows in Eq. (3.27). We want to use this equation to help us characterize the implicit basis of investment policy. To do so we concentrate on those investments, which are not replacement investments: these are those investments which will be concluded in excess of the difference $\widetilde{Inv}_{t+1} - \widetilde{Accr}_{t+1}$. Eq. (3.27) shows that a full distribution is being looked at exactly then when these investments are being financed by debt, thus when

$$\widetilde{Inv}_{t+1} - \widetilde{Accr}_{t+1} = \left(\underline{\widetilde{D}}_t - \underline{\widetilde{D}}_{t+1}\right)$$

is valid.

The full distribution results in that the equity's book value can change solely due to changes in the subscribed capital: if we enter in the condition of full distribution in the valuation equation (Theorem 3.17), then under Assumption 3.9 this results in

$$\begin{aligned}\underline{\widetilde{V}}^l_{t+1} &= \underline{\widetilde{V}}^l_t + \underline{e}^l_{t,t+1} - \underline{\widetilde{D}}_t + \underline{\widetilde{D}}_{t+1}\\ \underline{\widetilde{E}}^l_{t+1} &= \underline{\widetilde{E}}^l_t + \underline{e}^l_{t,t+1},\end{aligned}$$

which agrees with what we have stated. Apart from changes to the subscribed capital, the equity's book value remains constant through time.

With no further work, we can now assume that the equity's book value at time $t = 0$ is known. Thus, no random variable is being represented. From this we get

$$\begin{aligned}\underline{\widetilde{E}}^l_{t+1} &= \underline{E}^l_0 + \underline{e}^l_{0,1} + \ldots + \underline{e}^l_{t,t+1}\\ &= \underline{E}^l_0 + \underline{e}^l_{0,t+1}.\end{aligned}$$

for the book value of equity at time $t+1$. Since there are only deterministic quantities on the right-hand side, the book value of equity at time $t+1$ must be deterministic.

Let us now make use of the fact that the debt ratio $\underline{l}_t$ measured in book values is deterministic. The leverage ratio $\underline{L}_t$, which must be deterministic as well, can be deduced from the debt ratio with no further work. According to definition,

$$\widetilde{\underline{D}}_{t+1} = \underline{L}_{t+1}\left(\underline{E}_0^l + \underline{e}_{0,t+1}^l\right),$$

is valid for the book value of debt at time $t+1$, and from that it follows that the book value of debt is deterministic. If we bring this together with Assumption 3.7, we can determine that the market value of debt is deterministic. The firm is autonomously financed. These realizations can be summed up in the following theorem.

Theorem 3.18 (Market Value with Full Distribution) *If a firm is financed based on book values and simultaneously carries out a policy of full distribution, then the following equation is valid for the market value of the levered firm at all times:*

$$\widetilde{V}_t^l = \widetilde{V}_t^u + \sum_{s=t+1}^{T} \frac{\tau r_f \underline{L}_{s-1}\left(\underline{E}_0^l + \underline{e}_{0,s-1}^l\right)}{\left(1+r_f\right)^{s-t}}.$$

We need not repeat the proof here.

3.5.3 Replacement Investments

If a firm solely carries out investments in the scope of its accruals, it foregoes expansion investments and only takes on replacements investments. There are a lot of similarities here to the policy of full distribution just discussed. But it is not totally the same, as we will shortly make clear.

Definition 3.12 (Replacement Investment) A levered firm exclusively takes on replacement investments, if it only invests within the scope of accruals in each period,

$$\widetilde{Inv}_t = \widetilde{Accr}_t$$

for all $t > 0$.

The main consequence of this definition is the fact that the book value of the firm only changes when the subscribed capital changes. Entering in Eq. (3.27) under Assumption 3.12 brings us to

$$\begin{aligned}\widetilde{EBIT}_t(1-\tau) - \widetilde{FCF}_t^u &= \widetilde{Inv}_t - \widetilde{Accr}_t \\ &= 0.\end{aligned} \tag{3.28}$$

That means: If a firm exclusively takes on replacement investments, then there is no more difference between the profit after taxes of the unlevered firm and that amount that the unlevered firm would distribute to its owners. If we enter in this result into the valuation equation for the book value of the value of the firm (Theorem 3.17), then under Assumptions 3.9 there remains

$$\widetilde{\underline{V}}^l_{t+1} = \widetilde{\underline{V}}^l_t + \underline{e}^l_{t,t+1},$$

and we can recognize that the book value of the firm in fact only can change on the basis of changes in subscribed capital. Since we require that the book value of the firm is known at time $t = 0$, and does not represent a random variable, the following applies:

$$\begin{aligned}\widetilde{\underline{V}}^l_{t+1} &= \underline{V}^l_0 + \underline{e}^l_{0,1} + \ldots + \underline{e}^l_{t,t+1} \\ &= \underline{V}^l_0 + \underline{e}^l_{0,t+1}.\end{aligned}$$

Since there are only deterministic quantities on the right-hand side, the book value of the value of the firm must be deterministic at time $t + 1$.

If we now take advantage of the firm implementing a financing policy based on book values, then the following is valid for the book value of debt at time $t + 1$:

$$\widetilde{\underline{D}}_{t+1} = \underline{l}_{t+1}\left(\underline{V}^l_0 + \underline{e}^l_{0,t+1}\right).$$

It follows from this that this quantity is deterministic. In relation to Assumption 3.7, it again comes down to the realization that we are dealing with a firm where the financing policy is autonomous. Consequently, we have proven the following theorem.

Theorem 3.19 (Market Value with Replacement Investments) *If a firm is financed based on book values and exclusively carries out replacement investments, then the following equation is valid for the levered firm at each time:*

$$\widetilde{V}^l_t = \widetilde{V}^u_t + \sum_{s=t+1}^{T} \frac{\tau r_f \underline{l}_{s-1}\left(\underline{V}^l_0 + \underline{e}^l_{0,s-1}\right)}{\left(1 + r_f\right)^{s-t}}.$$

Long-Term Constant Amount of Debt In the section on autonomous financing, we concentrated on an (exacting) special case, which is mentioned in the literature as the Modigliani–Miller equation.[36] We also want to deal here with this case concerning the debt which continuously stays the same.

Theorem 3.20 (Modigliani–Miller Formula Based on Book Values) *The firm lives forever and the conditions of Theorem 3.19 are valid. The debt ratio remains*

[36]See Sect. 3.3.1.

constant through time. The following is then valid for the market value of the firm:

$$\widetilde{V}_t^l = \widetilde{V}_t^u + \tau \underline{l} \left(\underline{V}_0^l + \underline{e}_{0,t}^l \right).$$

We cannot recognize any essential difference from the original equation from Modigliani and Miller (see Theorem 3.7). The proof of the theorem is virtually trivial. Since the debt ratio as well as the book value of the value of the firm remain constant, the amount of debt is constant. With that the conditions of the Modigliani–Miller equation (Theorem 3.7) are met. And it is just that which must be shown.

3.5.4 Investment Policy Based on Cash Flows

It is not very often that firms exclusively carry out replacement investments, or have a policy of full distribution. They most often follow an investment policy, which is independent of the accruals. They will, for instance, make expansion investments or occasionally let the capacity of the firm shrink. The considerations of the two previous sections do not help us any further in these much more realistic cases. We have to develop new ideas. Let us start out looking at the investment policy and end up with accruals.

Concerning investment policy we want to follow the idea that the managers constantly reinvest an exogenously predetermined percentage of the cash flows. This percentage may be deterministic and already be fixed at time $t = 0$.

Definition 3.13 (Investments Based on Cash Flows) We define an investment policy as based on cash flows, if the investments for all future times $t > 0$ are a deterministic multiple of the free cash flows of the unlevered firm,

$$\widetilde{Inv}_t = \alpha_t \, \widetilde{FCF}_t^u.$$

You could of course get involved in linking the investment policy to the free cash flows of the levered firm, and thus work with the definition $\widetilde{Inv}_t = \alpha_t \, \widetilde{FCF}_t^l$. It does not matter in the end whether you are referring to the free cash flows of the unlevered firm or the levered firm. But we regard our procedure as being justified for the following reasons: if we want to value levered firms with their correct cost of capital, the unlevered firm only ever represents a reference point for us. This reference firm should differ neither with respect to its investment policy nor in regard to its accruals from the actual firm—as a rule a levered firm—to be valued, see our Assumption 3.2.[37] And Definition 3.13 sees to it that the investment policy is independent from the leverage.

[37] See Sect. 3.2.2.

Our assumption could likewise be viewed critically, because the investments $\widetilde{Inv}_t$ were already deducted from the cash flows $\widetilde{FCF}^u_t$. It would then practically be a relation, in which consideration is better given to the gross cash flows after taxes:

$$\widetilde{Inv}_t = \beta_t \left(\widetilde{GCF}_t - \tau \widetilde{EBT}_t \right).$$

But from Eq. (3.26) there results after a little reformulating for the unlevered firm

$$\widetilde{Inv}_t = \frac{\beta_t}{1 - \beta_t} \widetilde{FCF}^u_t .$$

We come to the following conclusion from this: If parameter $\beta \in (0,1)$ is seen as realistic, then α will typically be greater than zero, but not necessarily smaller than one. Furthermore, values of α are conceivable, which exceed the value of one.

We address ourselves to the accruals now. Provided that the congruence principle applies, the sum of accruals equals the sum of investment payments,

$$\sum_t \widetilde{Accr}_t = \sum_t \widetilde{Inv}_t .$$

For this expression the past and future sums need to be determined. However, this equation is not sufficient if more precise statements for the value of the company are needed.

In the literature, one differentiates between accruals which are discretionary and non-discretionary. Non-discretionary accruals have a definite functional correlation with the investment payments. Furthermore they are marked by a certain regularity. In the following, the non-discretionary accruals will be only those which result from a direct linear correlation to the amounts invested. This seems to be especially advisable if the accruals consist solely of depreciations and a straight-line depreciation is applied. Obviously, the congruence principle which we just mentioned is valid in this case as well.

Assumption 3.10 (Non-Discretionary Accruals) *Accruals are established from*

$$\widetilde{Accr}_t = \frac{1}{n} \left(\widetilde{Inv}_{t-1} + \ldots + \widetilde{Inv}_{t-n} \right).$$

If we want to value a firm at time $t = 0$, the investment expenses of the previous periods of time $t = -1$ to $t = -(n-1)$ must also be known. It should not be impossible to obtain this information.

The subsequent calculations show that the lack of discretionary accruals is not of critical importance for the development of a valuation equation. It is sufficient that the accruals linearly depend on investments the investment expenses $\widetilde{Inv}_{-1}$ through $\widetilde{Inv}_{t-n}$.

The Definition 3.13 and the Assumption 3.10 now suffice to prove the following theorem.

Theorem 3.21 (Investment Policy Based on Cash Flows) *The cash flows of the unlevered firm are weak auto-regressive and the firm follows a financing based on book values. There are only non-discretionary accruals and the investment policy is based on cash flows. The following is then valid for the market value of the levered firm:*

$$V_0^l = V_0^u + \tau r_f \sum_{t=0}^{T-1} \underline{l}_t \frac{\underline{V}_0^l + \underline{e}_{0,t} - \sum_{s=1-n}^{0} \frac{\min(n+s,t)}{n} Inv_s}{\left(1+r_f\right)^{t+1}} +$$
$$+\tau r_f \sum_{t=1}^{T-1} \frac{\alpha_t \operatorname{E}\left[\widetilde{FCF}_t^u\right]}{(1+k^{E,u})^t} \left(\frac{\frac{n}{n}\underline{l}_t}{1+r_f} + \frac{\frac{n-1}{n}\underline{l}_{t+1}}{\left(1+r_f\right)^2} + \ldots + \frac{\frac{1}{n}\underline{l}_{n+t-1}}{\left(1+r_f\right)^n} \right)$$

with $\underline{l}_s = 0$ *for* $s \geq T$.

Since this theorem's proof is very involved, we refer interested readers to the appendix.[38] The equation named in the current theorem is only formulated for time $t = 0$, and is nevertheless anything but pleasant to read. It can be generalized with considerable technical effort so that a result for $\widetilde{V}_t^l$ can be obtained. This representation certainly does not give any new insights. That is why we forego presenting it here.

Long-Term Constant Debt Ratios We also want to again examine here how the valuation equation changes when we make certain simplifications. To do so we particularly require that there is no resulting increase in subscribed capital and that the parameters α_t and $\underline{l}_t$ remain constant. We further suppose that the firm exists infinitely long. In contrast to Theorem 3.7, we do not, however, assume that the cash flows have a constant, or constantly growing, expectation. We can then, nevertheless, substantiate the outcome—which at first seems surprising and is by no means obvious—that a valuation formula, which is very similar to the Modigliani–Miller equation, is valid.

Theorem 3.22 (Adapted Modigliani–Miller Formula) *The conditions of Theorem 3.21 are valid. The firms exist perpetually. The debt ratio* $\underline{l}$ *and the investment parameter* α *are constant. The influence of past investments on the book value can be disregarded. The following is then valid for the market value of the firm:*

$$V_0^l = V_0^u \left(1 + \frac{n r_f - 1 + \left(1+r_f\right)^{-n}}{n r_f} \tau \alpha \underline{l} \right) + \tau D_0.$$

[38] See Sect. 6.2.

The proof is again found in the appendix.[39] In comparison to the original equation from Modigliani and Miller, two terms appear, which are easy to handle mathematically with all the technics in use today. But since it is, nevertheless, not readily understandable, we want to simplify it somewhat. For low interest rates, it appears that

$$\frac{nr_f - 1 + \left(1 + r_f\right)^{-n}}{nr_f} \approx \frac{(n+1)r_f}{2}$$

is valid.[40] With that a preliminary estimate of the order of magnitude of this term is easily possible.

Adjustment Formulas We also need adjustment formulas in the case of financing policy based on book values. Whoever wants to, for instance, work with the valuation equation of Theorem 3.21, can only do so if the cost of capital of the unlevered firm $k^{E,u}$ is known. We see two ways of obtaining this information if there is no reference firm available that is actually free of debt.

If we know all variables of the valuation equation besides $k^{E,u}$ of a levered reference firm, the cost of capital being sought after can be determined with the help of an iteration.[41] The fact that we cannot simply solve the valuation equation according to $k^{E,u}$, would then be a cosmetic blemish at best.

3.5.5 Example (Continued)

The Finite Case The duration of depreciation is $n = 2$. Under this condition the assumption that investments will be made exclusively at time $t = 1$ and not afterwards is useful,

$$\alpha_1 = 50\% \,, \quad \alpha_2 = \alpha_3 = 0\% \,.$$

---

[39]See Sect. 6.3.

[40]With help of a Taylor expansion the following holds:

$$\left(1 + r_f\right)^{-n} \approx 1 - nr_f + \frac{n(n+1)}{2} r_f^2$$

and from that immediately results

$$\frac{nr_f - 1 + \left(1 + r_f\right)^{-n}}{nr_f} \approx \frac{n+1}{2} r_f \,.$$

[41]In doing so, constant investment parameters α and constant debt ratios $\underline{l}$ would presumably be worked with within the framework of a practical application.

The book value of the levered firm at time $t = 0$ is

$$\underline{V}_0^l = 150.$$

For the debt ratios based on book values, we choose just those ratios, which were also used in the example of financing based on market values,

$$\underline{l}_0 = 50\% , \quad \underline{l}_1 = 20\% , \quad \underline{l}_2 = 0\% .$$

For simplicity's sake, we assume that in the previous periods there were no investments and there were no systematic increases in the subscribed capital,

$$Inv_{-1} = Inv_0 = 0, \quad \underline{e}_{0,2} = 0.$$

If we employ everything in the valuation equation according to Theorem 3.21, we then get

$$\begin{aligned} V_0^l &= V_0^u + \tau r_f \underline{V}_0^l \sum_{t=0}^{2} \frac{\underline{l}_t}{(1+r_f)^{t+1}} + \tau r_f \frac{\alpha_1 \operatorname{E}\left[\widetilde{FCF}_1^u\right]}{1+k^{E,u}} \left(\frac{\underline{l}_1}{1+r_f} + \frac{\frac{1}{2}\underline{l}_2}{(1+r_f)^2} \right) \\ &\approx 229.75 + 0.5 \cdot 0.1 \cdot 150 \cdot \left(\frac{0.5}{1.1} + \frac{0.2}{1.1^2} \right) + 0.5 \cdot 0.1 \cdot \frac{0.5 \cdot 100}{1.2} \cdot \frac{0.2}{1.1} \\ &\approx 234.77 . \end{aligned}$$

The Infinite Case As in the above example we assume that the debt ratio measured in book values remains constant. If we use

$$n = 2, \quad \alpha = 50\% , \quad \underline{l} = 50\% ,$$

then if there are no investments before $t = 0$ and with Theorem 3.22 we arrive at a firm value of

$$\begin{aligned} V_0^l &= V_0^u + \tau D_0 + \frac{n r_f - 1 + (1+r_f)^{-n}}{n r_f} \tau \alpha \underline{l} V_0^u \\ &= 500 + 0.5 \cdot 100 + \frac{2 \cdot 0.1 - 1 + (1+0.1)^{-2}}{2 \cdot 0.1} 0.5 \cdot 0.5 \cdot 0.5 \cdot 500 \\ &\approx 678.125 . \end{aligned}$$

3.5.6 Problems

1. Assume that the cash flows follow:

$$\widetilde{FCF}^u_{t+1} = \widetilde{FCF}^u_t + \varepsilon_{t+1},$$

where ε_{t+1} are independent and normally distributed with expectation zero and variance one. Cost of capital $k^{E,u}$ are constant, the firm follows an investment policy based in cash flows. There were no investments before $t = 0$ and there will be no increases in subscribed capital in the future. Furthermore, α does not depend on t.

   (a) Determine the distribution of the cash flows $\widetilde{FCF}^u_t$.
   (b) Write down the perpetual rent formula for the value of the unlevered firm $\widetilde{V}^u_t$. How is the value distributed?
   (c) [42] Write down a simple formula for the book value $\underline{\widetilde{V}}_t$. (You might have to look at the proofs...) How is the book value distributed?

   Hint: Any addition or any difference of two normally distributed random variables is again normally distributed. The expectation of the sum (or the difference) is the sum (or the difference) of the expectations. If both random variables are independent, then furthermore the variance of the sum is the sum of the variances.

2. Often people use the WACC approach and do not distinguish precisely between market and book values. This problem shows what can go wrong in the case of an infinite rent (i.e., constant expected cash flows).

   Assume that a firm is infinitely living, financed by book value, and follows an investment policy based in cash flows. There were no investments before $t = 0$ and there will be no increases in subscribed capital in the future. Furthermore, α as well as $\underline{l}$ do not depend on t.

   Compare the value of the unlevered firm financed by book value and market value. Let $\mathrm{E}[\widetilde{FCF}^u] = 100$, $r_f = 5\%$, $k^{E,u} = 15\%$, $n = 4$, $\underline{l} = 0.7$, $D_0 = 500$, $\alpha = 50\%$, and $\tau = 34\%$ and write down both values. Is it fair to evaluate a company financed by book values with WACC?

   Hint: Use the formula obtained from Problem 3 in Sect. 3.4.6 for the firm financed by market value. Notice that l_0 is not given.

3.6 Other Financing Policies

We see our task as examining every conceivable finance policy and deriving appropriate valuation equations. In this section we introduce three finance policies, which in our opinion are not as equally significant as those we have dealt with up to

[42]This problem is hard to solve.

now. Yet there will be situations in which the application of one of these three forms is called for. Throughout this section we will assume that debt is riskless.

3.6.1 Financing Based on Cash Flows

We want to discuss a fourth form of financing policy in this section that is based on the firm's free cash flows. If the free cash flows should happen to be high, then a lot of debt will be paid back. If in contrast, the cash flows turn out to be lower, debt redemption is abstained from. One such form of financing policy seems to us to be fully plausible with high leverage (at least for the time being).

One-Period Financing Policy As far as we know, a financing policy of this kind was only examined twice in the literature until now. That shows that considerable difficulties come up with the establishment of values of firms when it is supposed that financing based on cash flows is carried out over a longer period of time: the value of the firm is then dependent upon the price of certain exotic options. To keep these difficulties at a minimum, we observe a special case. The leverage should be based on free cash flows only in the first year; afterwards the amount of debt may remain constant. This leads to the following definition.[43]

Definition 3.14 A firm is financed based on cash flows if the debt develops

$$\widetilde{D}_t := \left(D_0 - \alpha\left(\widetilde{FCF}_1^l - r_f D_0\right)\right)^+$$

for $t \geq 1$. α is thereby a real number between zero and one, $\alpha \in (0, 1]$.

The definition reads as follows: The future amount of debt is established in that the initial amount is decreased by a random debt service. This random debt repayment is established as a part of that amount, which remains from the first year's free cash flow when the interest due has been subtracted. If the random redemption should be larger than the initial debt, then it is at most as large as this. The maximum condition is required so that negative amounts of debt are avoided.[44]

[43]The symbol X^+ is defined as

$$X^+ = \begin{cases} X & \text{if } X \geq 0, \\ 0 & \text{otherwise.} \end{cases}$$

[44]If full distribution is not insisted upon, one could interpret negative debt as retained earnings. In this case the maximum condition can be left out which simplifies the calculation. But notice that such a behavior is suboptimal since the company will pay corporate tax on interest obtained.

We can give a valuation equation for this case. To do so we use a put option on the value of the unlevered firm at time $t = 1$ with an exercise price of $\frac{1+\alpha r_f(1-\tau)}{\alpha d_1^u} D_0$. This put has the value Π. The following relation is then valid.

Theorem 3.23 *The firm lives until T and follows a financing policy based on cash flows. The cash flows of the unlevered firm are weak auto-regressive. Debt is riskless. The market value of a levered firm is then established from*

$$V_0^l = V_0^u + \frac{\tau r_f D_0}{1+r_f} + \tau\alpha d_1^u \left(1 - \frac{1}{\left(1+r_f\right)^{T-1}}\right) \Pi.$$

We refer readers, who want to grasp this somewhat difficult formula, to the appendix.[45]

The last theorem clarifies that for the valuation of the levered firm, it is necessary to trade a put with a determined exercise price. If this put is not traded, the valuation will not be successful. It is said in this case that the market is not complete.

Perpetual Annuity In general we cannot most likely assume that the put option required for the valuation of the firm where the financing is based on cash flows is traded. But the last theorem then has no practical relevance for valuation of firms. The derivation of a valuation equation that does not have to fall back on options is possible under a broader assumption.

Theorem 3.24 *The conditions of Theorem 3.23 are valid. In addition, the first period's debt is larger than zero, and finally, the expectation of the cash flows is constant. The market value of the levered firm is then established from*

$$V_0^l = \left(1 - \alpha\tau \frac{k^{E,u}}{1+k^{E,u}} \frac{1 - \frac{1}{\left(1+r_f\right)^{T-1}}}{1 - \frac{1}{(1+k^{E,u})^{T-1}}}\right) V_0^u + \frac{1 + (1+\alpha(1-\tau))r_f - \frac{1+\alpha(1-\tau)r_f}{\left(1+r_f\right)^{T-1}}}{1+r_f} \tau D_0.$$

The proof is again found in the appendix.[46]

Example (Finite Case Continued) We also want to calculate the firm value with financing based on cash flows in our example. To do so we suppose that at time $t = 0$ debt is

$$D_0 = 100$$

[45] See Sect. 6.4.

[46] See Sect. 6.4.

and the factor α amounts to exactly

$$\alpha = 1\,.$$

We are concentrating our attention on the put and next establish its exercise price. For this we need the dividend-price relation of the unlevered firm. Since we have already determined the cash flows as well as the values of the firm at time $t = 1$, this is easy to do. We get

$$d_1^u = \frac{\widetilde{FCF}_1^u(u)}{\widetilde{V}_1^u(u)} = \frac{\widetilde{FCF}_1^u(d)}{\widetilde{V}_1^u(d)} \approx 0.5692\,.$$

The exercise price of the put therefore comes to

$$\frac{1+\alpha r_f(1-\tau)}{\alpha d_1^u} D_0 \approx \frac{1+0.1\cdot(1-0.5)}{0.5692} 100 \approx 184.48\,.$$

The conditional payments of the put thus amount to

$$\widetilde{\Pi}_1 = \begin{cases} \left(\frac{1+\alpha r_f(1-\tau)}{\alpha d_1^u} D_0 - \widetilde{V}_1^u(u)\right)^+ = 0.00\,, & \text{if up in } t = 1 \\ \left(\frac{1+\alpha r_f(1-\tau)}{\alpha d_1^u} D_0 - \widetilde{V}_1^u(d)\right)^+ \approx 26.35\,, & \text{if down in } t = 1 \\ . \end{cases}$$

Since it is supposed that there is no free lunch in the market the fundamental theorem of asset pricing must hold for the put. This means

$$\Pi = \frac{\mathrm{E}_Q\left[\widetilde{\Pi}_1\right]}{1+r_f}.$$

Employing the appropriate risk-neutral probabilities from Fig. 3.1 gives

$$\Pi \approx \frac{0.0833\cdot 0.00 + 0.9167\cdot 26.35}{1.1} \approx 21.96\,.$$

We end up calculating the value of the levered firm with

$$\begin{aligned} V_0^l &= \widetilde{V}_0^u + \frac{\tau r_f D_0}{1+r_f} + \tau\alpha d_1^u\left(1 - \frac{1}{(1+r_f)^{T-1}}\right)\Pi \\ &\approx 229.75 + \frac{0.5\cdot 0.1\cdot 100}{1.1} + 0.5\cdot 0.5692\cdot 21.96\cdot 0.1736 \approx 235.38\,. \end{aligned}$$

For the case of an infinitely living firm financing based on cash flows requires the knowledge of a multiplicity of complicated derivatives. We believe that this assumption is far from being realistic to pursue this case.

3.6.2 Financing Based on Dividends

Distribution and Debt Redemption It is apparent with many corporations that the managers hold the dividends constant to be paid to the shareholders over a longer period of time. Such a policy has consequences for the firm's amount of debt. It emerges from Fig. 2.1 that there are only two uses for the free cash flow: distribution to the owners, or to serve the creditors with interest and debt repayments. In all of the financing policy variations discussed up to now, the debt redemption was exogenously set and followed a more or less realistic plan. Now we want to look at a new possibility and assume that the management determines the distribution. A look at Fig. 2.1 makes it clear that with a pre-given free cash flow, such a policy has consequences for debt redemption. If the managers subordinate the redemption of debt under the implemented policy of dividends in the way described, then we want to speak of financing based on dividends.

In relation to the equity approach, we made it clear that the shareholders of a levered firm receive payments at time t of (in the case of no default)[47]

$$\widetilde{Div}_t = \widetilde{FCF}^l_t - \widetilde{D}_{t-1} - \widetilde{I}_t + \widetilde{D}_t.$$

If the firm now tries to manage the amount of debt so that this exactly corresponds to the already determined dividends Div, then the following definition is useful.

Definition 3.15 A firm is financed based on dividends over n periods, when the development of debt meets the condition

$$\widetilde{D}_t := \left(Div - \widetilde{FCF}^l_t + \widetilde{D}_{t-1} + \widetilde{I}_t\right)^+$$

for all times $t \leq n$. The payments Div are then deterministic and correspond to the distributions to the shareholders at times $t \leq n$.

We could, in an analogous way to the financing based on cash flows, now again prove a theorem, which brings the value of the levered firm in proportion to the value of the unlevered firm and one option. But since we already stressed in the previous section that we regard such valuation equations as useless in practice, we want to look right away here at a special case.

Time Limitation of the Dividends Policy It does not make sense to assume that a policy of constant dividends can be carried out for a very long time. Firstly, that does not agree with the picture that can be empirically observed, and secondly, you

[47] See Eq. (3.22).

fall into a logical contradiction if you assume that constant dividends can be paid for all eternity from a taxable, levered firm. If, namely, the same dividends Div would really be continuously paid, then the market value of the levered firm would come to $\frac{Div}{r_f} + D_0$ at time $t = 0$. The tax advantages bound up with the financing policy would, it is true, be achieved, but never distributed to the shareholders and that could be a contradiction of the condition of transversality.

Constant Rate of Growth The same now applies for the method of financing based on dividends just as it did for the financing policy based on cash flows, namely that without simplifying assumptions we can only derive valuation equations with unpleasant options terms. For this reason, and only for this reason, we suppose that the amount of debt remains constant beyond time $t = n$, and the expected cash flows of the unlevered firm grow constantly with the rate g.

Theorem 3.25 *The firm implements a financing policy based on dividends over $n\widetilde{]}T$ periods, the cash flows of the unlevered firm are weak auto-regressive and debt is riskless. In addition, the amount of capital is continuously larger than zero up to the nth period. The expectation of the cash flows of the unlevered firm grows with the constant rate g. The market value of a levered firm is then established from*

$$V_0^l = \left(1 - \gamma^n \left(1 - \tau \left(1 - \frac{1}{(1+r_f)^{T-n}}\right)\right)\right) D_0 +$$
$$+ \left(1 - \gamma^n \left(1 - \tau \left(1 - \frac{1}{(1+r_f)^{T-n}}\right)\right) - \tau \left(1 - \frac{1}{(1+r_f)^T}\right)\right) \frac{Div}{r_f(1-\tau)} +$$
$$+ \left(\delta^n - \delta^T + \frac{\gamma^n - \delta^n}{\frac{\gamma}{\delta} - 1} \frac{k^{E,u} - g}{1+g} \left(1 - \tau \left(1 - \frac{1}{(1+r_f)^2}\right)\right)\right) \frac{V_0^u}{1 - \delta^T},$$

where $\gamma = \frac{1+r_f(1-\tau)}{1+r_f}$ *and* $\delta = \frac{1+g}{1+k^{E,u}}$.

You find the proof in the appendix.[48]

For the case of an infinite life span, the above equation is simplified to the extent that the factor δ^T then moves towards zero.

Example (Finite Case Continued) We again fall back upon the payment values of our example to establish the value of the firm for the case of financing based on dividends as well. We suppose that the firm at time $t = 1$ distributes a dividend of

$$Div = 150$$

[48] See Sect. 6.5.

and the firm does not change the amount of debt necessary to do so from $n = 1$ on. According to Definition 3.15, at future time $t = 1$ an amount of debt is required of

$$\widetilde{D}_1 = \left(Div - \widetilde{FCF}_1^u + (1 + r_f(1-\tau))\right)^+$$
$$= \begin{cases} 145 & \text{if up in } t = 1, \\ 165 & \text{if down in } t = 1. \end{cases}$$

The conditions of the theorem are obviously met with that; debt remains positive. Let us first establish the parameters γ and δ

$$\gamma = \frac{1 + r_f(1-\tau)}{1 + r_f} = \frac{1 + 0.1(1-0.5)}{1 + 0.1} \approx 0.9545\,,$$
$$\delta = \frac{1+g}{1+k^{E,u}} = \frac{1+0.1}{1+0.2} \approx 0.9167\,.$$

The value of the levered firm then results from the equation

$$V_0^l = \left(1 - \gamma\left(1 - \tau\left(1 - \frac{1}{(1+r_f)^2}\right)\right)\right) D_0 +$$
$$+ \left(\left(1 - \gamma\left(1 - \tau\left(1 - \frac{1}{(1+r_f)^2}\right)\right)\right) - \tau\left(1 - \frac{1}{(1+r_f)^3}\right)\right) \frac{Div}{r_f(1-\tau)} +$$
$$+ \left(\delta - \delta^3 + \frac{\gamma - \delta}{\frac{\gamma}{\delta} - 1} \frac{k^{E,u} - g}{1+g}\right) \frac{V_0^u}{1 - \delta^3}\,.$$

Entering all values known to us results in

$$V_0^l \approx 237.498\,.$$

We already mentioned that an eternally constant dividend could be a contradiction to transversality. That is why we will not evaluate our infinite example here. See the problem set for another infinite example.

3.6.3 Financing Based on Debt-Cash Flow Ratio

Dynamic Leverage Ratio The dynamic leverage ratio is a real number by which the cash flow is set in relation to the firm's debts,

$$L_t^d = \frac{\widetilde{D}_t}{\widetilde{FCF}_t^l}. \tag{3.29}$$

This ratio serves as a (simpler) criterion for the length of time in which the firm would be completely self-financed only using cash flows for debt redemption. We want to use this ratio to look at a sixth financing policy.

Definition 3.16 A firm is financed based on debt-cash flow ratios if these ratios are deterministic.

If a firm follows this debt schedule the following theorem can be verified. The proof can be found in the appendix.[49]

Theorem 3.26 (Debt-Cash Flow Ratio) *The firm implements a financing policy based on debt-cash flow ratios. The cash flows of the unlevered firm are weak auto-regressive and debt is riskless. The market value of a levered firm is then established from*

$$\widetilde{V}_t^l = \widetilde{V}_t^u + \widetilde{D}_t \sum_{s=t}^{T-1} \widetilde{L}_s^d \dots \widetilde{L}_{t+1}^d \left(\frac{\tau r_f}{1+r_f}\right)^{s+1-t} + \\ + \sum_{s=t+1}^{T-1} \left(\sum_{u=s}^{T-1} \widetilde{L}_u^d \dots \widetilde{L}_s^d \left(\frac{\tau r_f}{1+r_f}\right)^{u+1-s} \right) \frac{\mathrm{E}\left[\widetilde{FCF}_s^u | \mathcal{F}_t\right]}{(1+k^{E,u})^{s-t}}$$

where for the product $\widetilde{L}_s^d \dots \widetilde{L}_{t+1}^d = 1$ *holds if* $s = t$.

Infinite Lifetime If the firm exists infinitely long and if the dynamic leverage ratio remains constant, the following theorem can be shown.

Theorem 3.27 (Debt-Cash Flow Ratio in Infinite Lifetime) *The assumptions of Theorem 3.26 are valid. If the firm has an infinite lifetime and if the debt-cash flow ratio remains constant, then the firm value is given by*

$$\widetilde{V}_t^l = \left(1 + \frac{\tau r_f \widetilde{L}^d}{1 + r_f(1 - \tau \widetilde{L}^d)}\right) \widetilde{V}_t^u + \frac{\tau r_f}{1 + r_f(1 - \tau \widetilde{L}^d)} \widetilde{D}_t .$$

Example (Finite Case Continued) The debt-cash flow ratio will be constant

$$\widetilde{L}^d = 1 .$$

Debt at time $t = 0$ is

$$D_0 = 100 .$$

[49]See Sect. 6.6.

From the above theorems we have

$$V_0^l = V_0^u + D_0\left(\frac{\tau r_f}{1+r_f} + \left(\frac{\tau r_f}{1+r_f}\right)^2 + \left(\frac{\tau r_f}{1+r_f}\right)^3\right) +$$
$$+\left(\frac{\tau r_f}{1+r_f} + \left(\frac{\tau r_f}{1+r_f}\right)^2\right)\frac{\mathrm{E}\left[\widetilde{FCF}_1^u\right]}{1+k^{E,u}} + \frac{\tau r_f}{1+r_f}\frac{\mathrm{E}\left[\widetilde{FCF}_2^u\right]}{(1+k^{E,u})^2}.$$

This gives

$$V_0^l = 229.75 + 100\left(\frac{0.5\cdot 0.1}{1+0.1} + \left(\frac{0.5\cdot 0.1}{1+0.1}\right)^2 + \left(\frac{0.5\cdot 0.1}{1+0.1}\right)^3\right) +$$
$$+\left(\frac{0.5\cdot 0.1}{1+0.1} + \left(\frac{0.5\cdot 0.1}{1+0.1}\right)^2\right)\frac{100}{1+0.2} + \frac{0.5\cdot 0.1}{1+0.1}\frac{110}{(1+0.2)^2}$$
$$\approx 241.94$$

for the value of the levered firm.

Example (Infinite Case Continued) If the firm exists infinitely long and maintains a debt-cash flow ratio of

$$\widetilde{L}^d = 1,$$

then with debt of 100 at $t = 0$ the levered firm is worth

$$V_0^l = \left(1 + \frac{\tau r_f \widetilde{L}^d}{1+r_f(1-\tau\widetilde{L}^d)}\right)\widetilde{V}_t^u + \frac{\tau r_f}{1+r_f(1-\tau\widetilde{L}^d)}\widetilde{D}_t$$
$$= \left(1 + \frac{0.5\cdot 0.1\cdot 1}{1+0.1(1-0.5\cdot 1)}\right)500 + \frac{0.5\cdot 0.1}{1+0.1(1-0.5\cdot 1)}100$$
$$\approx 528.571\,.$$

3.6.4 Comparing Alternative Forms of Financing

In the previous sections, we discussed different forms of financing and their influences on the value of firms. In the case of autonomous financing, the evaluator knows the firm's future amount of debt $D_0, D_1, \ldots$. A valuation equation, which is possible under this assumption and delivers the correct value of the firm is the APV equation. If in contrast financing is based on market values, the evaluator knows the firm's future debt ratios $l_0, l_1, \ldots$ measured in market values. A valuation equation that results in the correct value of the firm under this condition is the WACC formula. In the case of financing based on book values, the future debt ratios $\underline{l}_0, \underline{l}_1, \ldots$ measured in book values are known to the evaluator. Which valuation equation is applied under this condition is dependent upon whether the firm follows a policy of full distribution, only takes on replacement investments or conditions its investments upon attained cash flows. With financing based on cash flows, the firm reduces its amount of debt—for a limited time—by a certain proportion of its free cash flows. Special valuation equations can be given that bear just this sort of financing calculation. Financing based on dividends are distinguished in that a firm pays constant dividends over a longer period of time.

Extent of Differences in Value In order to illustrate the way the different valuation equations work, we have used a standard example. Every reader, who has paid attention to our calculations can determine that the respective values of firms are not that dramatically different from each other. That brings up the question as to the practical relevance of those valuation equations either given or developed by us. It is after all conceivable that the differences in value of the forms of finance specified by us are relatively small. In this case, using any valuation formula you like and simply accepting the possible resultant valuation mistakes can be economically justified. It is, however, not now clear to us at all how you would have to go about confirming or refuting such an assertion if the firm lives longer than three periods or possesses different cash flows.

APV and WACC Autonomous financing and financing based on market values are particularly prominent forms of financing in the DCF literature, which is why we still want to spend some time on them here. In the first case we recommend the APV formula, and in the second case the WACC formula. "Mixed formulas" are derived in the literature that look like WACC formulas and are nevertheless appropriate to be applied for autonomous financing, or that look like APV formulas and still can be used for value-based financing.[50] From an academic viewpoint, such valuation formulas may be interesting, but they are not practically relevant. An autonomous evaluator supposes certain future amounts of debt. What sense is there then of the fiction of not knowing the amounts of debt (otherwise only the APV formula would be needed in order to value), but instead falling back upon the expected debt ratios in order to enter them into a WACC formula? It is likewise so for the opposite case. If an investor supposes future certain debt ratios, why should she fabricate not knowing them, and then instead access the expected amount of debt in order to put them into an APV formula? Whoever wants to get from A to B can either take the direct path or take the long way round. Economists normally avoid such long ways. We find it even more strange at the least to propagate such round about ways.

With autonomous financing the tax advantages determined by the terms of credit are certain, but with financing based on market values they are uncertain. Even

[50]See Wallmeier (1999) or Grinblatt and Titman (2002, chapter 13.2).

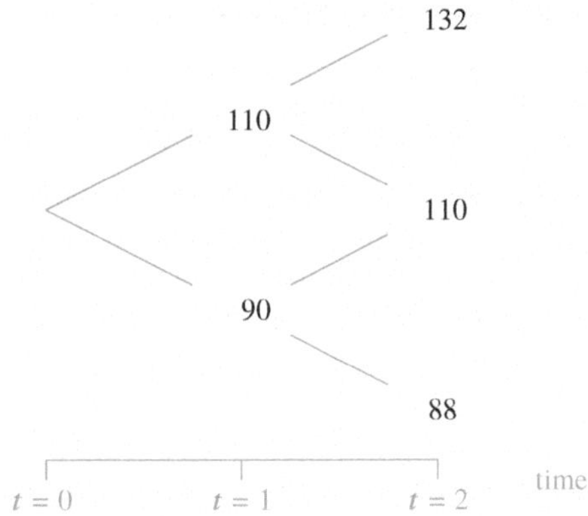

Fig. 3.13 Cash flows in future periods

if the expectations are identical to the tax savings,[51] certain payments are always worth more than uncertain payments from the point of view of risk-averse investors. It is thus completely plausible if one supposes that both assumptions do not necessarily lead to identical values of firms. This is not always adequately stressed in the literature. WACC and APV result in—at least with economic procedures—thoroughly different values of firms.

3.6.5 Problems

1. It is not necessary the case that the assumptions of Theorem 3.25 must violate transversality: show that for $n = T - 1$ and $n \to \infty$ the value of the levered firm satisfies

$$\lim_{n\to\infty} V_0^l = D_0 + \frac{Div}{r_f}$$

which is very intuitive since the company will pay a given dividend to the shareholders at any time in the future.

2. Assume an unlevered company has a lifetime $T = 2$ and its cash flows are given by the Fig. 3.13. Ignore default. The unlevered cost of capital are $k^{E,u} = 20\%$, any up- or down-movement has a probability 0.5. The riskless interest rate is $r_f = 10\%$, the tax rate is $\tau = 34\%$. The levered company has debt $D_0 = 0$ at time $t = 0$.
   (a) Write down a formula for the value of the levered firm if $\widetilde{D}_1(u)$ and $\widetilde{D}_1(d)$ are given.
   (b) Assume the firm has an expected debt $\mathrm{E}[\widetilde{D}_1] = 100$. Which debt schedule (i.e., what values of $\widetilde{D}_1(u)$ and $\widetilde{D}_1(d)$) yields the highest value of the levered firm?

[51] In our example that is not the case. This explains why the WACC value of the firm is greater than the APV value, even though the tax advantages in the first case are uncertain.

3.7 Further Literature

The first work on the valuation of tax advantages is already half a century old: compare Modigliani and Miller (1958) as well as Modigliani and Miller (1963). In their work both authors have also examined the case of the perpetual annuity. Sick (1990) was first to extensively use certainty equivalents (i.e., a martingale technique) to derive valuation formulas including taxes, although Ross (1987) examined the question mainly in a one-period setup.

The well-known formula of a perpetual rent first appeared in a book by Williams (1938, p. 72) but is still known as Gordon–Shapiro formula. Neither Williams nor Gordon/Shapiro did consider uncertainty. In the preceding setup our result might come close to the results from Feltham and Ohlson (1995).

The first two financing policies mentioned in this chapter are found in nearly every textbook on financing. See, for instance, Brealey et al. (2020, p. 254 (APV) and p. 508 (WACC)). We believe the designation "autonomous" goes back to Richter (1998).

Autonomous financing with an nonconstant amount of debt is shown for the first time in Myers (1974). Financing based on market values was examined for the first time by Miles and Ezzell (1980) as well as Miles and Ezzell (1985). However, both authors only succeeded in getting the proof which is named after them under the assumption of a constant leverage structure. A generalization is found in Löffler (2004). Arnold et al. (2015) have established results for a financing policy where the refinancing dates are given by multiples of a number greater than 1 (delayed financing). Dierkes and Schäfer (2016) looked at a policy where a firm combines both capital structure targets and predetermined debt levels. Barbi (2012) also used risk-neutral probabilities to derive general results for the tax shield.

Although a number of publications about financing based on market values later appeared (Harris and Pringle (1985) and Clubb and Doran (1995) are mentioned here as representative), they do not deal with any new financing. Financing based on cash flows was considered in Arzac (1996) and Löffler (2000).

Auto-regressive processes are covered in any textbook on time series analysis. Hamilton (1994) or Brockwell and Davis (2002) are a good source. Auto-regressive cash flows were introduced in a more general form by Lintner (1956) and Rubinstein (1976) and used by Ohlson (1979), Garman and Ohlson (1981), and Christensen and Feltham (2003). In Barberis et al. (1998) a violation of auto-regression was considered, although in a very different context. Our specific formulation of weak auto-regressive cash flows was first systematically examined in Laitenberger and Löffler (2006). That is also where theorems on the relation between cost of capital and conditional expected returns are found. Löffler (2002) points out the problem of the Modigliani–Miller adjustment. In an earlier discussion Fernández (2004), Fieten et al. (2005), and Cooper and Nyborg (2006) clarify the relation between Modigliani—Miller and Miles–Ezzell. The observations on financing based on book values are new, even if individual elements, such as the operating assets relation, are already known in the literature. Compare, for instance, Feltham and Ohlson (1995, S. 693f.) or Penman (2013, chapter 8).

The literature cited so far concentrated on discrete time models. There is a vast literature on continuous time models for the firm which we will not mention here.

References

Arnold S, Lahmann A, Schwetzler B (2015) (Re-)Financing policies and the value of debt-related tax shields. http://ssrn.com/paper=2602643. Accessed 8 Nov 2019

Arzac ER (1996) Valuation of highly leveraged firms. Financ Anal J 52:42–49

Barberis N, Shleifer A, Vishny R (1998) A model of investor sentiment. J Financ Econ 49:307–343

Barbi M (2012) On the risk-neutral value of debt tax shields. Appl Financ Econ 22:251–258

Brealey RA, Myers SC, Allen F (2020) Principles of corporate finance, 13th edn. McGraw-Hill, New York

Brockwell PJ, Davis RA (2002) Introduction to time series and forecasting, 2nd edn. Springer, New York

Christensen PO, Feltham GA (2003) Economics of accounting, vol I: information in markets. Kluwer, Boston and Dordrecht and London

Clubb CD, Doran P (1995) Capital budgeting, debt management, and the APV criterion. J Bus Financ Acc 22:681–694

Cooper IA, Nyborg KG (2006) The value of tax shield is equal to the present value of tax shields. J Financ Econ 81:215–225

Dierkes S, Schäfer U (2016) Corporate taxes, capital structure, and valuation: combining Modigliani/Miller and Miles/Ezzell. Rev Quant Financ Acc 48:363–383

Fazzari S, Hubbard RG, Petersen BC (1987) Finance constraints and corporate investment: response to Kaplan and Zingales. Working Paper 2387, NBER

Feltham GA, Ohlson JA (1995) Valuation and clean surplus accounting for operating and financial activities. Contemp Account Res 11:689–731

Fernández P (2004) The value of tax shields and the risk of the net increase of debt. http://ssrn.com/paper=506005

Fernández P (2005) Reply to 'Comment on the value of tax shields is not equal to the present value of tax shields'. Q Rev Econ Finance 45:188–192

Fieten P, Kruschwitz L, Laitenberger J, Löffler A, Tham J, Vélez-Pareja I, Wonder N (2005) Comment on 'The value of tax shields is not equal to the present value of tax shields'. Q Rev Econ Bus 45:184–187

Garman MB, Ohlson JA (1981) Valuation of risky assets in arbitrage-free economies with transaction costs. J Financ Econ 9:271–280

Grinblatt M, Titman SD (2002) Financial markets and corporate strategy, 2nd edn. Irwin, McGraw-Hill, Boston

Hamilton JD (1994) Time series analysis. Princeton University Press, Princeton

Harris RS, Pringle JJ (1985) Risk-adjusted discount rates: extensions from the average-risk case. J Financ Res 8:237–244

Ingersoll Jr JE (1987) Theory of financial decision making. Rowman & Littlefield, Totowa

Institut der Wirtschaftsprüfer in Deutschland (ed) (2013) WP Handbuch 2014: Wirtschaftsprüfung, Rechnungslegung, Beratung, vol II, 14th edn. IDW-Verlag, Düsseldorf

Kruschwitz L, Löffler A, Lorenz D, Scholze A (2015) Default triggers: does a liquidity-based default imply over-indebtedness and vice versa? Adv Quant Anal Financ Account 13:201–223

Laitenberger J, Löffler A (2006) The structure of the distributions of cash flows and discount rates in multiperiod valuation problems. OR Spectr 28:289–299

Lintner JV (1956) Distribution of incomes of corporations among dividends, retained earnings, and taxes. Am Econ Rev 46:97–113

Löffler A (2000) Tax shields in an LBO. http://ssrn.com/paper=217148
Löffler A (2002) WACC is not an expected return of the levered firm. http://ssrn.com/paper=340300
Löffler A (2004) Zwei anmerkungen zu wacc. Z Betriebswirt 74:933–942
Miles JA, Ezzell JR (1980) The weighted average cost of capital, perfect capital markets, and project life: a clarification. J Financ Quant Anal 15:719–730
Miles JA, Ezzell JR (1985) Reformulating tax shield valuation: a note. J Financ 40:1485–1492
Modigliani F, Miller MH (1958) The cost of capital, corporation finance, and the theory of investment. Am Econ Rev 48:261–297
Modigliani F, Miller MH (1963) Corporate income taxes and the cost of capital: a correction. Am Econ Rev 53:433–443
Myers SC (1974) Interactions of corporate financing and investment decisions: implications for capital budgeting. J Financ 32:211–220
Ohlson JA (1979) Risk, return, security-valuation and the stochastic behavior of accounting numbers. J Financ Quant Anal 14:317–336
Penman SH (2013) Financial statement analysis and security valuation, 5th edn. McGraw-Hill Irwin, New York
Richter F (1998) Unternehmensbewertung bei variablem Verschuldungsgrad. Z Bankrecht Bankwirtschaft 10:379–389
Ross SA (1987) Arbitrage and martingales with taxation. J Polit Econ 95:371–393
Rubinstein ME (1976) The valuation of uncertain income streams and the price of options. Bell J Econ Manag Sci 7:407–425
Sick GA (1990) Tax-adjusted discount rates. Manag Sci 36:1432–1450
Wallmeier M (1999) Kapitalkosten und Finanzierungsprämissen. Z Betriebswirt 69:1473–1490
Williams JB (1938) The theory of investment value. Harvard University Press, Cambridge

4 Personal Income Tax

We now shift gears. While in the last chapter we worked on the basis that the firm was taxed, but that the financiers were free from taxes, we now suppose that the financiers have to pay income tax, but that the firm is spared.

Certainly not all readers will think that it makes sense in the valuation of firms to take taxes due at the financiers' level into consideration. The appropriate textbooks at any rate like to leave out income tax all too well.[1] If, however, you keep in mind that income tax influences the consumption flow of private investors in every case, then there is hardly any reason why this tax is not taken into consideration in valuation of firms. Somebody who has acquired a firm will have other numbers to enter in on her income tax statements than someone who invests her money on the capital market. Just this fact itself speaks for including the income tax in the valuation of firms. The German profession of certified public accountants, for instance, officially decided in 1997 to advocate the consideration of income tax in valuation of firms.[2]

The reader can expect a timetable in this chapter very close in structure to the plan of action in the previous chapter. We will shortly recognize that despite clear differences, there exist enough similarities between corporate income tax and personal income tax to justify treating them structurally in the same way. So, surely to the surprise of some readers, we will again speak of levered and unlevered firms. We will use the same symbol for the tax rate and also look into the different firm policies again in order to value the resulting tax advantages of a levered firm versus an unlevered firm.

---

[1] The income tax is typically not gone into in detail. In the first edition of our book we were at least able to point to some textbooks that handled typically the case of an eternal annuity. While preparing the second edition it turned out that even these cases have been abolished in the literature. It seems that the inclusion of personal taxes fell out of favor.

[2] See Institut der Wirtschaftsprüfer in Deutschland (2000).

L. Kruschwitz, A. Löffler, *Stochastic Discounted Cash Flow*,
Springer Texts in Business and Economics,
https://doi.org/10.1007/978-3-030-37081-7_4

We will certainly not surprise our readers by the statement that considerable new ground is being broken with the inclusion of personal income tax in theory of valuation. The first work on WACC and APV appeared already half a century ago. In contrast, international literature on valuation of firms has very often ignored income tax on the level of the financiers up to present. We thus have considerably less literature on which to build. So being, this chapter cannot deal with the systematic presentation of available knowledge. We will, much rather, have to compile new results. In doing so, we cannot check to see if we are moving in the right direction by comparing our results with the outcomes of other papers. We thus see the following chapter not as an attempt at presenting already existing knowledge, but much rather as a contribution to the theoretical discussion of income tax and valuation of firms within the DCF theory.

4.1 Unlevered and Levered Firms

DCF theory, in essence, continually deals with the question as to how tax shields are appropriately valued. If talk of a tax advantage (or also of a tax disadvantage) is to be economically substantial, a reference point is needed against which the advantage (or disadvantage) can be measured. This reference point concerns a firm which pursues a very definite policy, a firm which we will say is unlevered.

4.1.1 "Leverage" Interpreted Anew

Do you remember the beginning of the previous chapter? We had supposed there that the firm has to pay taxes, but the financiers remained free from tax. We had made it clear there that a levered firm is less heavily burdened with taxes than is an unlevered. We had further yet considered that you can immediately understand what an unlevered firm is supposed to be without any further details, but much more detailed information is needed in order to exactly comprehend what a levered firm is.[3] We had agreed at the beginning of the previous chapter to refer to the non-debted firm as unlevered and to characterize the indebted firm with the adjective levered.

Reference Firm We are now dealing with a completely different tax situation. The firms remain free from tax, while the financiers will be enlisted to pay income tax. If you bear in mind that from the basis of income tax, dividends, and interest payments are the object of taxation, then a lot of income tax is due to a firm which has a policy of full distribution. An income taxes savings, in contrast, is expected if the firm only partially distributes the profits obtained to the financiers. Profit retention brings about a tax shield for the investors. It is therefore recommended to use the firm with full distribution as reference firm, since no other distribution activity makes

[3] See Sect. 3.1.

what we are talking about immediately clear. Whoever, in contrast, has to value a firm with partial distribution, must very precisely describe which share of the cash flows is to be withheld in which periods. It is completely clear, in contrast, what is designated by full distribution. Since more income tax has to be paid in the case of full distribution than in the case of reduced distribution, we will speak in the first case of an unlevered firm, and in the second of a levered firm.

Please observe that we use the terms levered differently in the current chapter than in the preceding chapter. Levered now no longer means indebted, but rather partial distribution. The capital structure of the firm does not play any role in this chapter. Leverage in the ongoing chapter relates solely to the question if and how much is retained in the firm. Although this may possibly be somewhat irritating for readers, we purposely chose the terminology in order to be able to make use of structural similarities in the previous chapter.

In the previous chapter a full retention policy was assigned to the unlevered and the levered firm as well. Any other possible retention policies were not object of our discussion. In this chapter we argue similarly. Now both companies, the unlevered (or full distributing) firm as well as the levered (or partially distributing) firm, are self-financed and therefore without debt. The financing policy is not object of our discussion. How financing and retention policy can be linked together will be the topic of the last chapter. Seen in this light, the unlevered firm of the previous and this chapter is identical: both are without debt and both fully distribute their cash flow to the owners.

If we interpret the notation anew in the sense explained here, then it should also apply that a firm with full distribution has the same value as a firm with partial distribution, as long as no taxes are imposed. That agrees with the theorem of Miller and Modigliani (1961) on the irrelevance of dividend policy. This theorem says that it does not matter when a firm distributes its earnings so long as taxes do not play a role.

Notation We will note the market value of the unlevered firm with $\widetilde{V}_t^u$ and the market value of the levered firm with $\widetilde{V}_t^l$, respectively. Please note that both firms are not indebted, hence both values coincide with the market value of the equity, respectively. And we will completely analogously use the symbol $\widetilde{FCF}_t^u$ for the post-tax free cash flows of the firm with full distribution, while the post-tax free cash flows of the firm with partial distribution are referred to by $\widetilde{FCF}_t^l$. Correspondingly, $\widetilde{Tax}_t^u$ has to do with the shareholders' taxes of a firm with full distribution, but $\widetilde{Tax}_t^l$ with the shareholders' income tax of a firm with partial distribution.

Notice another important difference between the previous and present chapters. Previously $\widetilde{FCF}_t^l$ described the free cash flow that accrued to all investors (to shareholders as well as to debt holders). Now, there are no debt holders. In contrast with the previous chapter, here the free cash flow exists only as payment flow, which accrues to the shareholders.

Positive Dividends If we work on the grounds that a firm's cash flows are dealing with payments from which the dividends to the owners are defrayed, then a further limitation results. If in the last chapter cash flows turned negative, it meant nothing more than that the financiers infused the firm with further equity. If this was no longer possible, we then spoke of default and in more than one section we specifically expanded upon the implications of such a situation. But negative payments do not make any sense in the case of dividends. Thus in the following we will presuppose that the (levered as well as the unlevered) firm's cash flows are always large enough so that the dividends cannot turn negative.

4.1.2 The Unlevered Firm

In this chapter firms with full distribution play the same role as firms without debt in the chapter on corporate taxes. We assume that firms with full distribution are just as seldom the case in economic reality as self-financed firms. Nonetheless, it is important to be able to value them. Just as we maintained in the last chapter that you can only value an indebted firm if you are also capable of valuing a firm that is self-financed, we can now maintain that you can only value a firm with partial distribution if you can find a way of valuing a firm with full distribution.

If the cost of equity and the free cash flows of a firm with full distribution are known, it is very simple to write down a correct valuation equation. To do this we first define the cost of equity.

Definition 4.1 (Cost of Equity) Cost of equity $\widetilde{k}_t^{E,u}$ of an unlevered firm are conditional expected returns

$$\widetilde{k}_t^{E,u} := \frac{\mathrm{E}\left[\widetilde{FCF}_{t+1}^u + \widetilde{V}_{t+1}^u | \mathcal{F}_t\right]}{\widetilde{V}_t^u} - 1.$$

Since these cost of equity are formally not different from the cost of equity of an unlevered firm according to Definition 3.1, the valuation equation for a firm with full distribution naturally results very easily. If we again assume that the cost of equity are deterministic, then the valuation equation looks exactly like the corresponding valuation equation for a fully self-financed firm according to Theorem 3.1.

Theorem 4.1 (Market Value of the Unlevered Firm) *If the cost of equity of the unlevered firm $k_t^{E,u}$ are deterministic, then the value of the firm, which fully distributes its free cash flows, amounts at time t to*

$$\widetilde{V}_t^u = \sum_{s=t+1}^{T} \frac{\mathrm{E}\left[\widetilde{FCF}_s^u | \mathcal{F}_t\right]}{\left(1 + k_t^{E,u}\right) \dots \left(1 + k_{s-1}^{E,u}\right)}.$$

We do, however, find it important to point out a fact that may take some time getting used to for one or more readers. The cost of equity $k^{E,u}$ are dealing with the cost of equity *post- taxes*, and not say *pre-taxes*! It is just as important for us to ascertain that we avoid every statement about the connection between the pre-tax and the post-tax cost of equity. We much rather see the cost of equity post-taxes as simply given. We will later come back to a likely relation between both quantities in still more detail.[4]

In the chapter on corporate income tax, it was necessary to be able to fall back upon a premise that we had designated as the assumption of weak auto-regressive cash flows.[5] In order to develop valuation equations and also, above all, adjustment equations, we used the Theorem 3.3 many times in the chapter on corporate tax. We then need a commensurate theorem when dealing with personal income tax. But in order to get the theorem, we first have to introduce the assumption on weak auto-regressive cash flows. Thus:

Assumption 4.1 (Weak Auto-Regressive Cash Flows) *There are real numbers g_t such that*

$$\mathrm{E}\left[\widetilde{FCF}^u_{t+1}|\mathcal{F}_t\right] = (1 + g_t)\,\widetilde{FCF}^u_t$$

is valid for the unlevered firm's cash flows.

Since we have already discussed the economic significance of this assumption above, we do not need to go into it again. Before we can begin with proving specific valuation equations, we have to complete a series of preparatory steps. We must first describe the tax which is at the center of this chapter's discussion in more detail. We must furthermore go into the question as to what happens to the fundamental theorem of asset pricing when we have to take personal income tax into consideration.

4.1.3 Income and Taxes

Economists usually describe a tax type by saying who pays the tax, how the tax base is established, and which tariff is to be applied. Individuals are always subject to tax.

Categories of Income In most countries of the world, income tax is measured according to an amount, that as a rule is not so easy to calculate since very detailed legal provisions must be observed. The core of this amount is comprised of the sum of the so-called income. For the present we will differentiate between the incomes of the owners and the creditors, although no creditors are present in our model yet.

---

[4]See Sect. 4.2.

[5]In regards see Assumption 3.1.

Table 4.1 From pre-tax gross cash flow to income

	Pre-tax gross cash flow	$\widetilde{GCF}_t$
−	Investment expenses	$\widetilde{Inv}_t$
=	Shareholder's unlevered taxable income	$\widetilde{GCF}_t - \widetilde{Inv}_t$
−	Retained earnings	$\widetilde{A}_t$
+	Reflux from retained earnings	$(1+\widetilde{r}_{t-1})\widetilde{A}_{t-1}$
=	Shareholder's levered taxable income	$\widetilde{GCF}_t - \widetilde{Inv}_t$ $-\widetilde{A}_t + (1+\widetilde{r}_{t-1})\widetilde{A}_{t-1}$

1. Owners' incomes can mean the firm's achieved earnings or the firm's dividends. If the firm's achieved earnings are taxed, and in fact taxed regardless of whether these earnings are distributed or withheld, then it is "accrued income" that forms the tax base. If, in contrast, the cash which the shareholders receive is the object of taxation, then "realized income" is spoken of. Income from shares, which are traded on capital markets, is always included in the second group.
2. When we speak of the creditors' incomes, we must think of interest. In many countries interest income and income from dividends are taxed differently.

Redemption of Capital Owners sometimes receive payments that do not have the character of dividends. Think of the repayment of capital in relation to capital reductions or the liquidation of firms. It is important not to mix such payments up with dividends since they are, as a rule, spared from the burden of income tax.

Earnings Retention It is possible to retain parts of the distributable cash flows in the firm. We write $\widetilde{A}_t$ for these earnings retention amounts. The earnings retention amounts are always non-negative. We proceed on the basis that these amounts are invested by the firm for one period at the (later more precisely described) interest rate of $\widetilde{r}_t$, to then be distributed to the financiers.

Table 4.1 describes how to get from the pre-tax gross cash flows of a firm to the levered taxable income. With that we get the term given in the last line of Table 4.1 for the financiers' taxable income. The owners must, however, still pay their taxes from this: the unlevered as well as the levered free cash flows result from the respective taxable income minus the tax payments.

In this figure the gross cash flows and the investment expenses are identical for the levered and the unlevered firm. The unlevered firm, however, does not have retained earnings.

Yield of the Retained Earnings Amounts Under what conditions does the firm invest the amount $\widetilde{A}_t$? To answer this question we want to recall that managers—independent of distribution policy—should institute every investment project with positive net present value. Investing the amount $\widetilde{A}_t$ in operating assets is as impossible as that of the principle repayment of debts or the mark-down of equity. The only remaining possibility is that of investing on the capital market.

Investing on the capital market can now turn out to be riskless, but it can also be risky. And one may suppose that it makes a difference as to which variants we abide by here. If personal income taxes are not (yet) taken into account we will, however, soon recognize that due to the fundamental theorem we do not have to take this into consideration. r_f shall denote the risk free interest rate before income tax is deducted. If the amount $\widetilde{A}_t$ is invested in riskless assets, then the following simply applies:

$$\widetilde{r}_t = r_f. \tag{4.1}$$

In case of a risky investment by the firm, the following happens: The firm invests the amount $\widetilde{A}_t$ and receives back the amount $(1 + \widetilde{r}_t)\widetilde{A}_t$ one period later. If the capital market is arbitrage free, then the reflux at time $t + 1$ must be just as great as the cash value on the money investment at time t. We use the fundamental theorem to determine this cash value. But since the investment is carried out by the firm and according to our conditions the firm does not pay taxes, we must apply the fundamental theorem here according to Theorem 2.2, which is valid in a world where companies do not pay taxes. The following results:

$$\widetilde{A}_t = \frac{\mathrm{E}_Q\left[(1+\widetilde{r}_t)\widetilde{A}_t|\mathcal{F}_t\right]}{1+r_f}.$$

With rules 2 and 5, we then get

$$\mathrm{E}_Q\left[\widetilde{r}_t|\mathcal{F}_t\right] = r_f. \tag{4.2}$$

That is a generalization of Eq. (4.1). In the following we will proceed from this relation.

Tax Rates for Interest and Dividends Just as with the firm tax, the tax rate is again linear. There are therefore neither exemptions nor exemption thresholds. As in the preceding section, the tax rate is certain as well as constant. We already clearly said in the previous chapter that this presents a heavy, but unfortunately necessary assumption. Furthermore, tax rates on dividends and interest differ: the tax rate on dividends will be denoted by τ^D, the tax rate on interest is τ^I. Although our firms are self-financed, this difference is of relevance in proving our fundamental theorem which will become clear in a moment.

We need to take the following into consideration: Let us assume that an investor has an amount of G at her disposal. There are two different possibilities to invest this sum securely. Either she could now keep G in his private means in order to acquire an asset of $G + \left(1 - \tau^I\right) r_f G$ for the course of one time period or she pays this into her company and invests it there. In this case her assets will at first increase to $G + r_f G$ during the next time period. Once distributed to the entrepreneur it is crucial as to how this additional cash flow is taxed. If the interest share of the additional cash flow is treated like a dividend, the investor will get $G + (1 - \tau^D) r_f G$ from the safe investment after income tax. Obviously this amount differs from $G + (1 - \tau^I) r_f G$ which we ascertained beforehand, unless, of course, the tax rate for interest and dividends happens to be identical. It is now quite easy to formulate a possibility for arbitrage from the disparity of the two values (even when considering only self-financed firms). This would make our model superfluous. To avoid this, we only have two possibilities.

1. We could assume that

$$\tau^I = \tau^D$$

applies.[6] Unfortunately it can easily empirically be verified that many industrial nations of the world do not currently match up to the identity we presumed. So we will not consider this particular option.
2. The second possibility consists in defining the assessment basis of the income tax in a different way than in our arbitrage example. For this purpose we need to define a capital market, which takes into account our considerations more precisely. We are assuming a fixed quantity of convertible assets to which we shall refer as basic assets.[7] One of these basic assets is risk free, all the others are risky. Additionally, every company and every investor can only dispose of a portfolio of these basic assets.

The formulation of such an assessment basis is thus crucial to the elimination of the arbitrage opportunities. Any investment in the capital market is geared to the portfolio of basic assets. Furthermore, payments from the risk free asset will always be taxed by τ^I, while payments from the risky asset will be taxed by τ^D. Such a definition has far reaching consequences. Let us assume an investor chooses to invest risk free not privately but rather into a company. Once the returns of this investment are distributed then the return will not be taxed as a dividend but will be treated like interest. Ultimately it can be traced back to the risk free basic assets. With such a definition of the assessment basis we avoid the arbitrage opportunity mentioned above.

Tax Equation Our model's income tax equation for shareholders can now be written principally in the form

$$\widetilde{Tax}_t^u = \tau^D \left(\widetilde{GCF}_t - \widetilde{Inv}_t \right)$$

for the unlevered firm.

[6] This assumption is found in Miller (1977) for instance.

[7] The use of basic assets is in keeping with common procedure in the financial mathematical literature, see Shreve (2004, section 1.2).

As far as the levered company is concerned, it is not quite as easy to deal with this issue. Much depends on how the amount $\widetilde{A}_t$ has been invested: because a risk free financial investment will be taxed differently as opposed to an investment of risky securities. In this chapter we shall assume that the retention investment will be risky. The owners of the levered firm together pay taxes in the amount of[8]

$$\widetilde{Tax}_t^l = \tau^D \left(\widetilde{GCF}_t - \widetilde{Inv}_t - \widetilde{A}_t + (1 + \widetilde{r}_{t-1})\widetilde{A}_{t-1} \right).$$

The two firms tax payments differ by one amount, which we, analogously to the chapter on firm tax, want to designate as tax shield.

Tax Shield If we want to determine the cash flows of the levered firm in t, we do not only have to observe the earnings retention at time t, but also the earnings retention from the previous period. In total the tax shield amounts to

$$\widetilde{Tax}_t^l - \widetilde{Tax}_t^u = \tau^D \left(-\widetilde{A}_t + (1 + \widetilde{r}_{t-1})\widetilde{A}_{t-1} \right).$$

In order to calculate the difference between the free cash flows of the two firms, we take into consideration that gross cash flows and capital repayments as well as investments all result in identical amounts in both firms. The one and only difference between the two firms is the single fact that one renounces all earnings retention measures, while the other institutes such measures, resulting in a different amount of income tax. We can then entirely concentrate on the retained earnings amounts and tax payments in calculating the difference between the free cash flows of the levered firm and the free cash flows of the unlevered firm,

$$\begin{aligned} \widetilde{FCF}_t^l - \widetilde{FCF}_t^u &= \left(\ldots - \widetilde{A}_t + (1 + \widetilde{r}_{t-1})\widetilde{A}_{t-1} - \widetilde{Tax}_t^l \right) - \left(\ldots - \widetilde{Tax}_t^u \right) \\ &= \left(1 - \tau^D \right) \left((1 + \widetilde{r}_{t-1})\widetilde{A}_{t-1} - \widetilde{A}_t \right). \end{aligned}$$

[8]Whereas if the retention is invested without risk, as you might expect, the equation will be formulated slightly differently. "Retention for a risk free investment" will only indicate that we are dealing with a portfolio with more risk free securities. As a result, the assessment basis for the income, which is taxed at a rate of τ^I, will correspondingly decrease. In the period that follows, it increases again by virtue of the repayment of the retention and the returns on interest. Thus we finally arrive at the following equation:

$$\widetilde{Tax}_t^l = \tau^D \left(\widetilde{GCF}_t - \widetilde{Inv}_t \right) + \tau^I \left(-\widetilde{A}_t + (1 + r_f)\, \widetilde{A}_{t-1} \right).$$

With the help of (4.2) and rule 5 we get for the expectation under risk-neutral probability

$$\mathrm{E}_Q\left[\widetilde{FCF}_t^l - \widetilde{FCF}_t^u|\mathcal{F}_{t-1}\right] = \left(1-\tau^D\right)\left(1+r_f\right)\widetilde{A}_{t-1} - \left(1-\tau^D\right)\mathrm{E}_Q\left[\widetilde{A}_t|\mathcal{F}_{t-1}\right]. \tag{4.3}$$

A tax shield then comes about if the firm does away with fully distributing the free cash flows.

4.1.4 Fundamental Theorem

In the last chapter we made thorough use of the fundamental theorem of asset pricing. We had already introduced this theorem in the first chapter of this book, since it is of such central importance for the derivation of valuation equations.

The fundamental theorem says that under the condition of an arbitrage free capital market, risk-neutral probabilities Q exist. Risk-neutral expectations can thus be discounted in a world without taxes with the riskless interest rate r_f. The correctness of this statement does not change if a corporate income tax is entered into the model. This is because in taxation, which is only affective at the level of the firm, the riskless interest is identical pre- and post-tax. But now we are dealing with taxation at the financiers' level. And whoever invests riskless money as a financier and is at the same time liable to pay taxes, no longer attains net returns in the amount of r_f, but rather a return in the amount of $r_f\left(1-\tau^I\right)$. What comes of the fundamental theorem under these conditions? Do risk-neutral probabilities Q still exist? And if so, how are risk-neutral expectations to be discounted?

For the value of any discretionary portfolio from risky and riskless assets as well the following theorem now applies.

Theorem 4.2 (Fundamental Theorem with Different Taxation of Dividends and Interest) *If the capital market with a personal income tax is free of arbitrage, the conditional probabilities Q can be chosen to the extent that the following result is valid:*

$$\widetilde{V}_t = \frac{\mathrm{E}_Q\left[\widetilde{FCF}_{t+1}^{post\text{-}tax} + \widetilde{V}_{t+1}|\mathcal{F}_t\right]}{1+r_f\left(1-\tau^I\right)}.$$

The tax rate for returns on interest is found in the denominator even if it includes assets with risky returns. This result is neither trivial nor is it immediately evident. Due to the fact that proofs like this cannot be found in the relevant literature, we nevertheless felt that we had no other option than to publish it here. For further information please refer to the appendix.[9] Now we shall continue to develop results analogous to the ones we have proved in the previous two chapters.

Theorem 4.3 (Williams/Gordon-Shapiro Formula) *If the cost of equity are deterministic and the assumption on weak auto-regressive cash flows holds, then for the value of the unlevered firm*

$$\widetilde{V}_t^u = \frac{\widetilde{FCF}_t^u}{d_t^u}$$

holds for deterministic d_t^u.

Theorem 4.4 (Equivalence of the Valuation Concepts) *If the cost of equity are deterministic and the assumption on weak auto-regressive cash flows holds, then the following is valid for all times $s > t$*

$$\frac{\mathrm{E}_Q\left[\widetilde{FCF}_s^u|\mathcal{F}_t\right]}{\left(1+r_f\left(1-\tau^I\right)\right)^{s-t}} = \frac{\mathrm{E}\left[\widetilde{FCF}_s^u|\mathcal{F}_t\right]}{\left(1+k_t^{E,u}\right)\ldots\left(1+k_{s-1}^{E,u}\right)}.$$

In terms of the value of equity of the unlevered firm, cost of equity and discount rates are the same. But the taxed interest rate $r_f\left(1-\tau^I\right)$ now appears in place of the riskless interest rate r_f. The cost of equity $k^{E,u}$ we are now dealing with is also a post-tax variable. We do, however, avoid establishing an explicit relation to the levered firm's pre-tax cost of equity here.

We do not really need to prove the two theorems here for a second time. Instead, we refer our readers to the applicable pages in the chapter on the corporate tax.[10]

4.1.5 Tax Shield and Distribution Policy

In this section we want to characterize the difference in value between an unlevered and a levered firm.

Let us begin with the firm with full distribution. From Theorem 4.1 in relation to (4.3), we immediately get the representation

$$\widetilde{V}_t^u = \frac{\mathrm{E}_Q\left[\widetilde{FCF}_{t+1}^u|\mathcal{F}_t\right]}{1+r_f\left(1-\tau^I\right)} + \ldots + \frac{\mathrm{E}_Q\left[\widetilde{FCF}_T^u|\mathcal{F}_t\right]}{\left(1+r_f\left(1-\tau^I\right)\right)^{T-t}}.$$

[9] See Sect. 6.7.

[10] See Sect. 6.1.

We get the value of a levered firm in the exact same way from

$$\widetilde{V}_t^l = \frac{\mathrm{E}_Q\left[\widetilde{FCF}_{t+1}^l|\mathcal{F}_t\right]}{1+r_f\left(1-\tau^I\right)} + \ldots + \frac{\mathrm{E}_Q\left[\widetilde{FCF}_T^l|\mathcal{F}_t\right]}{\left(1+r_f\left(1-\tau^I\right)\right)^{T-t}}.$$

Yet, we still have to think about how the free cash flows from the firm with partial distribution differ from those of the unlevered firm. We thereby regard the following principle: The first earnings retention takes place in t. It is economically unsuitable to forgo with distributions at the last time $t = T$. From that results $\widetilde{A}_T = 0$. If we compare the value of the levered and unlevered firm, we then get by applying the rules 4 as well as 5

$$\widetilde{V}_t^l = \widetilde{V}_t^u + \frac{\left(1-\tau^D\right)\mathrm{E}_Q\left[\left(1+r_f\right)\widetilde{A}_t - \widetilde{A}_{t+1}|\mathcal{F}_t\right]}{1+r_f\left(1-\tau^I\right)} + \ldots +$$
$$+ \frac{\left(1-\tau^D\right)\mathrm{E}_Q\left[\left(1+r_f\right)\widetilde{A}_{T-2} - \widetilde{A}_{T-1}|\mathcal{F}_t\right]}{1+r_f\left(1-\tau^I\right)^{T-t-1}} + \frac{\left(1-\tau^D\right)\mathrm{E}_Q\left[\left(1+r_f\right)\widetilde{A}_{T-1}|\mathcal{F}_t\right]}{\left(1+r_f(1-\tau^I)\right)^{T-t}}.$$

After some minimal reshuffling, the following results:

$$\widetilde{V}_t^l = \widetilde{V}_t^u + \frac{\left(1-\tau^D\right)\left(1+r_f\right)\widetilde{A}_t}{1+r_f\left(1-\tau^I\right)} + \frac{\mathrm{E}_Q\left[\frac{(1+r_f)(1-\tau^D)}{1+r_f(1-\tau^I)}\widetilde{A}_{t+1} - \left(1-\tau^D\right)\widetilde{A}_{t+1}|\mathcal{F}_t\right]}{1+r_f\left(1-\tau^I\right)} +$$
$$+ \ldots + \frac{\mathrm{E}_Q\left[\frac{(1+r_f)(1-\tau^D)}{1+r_f(1-\tau^I)}\widetilde{A}_{T-1} - \left(1-\tau^D\right)\widetilde{A}_{T-1}|\mathcal{F}_t\right]}{\left(1+r_f\left(1-\tau^I\right)\right)^{T-t}}.$$

This brings us to the conclusion

$$\widetilde{V}_t^l = \widetilde{V}_t^u + \left(1-\tau^D\right)\widetilde{A}_t + \frac{\tau^I\left(1-\tau^D\right)r_f\,\mathrm{E}_Q\left[\widetilde{A}_t|\mathcal{F}_t\right]}{1+r_f\left(1-\tau^I\right)} +$$
$$\ldots + \frac{\tau^I\left(1-\tau^D\right)r_f\,\mathrm{E}_Q\left[\widetilde{A}_{T-1}|\mathcal{F}_t\right]}{\left(1+r_f\left(1-\tau^I\right)\right)^{T-t}}. \tag{4.4}$$

This equation shows itself to be the personal income tax pendant to Eq. (3.11). In place of debt $\widetilde{D}_t$, $\left(1-\tau^D\right)\widetilde{A}_t$ simply enters in, that being the amount by which the maximum distribution to the financiers is reduced.

Alternative Retained Earnings Policies If we think the tax shields through to a consequential end, then we would have to advise every firm to hold off the distribution only so long as possible for tax reasons. There is nothing to object to this recommendation within the framework of our model. We could have also argued accordingly in the last chapter. It was the debt which brought a tax shield there. And it would have then made sense to recommend that the firm allow for the maximum debt ratio permissible. As we did there, we here refrain from such recommendations since we very well know that suitable advice is unreasonable if it is solely based on tax considerations. That is also why we want to master the situation differently here. We take the firm's distribution policy—just as we did the debt policy in the last chapter—as a given and question how it affects the value of the firm.

In the following we will more clearly analyze five distribution policies. Since distribution and retention are always complementary measures, we can naturally speak of alternative retention policies as well. This involves a phraseology in relation to the subsequent characterizations which can more easily be remembered.

1. With the *autonomous retention*, a certain amount is retained each period.
2. With the *cash flow based earnings retention*, a certain amount of the free cash flows is deducted each period.
3. With the *dividend based earnings retention*, the amounts to be deducted are so chosen that in the first n periods it comes to a distribution of a fixed dividend.
4. With the *market value based earnings retention*, the deducted amounts are so chosen that the relation of earnings retention and equity value remains deterministic.

Another potential dividend policy of relevance can be of consequence if we consider disbursement stoppages. In many countries statutory provisions allow that, at the very most, the earnings are distributed and nothing more. This applies as well even if the free cash flow should exceed this amount. Unfortunately, these disbursement stoppages are very difficult to manage. Therefore we will refrain from discussing them.

4.1.6 Example (Continued)

We also want to use the data from the two examples in the previous chapter in terms of the personal tax. We assume that the tax rates on dividend and interest will coincide and be denoted by τ. Since the expositions in this chapter almost completely formally correspond to those of the last, we could simply repeat the previous chapter's calculations here once again. we would just have to interpret the respective variables differently: with $\widetilde{FCF}_t^u$ as cash flows post income tax, $k^{E,u}$ as taxed cost of equity and τ as income tax rate, the calculations take shape for the finite as well as infinite example, but formally just as in the Sects. 2.2.3 and 3.1.3.

In the infinite case, we would—despite the formal agreement with the previous chapter's concept—indeed fumble into a trap. Analogously to Sect. 3.1.3, we could determine the risk-neutral probabilities $Q_1(d)$ and $Q_1(u)$ for a certain time period. Now the outcomes no longer agree with the values calculated for the infinite case in Sect. 3.1.3, because the fundamental theorems for the case of the corporate income tax and the personal income tax differ from each other. In the first case, the riskless interest r_f is to be calculated with, and in the other case it is the riskless tax interest $r_f(1-\tau)$. It now appears that with the data constellation we have chosen, the probabilities would be negative and that correlates to an arbitrage opportunity![11]

We will therefore suppose a cost of equity rate of $k^{E,u} = 15\,\%$ in the following. It can be seen that with such a cost of equity rate the arbitrage opportunity vanishes. With cost of equity in the amount of $k^{E,u} = 15\,\%$, the value of the unlevered firm in the infinite example amounts to

$$\begin{aligned} V_0^u &= \frac{\mathrm{E}\left[\widetilde{FCF}_1^u\right]}{1+k^{E,u}} + \frac{\mathrm{E}\left[\widetilde{FCF}_2^u\right]}{(1+k^{E,u})^2} + \frac{\mathrm{E}\left[\widetilde{FCF}_3^u\right]}{(1+k^{E,u})^3} \\ &= \frac{100}{1.15} + \frac{110}{1.15^2} + \frac{121}{1.15^3} \approx 249.692. \end{aligned}$$

The values of $\widetilde{V}_1^u$ and $\widetilde{V}_2^u$ have to be determined anew.

We can take the other original numerical values for the infinite example without restriction.

4.1.7 Problems

1. In Sect. 3.1.3 we were able to evaluate the risk-neutral probabilities $Q_1(d)$ and $Q_1(u)$ for the finite example.[12] Show that

$$Q_1(u) \approx -0.125, \qquad Q_1(d) \approx 1.125$$

   if a personal income tax with $\tau = 50\,\%$ is present.

   Verify that for $k^{E,u} = 15\,\%$ this arbitrage opportunity vanishes and determine $Q_1(u)$ and $Q_1(d)$. Determine $Q_2(dd)$, $Q_2(du)$, $Q_2(ud)$, and $Q_2(uu)$.
2. Prove that the tax shield $\widetilde{V}_t^l - \widetilde{V}_t^u$ in the case of the personal income tax satisfies

$$\widetilde{V}_t^l - \widetilde{V}_t^u = \frac{\mathrm{E}_Q\left[\widetilde{V}_{t+1}^l - \widetilde{V}_{t+1}^u | \mathcal{F}_t\right]}{1+r_f(1-\tau^I)} + (1-\tau^D)\frac{\mathrm{E}_Q\left[(1+r_f)\widetilde{A}_t - \widetilde{A}_{t+1} | \mathcal{F}_t\right]}{1+r_f(1-\tau^I)}.$$

3. Similar to problem 4 show that the main valuation Eq. (4.4) can be written as

$$\widetilde{V}_t^l = \widetilde{V}_t^u + \frac{1-\tau^D}{1-\tau^I}\widetilde{A}_t + \frac{\tau^I\left(1-\tau^D\right)}{1-\tau^I}\sum_{s=t+1}^{T}\frac{\mathrm{E}_Q\left[\widetilde{A}_s - \widetilde{A}_{s-1} | \mathcal{F}_t\right]}{\left(1+r_f\left(1-\tau^I\right)\right)^{s-t}}.$$

[11] For details see problem 1.

[12] See Sect. 3.1.3.

4.2 Excursus: Cost of Equity and Tax Rate

Statement of the Problem In this section we will go into the question which until now has been left out. The question goes: How do a firm's cost of equity change when the income tax rate changes? And further: What can we say about the value of a fully self-financed firm as function of the income tax rate? In all our expositions up to now, we kept the tax rates constant. We did not want to clarify how a firm's market value behaved with a different tax rate. In this section it will be seen why we constantly avoided this question.

Whoever wants to investigate the relation between tax rate and value of the firm has to grapple with two problems. On the one hand, she has to analyze the influence of the tax rate on the cash flow, and on the other hand, the influence of the tax rate on the cost of equity. The first problem mentioned is not considered particularly difficult in the literature, which is why it generally does not get much attention. The question as to how the cost of equity react to changes in the tax rate, in contrast, deserves much more consideration. We will limit ourselves to the case of the eternal return in our subsequent analysis. The reasons for doing so will soon be clear. To simplify matters, we are operating in this section on the basis that both income types are burdened by income tax in the same way. The tax rate will be denoted by τ.

Influence on Cash Flows We presuppose expected cash flows remain equal. We further assume that no changes of the drawn capital and no investments result during the entire duration. Thus the free cash flow is dealing with an amount that can be easily calculated as product of the gross cash flow and the term $1 - \tau$,

$$\widetilde{FCF}_t^u = \widetilde{GCF}_t(1 - \tau). \tag{4.5}$$

Influence on Cost of Equity In connection to a work by Johansson (1969), a declaration on the functional relation between the cost of equity (post-tax) and the tax rate is often made in the literature,[13] which can be formulated as follows: the post-tax cost of equity $k^{E,u}$ is dependent linearly on tax rate τ; there is then a number k^E, so that

$$k^{E,u} = k^E(1 - \tau) \tag{4.6}$$

[13]Johansson addressed the question, indeed in more scope, as to if the formula notated below is in fact applicable. He clearly pointed out in response that a series of conditions must be satisfied here. One typically finds this relation in examples and not in a chapter on theory, as, for example, in Hillier et al. (2008, Example 14.5, page 520) or in texts dealing with practical issues as Institut der Wirtschaftsprüfer in Deutschland (2008, section 4.4.2.5) (in German).

is valid. k^E is also referred to as "pre-tax cost of equity," although this interpretation is not necessary for our argument. We ourselves have always very wisely forgone asserting such a relation.

Equation (4.5) now leads in connection to Eq. (4.6) to the familiar outcome of the income tax being completely redundant under the conditions assumed here. It simply cancels from the valuation equation,[14]

$$\widetilde{V}_t = \frac{\widetilde{FCF}_t^u}{k^{E,u}} = \frac{\widetilde{GCF}_t(1-\tau)}{k^E(1-\tau)} = \frac{\widetilde{GCF}_t}{k^E}. \tag{4.7}$$

But our discussion concerns a deeper matter. We want to critically analyze the linear relation (4.6).

Stochastic Structure of the Cash Flows There is a strong relation between the cost of equity and the risk-neutral probability measure Q.

We always stressed that earlier as well. The relation which we want to call attention to here once again is particularly well expressed in Theorems 3.3 and 4.4. If, as now in Eq. (4.6), a statement on the dependence of the cost of equity on the tax rate is made, then that also implies a relation between risk-neutral probabilities and the tax rate.

We want to show with help from an example that this relation can lead to a dramatic problem. In order to more exactly characterize the stochastic structure of the future gross cash flows, we use our example of an infinitely long living firm. We now assume that the gross cash flows $\widetilde{GCF}_t$ of the firm evolve according to Fig. 2.3.

In order to show that the free cash flows as modelled are in fact weak auto-regressive, we have to make it clear how the conditioned expectation $\mathrm{E}[\cdot|\mathcal{F}_t]$ is calculated. At time t the cash flow $\widetilde{GCF}_t$ is already known, and that is why the uncertainty can only relate the subsequent movement u or d. We thus have in

[14]There was a heated discussion in the German literature about this relation, which has found a way to enter into the documents of the Institute of Certified Public Accountants, the German association of CPAs ("Institut der Wirtschaftsprüfer" or IdW). You read, for instance, in Institut der Wirtschaftsprüfer in Deutschland (2013, II. Band, Teil A, Rz. 195): "... 1983 it was still assumed that a number of cases could forgo the (explicit) inclusion of the investor's tax burden, since it has no affect upon the firm's value." The Institute of Certified Public Accountants, however, gave up this position in 1997. Since then an income tax rate of 35% has been used, if no other income tax rate can be identified, see here Institut der Wirtschaftsprüfer in Deutschland (2000) as well as Institut der Wirtschaftsprüfer in Deutschland (2013, II.Band, Teil A, Rz. 117).

connection to rule 2

$$
\begin{aligned}
\mathrm{E}\left[(1-\tau)\widetilde{GCF}_{t+1}|\mathcal{F}_t\right] &= (1-\tau)\,\mathrm{E}\left[\widetilde{GCF}_{t+1}|\mathcal{F}_t\right] \\
&= (1-\tau)\,P(u)\,u\,\widetilde{GCF}_t + (1-\tau)\,P(d)\,d\,\widetilde{GCF}_t \\
&= \Big(\underbrace{P(u)u + P(d)d}_{:=1+g}\Big)(1-\tau)\widetilde{GCF}_t. \qquad (4.8)
\end{aligned}
$$

Because of (4.5) that is exactly the assumption of weak auto-regressive cash flows.

An Arbitrage Opportunity Now we do not only suppose the existence of one, but also of two firms. Both should be without debt and pursue a policy of full distribution. For the parameters u,d in the first firm

$$P(u)u + P(d)d = 1 \qquad \Longrightarrow \qquad g = 0$$

should be valid. The value of the firm at time t is denoted by $\widetilde{V}_t$. For the sake of simplicity, we designate the cost of equity when taxes are neglected with k; they should remain constant in time.

The second firm should also possess gross cash flows with the stochastic structure as in Fig. 2.3. If the cash flows grow in the first firm (that is, move up), then they also grow in the second firm. If they fall in the first firm, then they also sink in the second. It can thus be determined that the cash flows of the two firms are perfectly correlated. We will denote the cash flows of the second firm with $\widetilde{GCF}'_t$. The factors u',d' are different from those of the first firm, but

$$P(u)u' + P(d)d' = 1 \qquad \Longrightarrow \qquad g' = 0$$

should again be valid. Because of this connection, the gross cash flows do not point to any expected growth in either case. The second firm's cost of equity rate when taxes are neglected is k' and the firm's value in t is denoted with $\widetilde{V}'_t$.

The investor can continue selling or acquiring riskless bonds, which at time t have the value B_t. When taxes are left out, the bonds promise a return in the amount of r_f, the riskless interest rate.

We use an idea reasonably well known in the literature, that of the so-called pricing by duplication. This way we will be able to uncover a relationship between the value of the two firms, $\widetilde{V}_t$ and $\widetilde{V}'_t$, and so too between the cost of equity k and k'. This relationship is based on the idea that a portfolio can be put together from shares from the first company and the riskless bond, the cash flows of which do not differ from the payments with which an owner from the second firm can plan.

For that purpose we make up a portfolio which at time t includes exactly n_B riskless bonds and n_V shares of the first firm. We choose the numbers n_B and n_V in such a way that, independently from the state which manifests at time $t+1$, the equation

$$n_B B_t \left(1 + r_f(1-\tau)\right) + n_V \left(\widetilde{GCF}_{t+1}(1-\tau) + \widetilde{V}_{t+1}\right) = \widetilde{GCF}'_{t+1}(1-\tau) + \widetilde{V}'_{t+1}$$

is satisfied. With the help of (4.7), applied to both firms, the equation can be simplified to

$$n_B B_t \left(1 + r_f(1-\tau)\right) + n_V \left(1 + k_{t+1}(1-\tau)\right) \widetilde{V}_{t+1} = \left(1 + k'_{t+1}(1-\tau)\right) \widetilde{V}'_{t+1}.$$

In the period following from the end of time t, there are exactly two possible directions (up or down) along the cash flow path in the binomial model. That is why the above condition can be resolved in a system of two equations, which must be simultaneously satisfied: in the case of an up movement

$$\left(1 + r_f(1-\tau)\right) n_B B_t + u\left(1 + k(1-\tau)\right) n_V \widetilde{V}_t = u'\left(1 + k'(1-\tau)\right) \widetilde{V}'_t$$

must be valid, while in the case of a down movement

$$\left(1 + r_f(1-\tau)\right) n_B B_t + d\left(1 + k(1-\tau)\right) n_V \widetilde{V}_t = d'\left(1 + k'(1-\tau)\right) \widetilde{V}'_t$$

must be satisfied. Both equations make up a linear system, which can be unequivocally resolved according to variables n_B and n_V,

$$\begin{aligned} n_B &:= \frac{\widetilde{V}'_t}{B_t} \frac{(u-u')(1+k'(1-\tau))}{u(1+r_f(1-\tau))} \\ n_V &:= \frac{\widetilde{V}'_t}{\widetilde{V}_t} \frac{u'(1+k'(1-\tau))}{u(1+k(1-\tau))}. \end{aligned}$$

All variables are uncertain. They depend upon the firm value in t.

Since the portfolio ex constructione at time $t+1$ generates the same payments as the second firm, it has to have the same price under the arbitrage free conditions as this has,

$$n_B B_t + n_V \widetilde{V}_t = \widetilde{V}'_t. \tag{4.9}$$

If we employ the solutions for n_B and n_V in the solution at hand, then we get a valuation equation for the second firm. In so doing $\widetilde{V}'_t$ cancels out and we get a functional relation between the cost of equity k of the first firm and k' of the second. It reads as follows:

$$\frac{u-u'}{1+r_f(1-\tau)} + \frac{u'}{1+k(1-\tau)} = \frac{u}{1+k'(1-\tau)}. \tag{4.10}$$

A possible economic interpretation of this equation could consist of the cost of equity $1 + k'(1 - \tau)$ being established as harmonic mean of the cost of equity $1 + r_f(1 - \tau)$ and $1 + k(1 - \tau)$, whereby this harmonic mean is weighted with the parameters of the up and down movement.

The following is decisive for this equation: it must be valid for all conceivable tax rates τ. But that does not work. In addition to the trivial solution $\tau = 1$ the value $\tau = 0$ will yield a relation between k and k'. Hence, $\tau = 0$ and $\tau = 1$ solve the above equation already. But, a simple rearrangement shows that (4.10) is a quadratic equation in τ that cannot have more than two solutions! The equation cannot be satisfied for a single further τ.

That is a violation of the no arbitrage principle, a principle we always uphold. If namely, the cost of equity do not fulfill the given relation (4.10), then that means nothing more than that the relation of the firm values (4.9) is also not valid—and a free lunch can easily be construed from there. Depending upon whether

$$n_B B_t + n_V \widetilde{V}_t > \widetilde{V}_t' \qquad \text{or} \qquad n_B B_t + n_V \widetilde{V}_t < \widetilde{V}_t'$$

is valid, you must either go short or long with the shares of the second firm and cover this transaction with the bond and the shares of the first firm.

We had posed the question as to what connection existed between cost of equity and the tax rate. Until now, this question was always left out of our considerations. In order to answer the question, we fall back upon a concept which is very popular in applied work. This concept produces a simple linear relation between the cost of equity and the tax rate. We could show that the unlimited application of the appropriate equation results in an arbitrage opportunity. We are thus left with the following realization: whoever wants to know how cost of equity react to the changes in the tax rate, may not rely on Eq. (4.6). The DCF theory simply does not give any answer here. And that is exactly why we have until now deliberately avoided the question.

4.2.1 Problems

The following problems are devoted to the understanding of the arbitrage opportunity revealed in this section.

1. One particular feature of our tax system in that section was that only dividends were taxed. Assume now that also capital gains are taxed. In particular, we assume that the capital gains (even if they are not realized!) also add to the tax base, i.e., instead of (4.5) we assume

$$\widetilde{FCF}_t^u = \widetilde{GCF}_t - \tau\left(\widetilde{GCF}_t + \underbrace{\widetilde{V}_t^u - \widetilde{V}_{t-1}^u}_{\text{unrealized capital gain}}\right).$$

Such a tax system is also called neutral tax system or taxation of economic rent. Show that if the value of the assets remain unchanged by the tax rate the cost of equity have to satisfy

$$k^{\text{post-tax}} = k^{\text{pre-tax}}(1-\tau).$$

Remark It can be shown that if this system is free of arbitrage pre-tax it will remain free of arbitrage post-tax.

2. This problem derives a possible relation between company value and tax rate without violating the arbitrage principle.

   Assume that the risk-neutral probability measure Q does not change with the tax rate τ and that the cash flows form a perpetual rent (no growth). We further assume that the company has constant pre-tax cost of equity $k^{\text{pre-tax}}$. Using Theorem 4.2, derive an equation for post-tax value of the unlevered firm that explicitly contains $k^{\text{pre-tax}}$.

   Hint: The heart of the solution is the precise definition of a pre-tax cost of equity. Make certain that

$$\frac{\mathrm{E}_Q\left[\widetilde{GCF}_s|\mathcal{F}_t\right]}{\left(1+r_f\right)^{s-t}} = \frac{\mathrm{E}\left[\widetilde{GCF}_s|\mathcal{F}_t\right]}{(1+k^{\text{pre-tax}})^{s-t}}$$

   is a good choice.
3. The (pre-tax) gross cash flows from two companies follow the binomial tree as in Fig. 2.3 and let $FCF_0 = 100$, $g = 0$, $r_f = 5\,\%$, $k = 15\,\%$, $u = 10\,\%$, and $u' = 20\,\%$.
   a. Consider the first company having cost of equity k. Determine the risk-neutral probabilities $Q_1(u)$ and $Q_1(d)$.
   b. Use the arbitrage argument above to determine k'.
   c. Assume that for the first company the post-tax cost of equity are given as $(1-\tau)k$. Determine the risk-neutral probabilities depending on τ.
   d. Now assume that for the second company the post-tax cost of equity are given as $(1-\tau)k'$. Calculate again the risk-neutral probabilities depending on τ. Does the result coincide with c)?

   Hint: You might consult the finite example from Sect. 3.1.3 on how to calculate $Q_1(u)$ and $Q_1(d)$.

4.3 Retention Policies

In the following we will analyze alternative forms of the earnings retention policies. With one exception, it essentially deals with such strategies in which the scale of the earnings withholding is uncertain.

4.3.1 Autonomous Retention

The free cash flow of the unlevered firm can be either fully or partially distributed. We will now examine the most simple form of a retention policy. It is distinguishable in that the firm, on principle, annually holds back a certain amount of the maximally distributable cash flows.

Definition 4.2 (Autonomous Retention) A firm is following autonomous retention policy if the retention is deterministic.

The value of a firm which follows this policy is easy to calculate. We employ Definition 4.2 in Eq. (4.4) and get

Theorem 4.5 (Autonomous Retention) *In the case of an autonomous retention, the following is valid:*

$$\widetilde{V}_t^l = \widetilde{V}_t^u + \left(1 - \tau^D\right) A_t + \frac{\tau^I \left(1 - \tau^D\right) r_f A_t}{1 + r_f \left(1 - \tau^I\right)} + \ldots + \frac{\tau^I \left(1 - \tau^D\right) r_f A_{T-1}}{\left(1 + r_f \left(1 - \tau^I\right)\right)^{T-t}}.$$

Eternally Living Firm with Autonomous Retention If the firm pursues the autonomous retention in such a way so that A_t does not change in time, the last statement is simplified. We furthermore suppose at the same time that the firm lives infinitely. Notice that the value of the tax shield in Theorem 4.6 does not depend from the tax rate if $\tau^D = \tau^I$.

Theorem 4.6 (Constant Retention) *The firm lives on forever. For constant A, the following applies:*

$$\widetilde{V}_t^l = \widetilde{V}_t^u + \frac{1 - \tau^D}{1 - \tau^I} A.$$

The proof of this statement is straightforward.

Example Let us turn to our finite example. The amounts of retention with the levered firm are exactly

$$A_0 = 10, \quad A_1 = 20, \quad A_2 = 0.$$

With that we get

$$\begin{aligned} V_0^l &= V_0^u + (1-\tau)A_0 + \frac{\tau(1-\tau)r_f A_0}{1+r_f(1-\tau)} + \frac{\tau(1-\tau)r_f A_1}{(1+r_f(1-\tau))^2} \\ &= 249.692 + (1-0.5)\cdot 10 + \frac{0.5\cdot(1-0.5)\cdot 0.1\cdot 10}{1+0.1\cdot(1-0.5)} + \frac{0.5\cdot(1-0.5)\cdot 0.1\cdot 20}{(1+0.1\cdot(1-0.5))^2} \\ &\approx 255.383 \end{aligned}$$

for the value of the levered firm.

In order to establish the value of the levered firm in the infinite example, assuming $A = 10$ and using the statement from Theorem 4.6 we get

$$V_0^l = V_0^u + A = 510\,,$$

which is independent from the tax rate as mentioned earlier.

4.3.2 Retention Based on Cash Flow

The next policy concerns the case where a fraction of the distributable cash flow is retained.

Definition 4.3 (Retention Based on Cash Flows) A firm is following an earnings retention policy based on cash flows if the retention is a determinate multiple of the free cash flow of the unlevered firm,

$$\widetilde{A}_t = \alpha_t \, \widetilde{FCF}_t^u .$$

α_t is a number greater than zero.

The value of a firm which follows this policy is easy to calculate. We employ Definition 4.3 in Eq. (4.4) and get

$$\begin{aligned} \widetilde{V}_t^l &= \widetilde{V}_t^u + \left(1-\tau^D\right)\widetilde{A}_t + \frac{\mathrm{E}_Q\left[\tau^I r_f\left(1-\tau^D\right)\widetilde{A}_t|\mathcal{F}_t\right]}{1+r_f\left(1-\tau^I\right)} + \ldots + \frac{\mathrm{E}_Q\left[\tau^I r_f\left(1-\tau^D\right)\widetilde{A}_{T-1}|\mathcal{F}_t\right]}{\left(1+r_f\left(1-\tau^I\right)\right)^{T-t}} \\ &= \widetilde{V}_t^u + \left(1-\tau^D\right)\alpha_t\widetilde{FCF}_t^u + \frac{\tau^I r_f\left(1-\tau^D\right)\alpha_t\widetilde{FCF}_t^u}{1+r_f\left(1-\tau^I\right)} + \\ &\quad + \frac{\tau^I r_f\left(1-\tau^D\right)}{1+r_f\left(1-\tau^I\right)}\left(\frac{\mathrm{E}_Q\left[\alpha_{t+1}\widetilde{FCF}_{t+1}^u|\mathcal{F}_t\right]}{1+r_f\left(1-\tau^I\right)} + \ldots + \frac{\mathrm{E}_Q\left[\alpha_{T-1}\widetilde{FCF}_{T-1}^u|\mathcal{F}_t\right]}{\left(1+r_f\left(1-\tau^I\right)\right)^{T-t-1}}\right). \end{aligned}$$

All we need to do now is to use Theorem 4.4, and the following statement is already proven.

Theorem 4.7 (Cash Flow-Retention) *In the case of a retention based on cash flows, the following is valid:*

$$\widetilde{V}_t^l = \widetilde{V}_t^u + \frac{(1+r_f)\left(1-\tau^D\right)\alpha_t \widetilde{FCF}_t^u}{1+r_f\left(1-\tau^I\right)} + \\ + \frac{\tau^I r_f\left(1-\tau^D\right)}{1+r_f\left(1-\tau^I\right)}\left(\frac{\mathrm{E}\left[\alpha_{t+1}\widetilde{FCF}_{t+1}^u|\mathcal{F}_t\right]}{1+k^{E,u}} + \ldots + \frac{\mathrm{E}\left[\alpha_{T-1}\widetilde{FCF}_{T-1}^u|\mathcal{F}_t\right]}{(1+k^{E,u})^{T-t}}\right).$$

Eternally Living Firm with Constant Retention If the firm pursues the retention based on cash flow in such a way so that the share percentage $\alpha > 0$ does not change in time, the last statement is simplified. True, we only arrive at this simplification if we suppose at the same time that the firm lives infinitely. Otherwise it is so that $\alpha_T = 0$ is necessarily valid, and then a constant retention rate can no longer be spoken of. The subsequent statement applies under these conditions.

Theorem 4.8 (Constant Retention Rate) *The firm lives on forever. For constant α, the following applies:*

$$\widetilde{V}_t^l = \left(1 + \frac{\tau^I r_f\left(1-\tau^D\right)\alpha}{1+r_f\left(1-\tau^I\right)}\right)\widetilde{V}_t^u + \frac{(1+r_f)\left(1-\tau^D\right)\alpha}{1+r_f\left(1-\tau^I\right)}\widetilde{FCF}_t^u.$$

The proof of this statement is simple. We only need to employ the constant retention rate,

$$\begin{aligned}\widetilde{V}_t^l &= \widetilde{V}_t^u + \frac{(1+r_f)\left(1-\tau^D\right)\alpha\widetilde{FCF}_t^u}{1+r_f\left(1-\tau^I\right)} + \frac{\tau^I r_f\left(1-\tau^D\right)\alpha}{1+r_f\left(1-\tau^I\right)}\sum_{s=t+1}^{\infty}\frac{\mathrm{E}\left[\widetilde{FCF}_s^u|\mathcal{F}_t\right]}{(1+k^{E,u})^{s-t}} \\ &= \widetilde{V}_t^u + \frac{(1+r_f)\left(1-\tau^D\right)\alpha\widetilde{FCF}_t^u}{1+r_f\left(1-\tau^I\right)} + \frac{\tau^I r_f\left(1-\tau^D\right)\alpha}{1+r_f\left(1-\tau^I\right)}\widetilde{V}_t^u.\end{aligned}$$

And that was it. q.e.d.

Example Let us turn again to our finite example. The retention coefficients with the levered firm are exactly

$$\alpha_0 = 0\,\%, \quad \alpha_1 = 10\,\%, \quad \alpha_2 = 20\,\%.$$

With that we get

$$
\begin{aligned}
V_0^l &= V_0^u + \frac{(1+r_f)\,(1-\tau)\alpha_0 FCF_0^u}{1+r_f(1-\tau)} + \frac{\tau r_f(1-\tau)}{1+r_f(1-\tau)}\left(\alpha_1 \frac{\operatorname{E}\left[\widetilde{FCF}_1^u\right]}{1+k^{E,u}}\right.\\
&\quad\left.+\alpha_2 \frac{\operatorname{E}\left[\widetilde{FCF}_2^u\right]}{(1+k^{E,u})^2}\right)\\
&= 249.692 + 0 + \frac{0.5\cdot 0.1\cdot(1-0.5)}{1+0.1\cdot(1-0.5)}\cdot\left(0.1\cdot\frac{100}{1+0.15} + 0.2\cdot\frac{110}{(1+0.15)^2}\right)\\
&\approx 250.295
\end{aligned}
$$

for the value of the levered firm.

In order to establish the value of the levered firm in the infinite example, we use the statement from Theorem 4.8 and get

$$
\begin{aligned}
V_0^l &= \left(1+\frac{\tau r_f(1-\tau)}{1+r_f(1-\tau)}\alpha\right)V_0^u + \frac{(1+r_f)\,(1-\tau)\alpha}{1+r_f(1-\tau)} FCF_0^u\\
&= \left(1+\frac{0.5\cdot 0.1\cdot(1-0.5)}{1+0.1\cdot(1-0.5)}\cdot 0.5\right)\cdot 500 + \frac{(1+0.1)\cdot(1-0.5)\cdot 0.5}{1+0.1\cdot(1-0.5)}\cdot 100\\
&\approx 558.333\,.
\end{aligned}
$$

4.3.3 Retention Based on Dividends

Valuation Equation We now want to look at a retention policy in which a prescribed dividend (pre-tax) is distributed for a period of n years. At the end of this period, the firm should change over to a policy of full distribution. We will expect in the following that all decisions about the firm's investment policy have already been made. But then the firm cannot pay out any dividends if the free cash flow is not large enough. It is thus recommended requiring that the free cash flow is higher or at worst the same as the planned dividend. If the two amounts do not agree, then the difference is withheld. The reflux from this difference is then available as additional distribution potential at time $t+1$.

Definition 4.4 (Retention Based on Dividends) A firm is following a retention policy based on dividends if a prescribed certain pre-tax dividend should be payed in the first $n \widetilde{l} T$ periods,

$$\widetilde{A}_t = \left(\frac{1}{1-\tau^D} \widetilde{FCF}_t^u + (1+r_{t-1})\widetilde{A}_{t-1} - Div_t \right)^+$$

for all $t = 1, \ldots, n$.

Readers who still remember details from Sects. 3.6.1 and 3.6.2 of the previous chapter will hardly be surprised by the assertion that a general valuation equation is only possible through the inclusion of derivatives which we believe are not always traded in the market. Such complications can only be avoided if we introduce an additional assumption.

Assumption 4.2 (Non-negative Retention) *At no time does the prescribed dividend policy lead to the retention amount being negative,*

$$\frac{1}{1-\tau^D} \widetilde{FCF}_t^u \geq Div_t \qquad \forall t \leq n.$$

The maximum function in Definition 4.4 is superfluous under this simplified assumption, and we can prove that the following statement is valid.

Theorem 4.9 (Retention Based on Dividends) *The following applies in the case of a retention based on dividends, if the dividend is not greater than the free cash flow of the unlevered firm for all times before T,*

$$\widetilde{V}_u^l = \widetilde{V}_t^u + \tau^I \left(1-\tau^D\right) \left(\frac{1+r_f}{1+r_f\left(1-\tau^I\right)} \right)^{n-t+1} \widetilde{A}_t +$$
$$+\tau^I r_f \sum_{v=t+1}^{n} \left(\frac{\mathrm{E}\left[\widetilde{FCF}_v^u | \mathcal{F}_t\right]}{(1+k^{E,u})^{v-t}} - \frac{(1-\tau^D) Div_v}{(1+r_f(1-\tau^I))^{v-t}} \right) \cdot \left(1 + \left(\frac{1+r_f}{1+r_f(1-\tau^I)}\right)^{n+1-v}\right).$$

The proof is found in the appendix. In our opinion it does not make sense to generalize the above statement to the case of an infinitely long living firm with an eternally constant dividend ($n \to \infty$), since we otherwise fall into conflict with the assumption of transversality. We already pointed this out in a similar context in Sect. 3.6.2.

Example Let us work on the basis that the firm will pay the following pre-tax dividend:

$$A_0 = 0, \quad Div_1 = Div_2 = 40.$$

If the tax rate amounts to 50%, Assumption 4.2 is satisfied. Under these conditions we get the following for the value of the levered firm:

$$V_0^l = V_0^u + \tau r_f \left(\frac{\mathrm{E}\left[\widetilde{FCF}_1^u\right]}{1+k^{E,u}} - \frac{(1-\tau)Div_1}{1+(1-\tau)r_f} \right) \left(1 + \left(\frac{1+r_f}{1+(1-\tau)r_f} \right)^2 \right) +$$
$$+ \tau r_f \left(\frac{\mathrm{E}\left[\widetilde{FCF}_2^u\right]}{(1+k^{E,u})^2} - \frac{(1-\tau)Div_2}{(1+(1-\tau)r_f)^2} \right) \left(1 + \frac{1+r_f}{1+(1-\tau)r_f} \right)$$

and from that

$$V_0^l = 249.692 +$$
$$+ 0.1 \cdot 0.5 \cdot \left(\frac{100}{1+0.15} - \frac{(1-0.5)\cdot 40}{1+(1-0.5)\cdot 0.1} \right) \cdot \left(1 + \left(\frac{1+0.1}{1+(1-0.5)\cdot 0.1} \right)^2 \right) +$$
$$+ 0.1 \cdot 0.5 \cdot \left(\frac{110}{(1+0.15)^2} - \frac{(1-0.5)\cdot 40}{(1+(1-0.5)\cdot 0.1)^2} \right) \cdot \left(1 + \frac{1+0.1}{1+(1-0.5)\cdot 0.1} \right).$$

That results in

$$V_0^l \approx 263.472$$

for the levered firm.

4.3.4 Retention Based on Market Value

Valuation Equation A retention policy could take on the following form: the managers withhold a certain share of the value of the levered firm every year. However, much more value that firm has, that much more is retained. Hiding behind that could be the strategy of internally financing the growth of the firm with invariable intensity.

Definition 4.5 (Retention-Value Ratio) The firm is following a retention policy based on market values if the relation of retention and value of the firm

$$\tilde{l}_t = \frac{\widetilde{A}_t}{\widetilde{V}_t^l}$$

is deterministic.

We again use the symbol for leverage here, since, as we shall soon see, an equation equivalent to the WACC approach can be proven with the help of this quotient. This justifies the designation of this retention policy.

Theorem 4.10 (Retention Based on Market Values) *In the case of a retention policy based on market values, the following is valid for the levered firm that bears no debt*

$$\widetilde{V}_t^l = \sum_{s=t+1}^{T} \frac{\mathrm{E}\left[\prod_{h=t+1}^{s-1} \left(1 - \left(1 - \tau^D\right) l_h\right) \widetilde{FCF}_s^u | \mathcal{F}_t\right]}{\prod_{h=t}^{s-1} \left(1 + k_h\right)},$$

whereby

$$1 + k_h = \left(1 + k^{E,u}\right) \left(1 - \frac{\left(1 + r_f\right)\left(1 - \tau^D\right)}{1 + r_f\left(1 - \tau^I\right)} l_h\right).$$

The last equation looks a bit like the Miles–Ezzell formula.[15] In order to prove Theorem 4.10, we notate Eq. (4.4) for $\widetilde{V}_{t+1}^l$,

$$\widetilde{V}_{t+1}^l - \widetilde{V}_{t+1}^u = \left(1 - \tau^D\right) \widetilde{A}_{t+1} + \frac{\mathrm{E}_Q\left[\tau^I r_f \left(1 - \tau^D\right) \widetilde{A}_{t+1} | \mathcal{F}_{t+1}\right]}{1 + r_f\left(1 - \tau^I\right)} + \ldots$$
$$+ \frac{\mathrm{E}_Q\left[\tau^I r_f \left(1 - \tau^D\right) \widetilde{A}_{T-1} | \mathcal{F}_{t+1}\right]}{\left(1 + r_f\left(1 - \tau^I\right)\right)^{T-t-1}},$$

out of which with the rule for the iterated expectation

$$\frac{\mathrm{E}_Q\left[\widetilde{V}_{t+1}^l - \widetilde{V}_{t+1}^u | \mathcal{F}_t\right]}{1 + r_f\left(1 - \tau^I\right)} = \frac{\mathrm{E}_Q\left[\left(1 - \tau^D\right) \widetilde{A}_{t+1} | \mathcal{F}_t\right]}{1 + r_f\left(1 - \tau^I\right)} +$$
$$+ \frac{\mathrm{E}_Q\left[\tau^I r_f \left(1 - \tau^D\right) \widetilde{A}_{t+1} | \mathcal{F}_t\right]}{\left(1 + r_f\left(1 - \tau^I\right)\right)^2} + \ldots + \frac{\mathrm{E}_Q\left[\tau^I r_f \left(1 - \tau^D\right) \widetilde{A}_{T-1} | \mathcal{F}_t\right]}{\left(1 + r_f\left(1 - \tau^I\right)\right)^{T-t}}$$

results. If we now add the expression $\frac{\mathrm{E}_Q\left[\tau^I r_f (1-\tau^D)\widetilde{A}_t - (1-\tau^D)\widetilde{A}_{t+1} | \mathcal{F}_t\right]}{1+r_f(1-\tau^I)} + \left(1 - \tau^D\right) \widetilde{A}_t$ to both sides, then we can again under application of (4.4) bring the above equation

[15] See Theorem 3.14.

into the form

$$\frac{\mathrm{E}_Q\left[\widetilde{V}^l_{t+1}-\widetilde{V}^u_{t+1}+\left(1-\tau^D\right)\left(1+r_f\right)\widetilde{A}_t-\left(1-\tau^D\right)\widetilde{A}_{t+1}|\mathcal{F}_t\right]}{1+r_f\left(1-\tau^I\right)}=\widetilde{V}^l_t-\widetilde{V}^u_t.$$

With the help of the fundamental Theorem 4.2, we can eliminate $\widetilde{V}^u_t$ and $\widetilde{V}^u_{t+1}$ from the last equation for the unlevered firm and get

$$\widetilde{V}^l_t=\frac{\mathrm{E}_Q\left[\widetilde{V}^l_{t+1}+\widetilde{FCF}^u_{t+1}-\left(1-\tau^D\right)\widetilde{A}_{t+1}|\mathcal{F}_t\right]}{1+r_f\left(1-\tau^I\right)}+\frac{\left(1-\tau^D\right)\left(1+r_f\right)\widetilde{A}_t}{1+r_f\left(1-\tau^I\right)}.$$

Since the retention-value ratio is deterministic, we have

$$\widetilde{V}^l_t-\frac{\left(1-\tau^D\right)\left(1+r_f\right)l_t\widetilde{V}^l_t}{1+r_f\left(1-\tau^I\right)}=\frac{\mathrm{E}_Q\left[\widetilde{V}^l_{t+1}+\widetilde{FCF}^u_{t+1}-\left(1-\tau^D\right)l_{t+1}\widetilde{V}^l_{t+1}|\mathcal{F}_t\right]}{1+r_f\left(1-\tau^I\right)}.$$

We now divide by the factor $\left(1-\frac{(1-\tau^D)(1+r_f)}{1+r_f(1-\tau^I)}l_t\right)$ and get the recursion equation

$$\widetilde{V}^l_t=\frac{\mathrm{E}_Q\left[\left(1-\left(1-\tau^D\right)l_{t+1}\right)\widetilde{V}^l_{t+1}+\widetilde{FCF}^u_{t+1}|\mathcal{F}_t\right]}{1+r_f\left(1-\tau^I\right)-\left(1-\tau^D\right)\left(1+r_f\right)l_t}.$$

If we apply this repeatedly, the following then results:[16]

$$\widetilde{V}^l_t=\sum_{s=t+1}^{T}\frac{\mathrm{E}_Q\left[\prod_{h=t+1}^{s-1}\left(1-\left(1-\tau^D\right)l_h\right)\widetilde{FCF}^u_s|\mathcal{F}_t\right]}{\prod_{h=t}^{s-1}\left(1+r_f\left(1-\tau^I\right)-\left(1-\tau^D\right)\left(1+r_f\right)l_h\right)}.$$

With the help of statement Theorem 4.4, the following ensues:

$$\widetilde{V}^l_t=\sum_{s=t+1}^{T}\frac{\mathrm{E}\left[\prod_{h=t+1}^{s-1}\left(1-\left(1-\tau^D\right)l_h\right)\widetilde{FCF}^u_s|\mathcal{F}_t\right]}{\prod_{h=t}^{s-1}\left((1+k^{E,u}_h)(1-\frac{(1+r_f)(1-\tau^D)}{1+r_f(1-\tau^I)}l_h)\right)}.$$

That is the assertion of the statement. q.e.d.

Example We assume a retention-value ratio constant in time of

$$l_0=l_1=l_2=10\%\,.$$

[16]By definition, $\prod_{s=t+1}^{t}x_s=1$.

The following then results for the cost of equity:

$$k_t = (1 + k_t^{E,u}) \left(1 - \frac{(1 + r_f)(1 - \tau)}{1 + r_f(1 - \tau)} l_h\right) - 1$$
$$= (1 + 0.15) \cdot \left(1 - \frac{(1 + 0.1) \cdot (1 - 0.5)}{1 + 0.1 \cdot (1 - 0.5)} \cdot 0.1\right) - 1 \approx 8.976\%\,.$$

With that we get the value of the levered firm with

$$V_0^l = \frac{\mathrm{E}\left[\widetilde{FCF}_1^u\right]}{1+k} + \frac{(1-(1-\tau)l_1)\,\mathrm{E}\left[\widetilde{FCF}_2^u\right]}{(1+k)^2} + \frac{(1-(1-\tau)l_1)(1-(1-\tau)l_2)\,\mathrm{E}\left[\widetilde{FCF}_3^u\right]}{(1+k)^3}$$
$$\approx \frac{100}{1+0.08976} + \frac{(1-(1-0.5)\cdot 0.1)110}{(1+0.08976)^2} + \frac{(1-(1-0.5)\cdot 0.1)^2 \cdot 121}{(1+0.08976)^3}$$
$$\approx 264.137\,.$$

In the infinite example, we again use

$$l_s = 10\,\%$$

resulting in

$$k_s = (1 + k_s^{E,u}) \left(1 - \frac{(1 + r_f)(1 - \tau)}{1 + r_f(1 - \tau)} l_s\right) - 1$$
$$= (1 + 0.2) \left(1 - \frac{(1 + 0.1) \cdot (1 - 0.5)}{1 + 0.1 \cdot (1 - 0.5)} 0.1\right) - 1 \approx 0.13714\,.$$

We thus get

$$V_0^l = \sum_{t=1}^{\infty} \frac{\mathrm{E}\left[(1-(1-\tau)l)^{t-1}\widetilde{FCF}_t^u\right]}{(1+k)^t}$$
$$= \frac{1}{1-(1-\tau)l} \frac{\mathrm{E}\left[\widetilde{FCF}_1^u\right]}{\frac{1+k}{1-(1-\tau)l} - 1}$$
$$= \frac{\mathrm{E}\left[\widetilde{FCF}_1^u\right]}{k + (1-\tau)l}$$
$$= \frac{100}{0.13714 + (1-0.5)\cdot 0.1} = 534.351\,.$$

4.3.5 Problems

1. Look at the example of the unlevered firm in this section. Assume that funds in the firm are invested risky. Let $A_0 = 0$. What are the highest possible retentions at times $t = 1,2$? What value does the firm have if it institutes these retentions?
2. Consider the case where retention is invested in riskless assets. Write down the valuation equation similar to (4.4). Determine the value of the levered and eternally living company if the firm follows an autonomous retention with constant A_t.

4.4 Further Literature

The literature on personal income tax is few and far between. Miller and Modigliani (1961) dividends story is a predecessor of our handling of tax shield and distribution policy. Miller (1977) investigated an equilibrium model where a corporate and a personal income tax are present. The papers by Sick (1990), Taggart Jr. (1991), and Rashid and Amoaku-Adu (1995) considered personal income taxes in a valuation setup. The relation between tax and arbitrage (and in particular a fundamental theorem with income taxes) is also developed in a paper by Jensen (2009). Lally (2000) develops the DCF valuation implications with personal and corporate income tax where an imputation system is applicable. Fernández (2004) discusses the effect of different retention policies on the firm value.

The so-called "lock-in-effect" designates a situation where the owner of a company retains parts of the distributable cash flows due to personal income tax savings. If the tax rate differs across individuals people with high tax brackets hold assets with low dividends and people with low tax brackets hold assets with high dividend yields. This "clientele effect" is widely discussed in the literature.

References

Fernández P (2004) The value of tax shields and the risk of the net increase of debt. http://ssrn.com/paper=506005

Gallmeyer MF, Srivastava S (2011) Arbitrage and the tax code. Math. Financ Econ 4:183–221

Hillier D, Grinblatt M, Titman SD (2008) Financial markets and corporate strategy: European edition. McGraw-Hill Irwin, London

Institut der Wirtschaftsprüfer in Deutschland (2000) IDW Standard: Grundsätze zur Durchführung von Unternehmensbewertungen (IDW S 1) (Stand: 28.06.2000). Die Wirtschaftsprüfung 53:825–842

Institut der Wirtschaftsprüfer in Deutschland (2008) IDW Standard: Grundsätze zur Durchführung von Unternehmensbewertungen [IDW S 1] (Stand: 02.04.2008). Die Wirtschaftsprüfung (Supplement) 3:68–89

Institut der Wirtschaftsprüfer in Deutschland (ed) (2013) WP Handbuch 2014: Wirtschaftsprüfung, Rechnungslegung, Beratung, vol II, 14th edn. IDW-Verlag, Düsseldorf

Jensen BA (2009) Valuation before and after tax in the discrete time, finite state no arbitrage model. Ann Finance 5:91–123

Johansson SE (1969) Income taxes and investment decisions. Swed J Econ 71:103–110
Lally M (2000) Valuation of companies and projects under differential personal taxation. Pac Basin Financ J 8:115–133
Miller MH (1977) Debt and taxes. J Financ 32:261–275
Miller MH, Modigliani F (1961) Dividend policy, growth and the valuation of shares. J Bus 34:411–433
Rashid M, Amoaku-Adu B (1995) The cost of capital under conditions of personal taxes and inflation. J Bus Financ Acc 22:1049–1062
Shreve SE (2004) Stochastic calculus for finance I: the binomial asset pricing model. Springer, New York
Sick GA (1990) Tax-adjusted discount rates. Manag Sci 36:1432–1450
Taggart Jr RA (1991) Consistent valuation and cost of capital expressions with corporate and personal taxes. Financ Manag 20:8–20

5 Corporate and Personal Income Tax

In the last chapter of this book we would like to look into the question of how to evaluate a firm if taxes are raised both at the investor and at the company level. Attentive readers of Chaps. 2 and 3 might expect a discussion on different strategies of financing policy (Chap. 2) and of dividend policy (Chap. 3). But, we are not going to do this. We will also, however, not dwell on the innumerable variations of possible combinations in this context, rather we will restrict ourselves to a manageable example. At the end, we will only discuss how to proceed in the cases of further possible financing and dividend policies.

5.1 Assumptions

In this chapter we will define an unlevered company as a company, which fulfills the following two conditions. First, it has to be entirely self-financed, and second, it has to distribute all free cash flow to the shareholders. If even one of the attributes does not apply, then we will switch to discussing a levered company. Like in Chaps. 2 and 3 we will refer to the symbols u and l to distinguish either one case or the other.

In what follows we will begin by characterizing a tax system, which will be used in our example.

Corporate Income Tax The corporate income tax will possess the attributes we mentioned in Chap. 2: The tax is measured by the company's profit. The tax scale will be linear and the tax rate, which we will designate with τ^C is independent on time. Furthermore, taking out loans at time $t-1$ provides a tax advantage. This advantage will be equal to the product of tax scale and interest, $\tau^C \widetilde{I}_t$.

L. Kruschwitz, A. Löffler, *Stochastic Discounted Cash Flow*,
Springer Texts in Business and Economics,
https://doi.org/10.1007/978-3-030-37081-7_5

Personal Income Tax The personal income tax will follow the same model as in Chap. 3. On an assessment basis we are dealing with dividends and interest. Both will be taxed differently, the dividends with a tax rate of τ^D and the interest with a rate of τ^I. Such a strongly diverging treatment of income categories exists in several industrial nations. Both of the tax scales are linear and the tax rate is independent on time. In case the company does not pay out its entire free cash flow a tax advantage in the amount of $\widetilde{A}_t$ will result due to the retention.

Interaction of Both Taxes As we excluded one of the two tax types in Chaps. 2 and 3 we did not have to deal with the question of how to pattern an interaction of both types. It is obvious that here is a problem we have to discuss. For this purpose we shall put ourselves into the position of a shareholder whose earnings consist only of dividends. However, in order to be able to distribute dividends, the company in which the shareholder is involved, has to first yield profits. These profits are liable to corporate taxes. Consequently, the distribution to the shareholder will therefore already have been subject to initial taxes. Naturally the company can only distribute that amount of money that remains after corporate taxes. If the shareholder now has to pay personal income tax as well, the tax authorities will essentially have access to the dividend once again.

The legislator will have two ways to deal with the situation. Either he accepts that the income tax, which the company has already paid (entirely or in part), is considered just as a first installment, in which case we can talk about indirect relief,[1] or the legislator does not provide for such an allowance. This last option would imply a double taxation of dividends.[2] Occasionally political entities try to combine both concepts. As a general rule this is achieved with a milder dose of taxation of the dividends, especially when compared to the taxation applied to interest.[3]

In our examples we will assume the classical system with a two-tier rate of taxation for dividends and interest. Further comments as to the question of how to proceed in the case of different indirect relief policies or financial systems are discussed in Cooper and Nyborg (2004), Husmann et al. (2006), and Lally (2000).

5.2 Identification and Evaluation of Tax Advantages

Gross and Free Cash Flows Our intention consists in evaluating the tax advantages of the levered company, especially compared with those of the unlevered company. Again this can be achieved in two steps as in the preceding chapters. In the first step we will identify the tax advantages in t. In a second step we will

[1] In Italy, Japan, and New Zealand, for example, a form of indirect relief has been in use as of 2004.

[2] In 2004, the "classical system" was adopted in Belgium, Denmark, and the USA.

[3] In 2004, adequate solutions to this problem were in existence in Germany, the Netherlands, and Greece.

Fig. 5.1 From pre-tax gross cash flows to post-tax free cash flow

	Gross cash flow before taxes	$\widetilde{GCF}_t$
–	Corporate income taxes	$\widetilde{Tax}_t^C$
–	Investment expenses	$\widetilde{Inv}_t$
–	Interest (Creditor's taxable income)	$\widetilde{I}_t$
–	Debt repayments	$-\widetilde{D}_t + \widetilde{D}_{t-1}$
–	Retained earnings	$\widetilde{A}_t$
+	Reflux from retained earnings	$(1+\widetilde{r}_{t-1})\widetilde{A}_{t-1}$
–	Shareholder's personal income tax	$\widetilde{Tax}_t^P$
=	Shareholder's levered post-tax cash flow	$\widetilde{FCF}_t^l$

evaluate these future tax advantages at the point in time of evaluation. To identify the amount of the tax advantages accurately it is advisable to examine Fig. 5.1.

It specifies how to get from the gross cash flow to the free cash flow of the levered company. According to our assumption, the gross cash flow of the levered company involves the same amount as the gross cash flow of the unlevered company. The same applies to the investment expenses. Notice that (as in Chap. 3) $\widetilde{FCF}_t^l$ in Fig. 5.1 does not represent the entire payments of the investors but rather only the payments to the shareholders.

Tax Shields Let us now have a look at the distributions of the levered company. We intend to compare these payments with those of an unlevered company. The unlevered company is able to pay the following amount to the shareholders:

$$\widetilde{FCF}_t^u = \widetilde{GCF}_t - \widetilde{Tax}_t^{C,u} - \widetilde{Inv}_t - \widetilde{Tax}_t^{P,u} . \tag{5.1}$$

Due to the indebtedness of the levered company the payments to the shareholders will diminish. In addition, a part of the cash flow is withheld. The following equation for the payments to the shareholders of the levered company can be derived from Fig. 5.1:

$$\widetilde{FCF}_t^l = \widetilde{FCF}_t^u - \widetilde{I}_t + \widetilde{D}_t - \widetilde{D}_{t-1} - \widetilde{A}_t + (1+\widetilde{r}_{t-1})\widetilde{A}_{t-1} \\ + \widetilde{Tax}_t^{C,u} - \widetilde{Tax}_t^{C,l} + \widetilde{Tax}_t^{P,u} - \widetilde{Tax}_t^{P,l} . \tag{5.2}$$

Here we can find two tax shields, a corporate income tax shield and a personal income tax shield. In our example we want to focus on a case in which both the indebtedness and the retention are constant over a specified period of time. Hence the following always applies:

$$\widetilde{D}_t = D, \quad \widetilde{A}_t = A . \tag{5.3}$$

Now, let us address the tax shields.

The earnings before taxes determine the corporate income tax. Consequently, analogously to Chap. 2, the following applies:

$$\begin{aligned}
\widetilde{Tax}_t^{C,l} &= \tau^C \widetilde{EBT}_t^l \\
&= \tau^C \left(\widetilde{EBT}_t^u - r_f D + \widetilde{r}_{t-1} A\right) \\
&= \widetilde{Tax}_t^{C,u} - \tau^C r_f D + \tau^C \widetilde{r}_{t-1} A .
\end{aligned}$$

The personal income tax follows the classical system and is geared to distribution. If we take a closer look at the basic assets, we can see that the shareholder's tax base of the levered company decreases by the amount of the interest payments and increases by the amount of the proceeds from the retention. Looking at the creditors, however, the tax advantages based on borrowing need to be added. But these are partly with risk and partly without risk. Thus the appropriate tax rate has to be used as follows:

$$\begin{aligned}
\widetilde{Tax}_t^{P,l} &= \widetilde{Tax}_t^{P,u} - \tau^I r_f D + \tau^D \widetilde{r}_{t-1} A + \tau^I \tau^C r_f D - \tau^D \tau^C \widetilde{r}_{t-1} A \\
&= \widetilde{Tax}_t^{P,u} - \tau^I \left(1 - \tau^C\right) r_f D + \tau^D \left(1 - \tau^C\right) \widetilde{r}_{t-1} A .
\end{aligned}$$

Finally, both equations add up to the entire tax shield of the levered company.[4] For this purpose we will concentrate on Eq. (5.2) and will take advantage of the fact that indebtedness and distribution remain unchanged over time,

$$\begin{aligned}
\widetilde{FCF}_t^l &= \widetilde{FCF}_t^u - r_f D + \widetilde{r}_{t-1} A + \widetilde{Tax}^{C,u} - \widetilde{Tax}^{C,l} + \widetilde{Tax}^{P,u} - \widetilde{Tax}^{P,l} \\
&= \widetilde{FCF}_t^u - \left(1 - \tau^I\right)\left(1 - \tau^C\right) r_f D + \left(1 - \tau^D\right)\left(1 - \tau^C\right) \widetilde{r}_{t-1} A \\
\mathrm{E}_Q\left[\widetilde{FCF}_t^l | \mathcal{F}_{t-1}\right] &= \mathrm{E}_Q\left[\widetilde{FCF}_t^u | \mathcal{F}_{t-1}\right] + \left(1 - \tau^D\right)\left(1 - \tau^C\right) r_f A \\
&\quad - \left(1 - \tau^I\right)\left(1 - \tau^C\right) r_f D .
\end{aligned}$$

The difference of both equations is now easy to determine. All we need to do is to make use of the fundamental theorem (4.2), which applies to the levered as well as to the unlevered companies.

Again we have to take into account an important detail that we have already mentioned in the previous chapter. We designated the cash flow of the unlevered company, thus this company that conducts a full dividend policy, with $\widetilde{FCF}_t^u$. We already pointed out that this merely concerns the cash flow, which accrues to the owners. Hence, the payments (interest and/or amortization) for the creditors have not been included up to now. In order to determine not only the value of equity but

[4] The argumentation is equivalent to the Eq. (4.2) on page 147.

moreover the value of the entire company, we need to take into consideration the payments to all investors. It would not be correct to focus just on $\widetilde{FCF}_t^u$.

Here we technically have two possibilities: On the one hand we could concentrate on the income of the owner and subsequently add $\widetilde{D}_t$. On the other hand we could calculate the payments to all financiers. This can be obtained by adding the interest payments to those accrued from amortization and to the $\widetilde{FCF}_t^u$. And then we subtract the personal income tax, which the creditors have to pay. Both methods lead to the same result. This is due to the fundamental theory of asset pricing. Correspondingly this applies to the levered company as well.

According to this, the difference between the values of the companies concerned is equal to the sum of the discounted tax shields plus the market value of the debt,

$$\begin{aligned}
\widetilde{V}_t^l &= \widetilde{V}_t^u + D + \sum_{s=t+1}^{\infty} \frac{\mathrm{E}_Q\left[\left(1-\tau^D\right)\left(1-\tau^C\right) r_f A - \left(1-\tau^I\right)\left(1-\tau^C\right) r_f D | \mathcal{F}_t\right]}{\left(1+r_f\left(1-\tau^I\right)\right)^{s-t}} \qquad (5.4)\\
&= \widetilde{V}_t^u + D + \sum_{s=t+1}^{\infty} \frac{\left(1-\tau^D\right)\left(1-\tau^C\right)}{\left(1+r_f\left(1-\tau^I\right)\right)^{s-t}} r_f A - \sum_{s=t+1}^{\infty} \frac{\left(1-\tau^I\right)\left(1-\tau^C\right)}{\left(1+r_f\left(1-\tau^I\right)\right)^{s-t}} r_f D \\
&= \widetilde{V}_t^u + D + \frac{\left(1-\tau^D\right)\left(1-\tau^C\right)}{r_f\left(1-\tau^I\right)} r_f A - \frac{\left(1-\tau^I\right)\left(1-\tau^C\right)}{r_f\left(1-\tau^I\right)} r_f D \\
&= \widetilde{V}_t^u + \frac{\left(1-\tau^D\right)\left(1-\tau^C\right)}{1-\tau^I} A + \tau^C D .
\end{aligned}$$

This describes a more general view of the findings of the precedent chapters (Modigliani–Miller-Theorem 3.7 and Theorem 4.6).

5.3 Conclusion

In the previous paragraph we evaluated a company assuming that taxes are raised at the company's level as well as at the investor's level. We could formulate a simple valuation equation under the special conditions concerning the lifespan of the company as well as its debt and dividend policies. The question remains how to proceed if the debt and dividend policies seriously deviate from the conditions which we had originally assumed.

For this purpose we will analyze the Eq. (5.4). It permits us (according to the special assumptions which we have made) to make a statement of appraisal on the difference in value between the levered and unlevered company. Given different assumptions concerning the debt and dividend policies, one can also easily modify the equation. One only has to identify the tax advantages, which are associated with specific debt and dividend policies to determine the corresponding equation. The expected values in such an equation would be valid for the future amounts of debt $\widetilde{D}_t$ and the future amounts of retention $\widetilde{A}_t$. But in any case they have to be calculated with the risk neutral probability measure Q. And since the person who, in practice, has to evaluate a company is usually unaware of this measure we would have an elegant but, nevertheless, useless valuation equation.

In a first step in acquiring a valuation equation (while taking into account the subjective probability measure) it is important to formulate a linear correlation between the future amounts of debt $\widetilde{D}_t$ and the future amounts of retention $\widetilde{A}_t$ as well as the cash flow of the unlevered company $\widetilde{FCF}^u_t$.[5] If we cope with this task fairly successfully the valuation equation can be expressed by the following formula:

$$V_0^l = V_0^u + x_0 D_0 + x_0' A_0 + \frac{x_1 \operatorname{E}_Q\left[\widetilde{FCF}^u_1\right]}{\left(1 + r_f\left(1 - \tau^I\right)\right)^2} + \cdots + \frac{x_{T-1} \operatorname{E}_Q\left[\widetilde{FCF}^u_{T-1}\right]}{\left(1 + r_f\left(1 - \tau^I\right)\right)^T}.$$

In this case we need to assume that current amount of debt and current amount of retention are given as known factors. The parameter x_t are the expressions of any deterministic variables, which describe the linear correlation between the amounts of debt and the amounts of retention on the one hand, and the cash flow of the unlevered firm on the other hand. Unfortunately we cannot characterize them more precisely in our final general view. With this we will have retraced the evaluation of the tax shield to an ascertainment of expected values of future cash flow under Q.

Finally, we need to eliminate the risk neutral probability measure. For this we avail ourselves in a second step of the assumption that the free cash flow of the unlevered company is going to be weak auto-regressive. Under these conditions the cost of capital of the unlevered company imply suitable discount rates. Finally, we can ascertain realistic valuation equations, which rely just on known variables (subjectively expected cash flow, cost of capital of the unlevered company, tax rates, and interest rates).

Consequently, if we proceed in the described manner, we will be able to evaluate companies operating with other financing and dividend policies. Initially we always have to identify the ensuing tax advantages. Subsequently the future amounts of debt $\widetilde{D}_t$ and the future amounts of retention $\widetilde{A}_t$ need to be linked to the future cash flow of the unlevered company with a linear correlation. Afterwards we can evaluate the expected values of this cash flow in that the cost of capital of the unlevered company can also be used as discount rates.

But the limits of our approach are quite in evidence. Every time we fail to construct a linear correlation the concept collapses. Such situations are easy to imagine. One just has to think of cases in which the future investments of a company follow a stochastic process which is independent of the cash flow and in which the manager commit themselves to trade the investments exclusively on the equity. In such a case it would not be possible to depict the future amounts of debt with the cash flows in a linear correlation. And our approach would not reap the desired

[5] For a similar approach in continuous time see Grinblatt and Liu (2008), chapter 1.C.

result in which the tax shield is determined solely by the cost of capital and the subjectively expected values of future cash flows.

5.4 Problem(s)

1. Evaluate the value of the levered company in the infinite example using all our assumptions (from autonomous debt and retention) so far.

References

Cooper IA, Nyborg KG (2004) The value of tax shield is equal to the present value of tax shields. http://ssrn.com/paper=625001

Grinblatt M, Liu J (2008) Debt policy, corporate taxes, and discount rates. J Econ Theory 141:225–254

Husmann S, Kruschwitz L, Löffler A (2006) WACC and a generalized tax code. Eur J Finance 12:33–40

Lally M (2000) Valuation of companies and projects under differential personal taxation. Pac Basin Finance J 8:115–133

Proofs

6

6.1 Williams/Gordon–Shapiro Formula (Theorem 3.2) and Equivalence of Valuation Concepts (Theorem 3.3)

We start with the proof of Theorem 3.2. From the valuation equation (Theorem 3.1) and the Assumption 3.1

$$\begin{aligned}
\widetilde{V}_t^u &= \sum_{s=t+1}^{T} \frac{\mathrm{E}\left[\widetilde{FCF}_s^u | \mathcal{F}_t\right]}{\left(1+k_t^{E,u}\right)\dots\left(1+k_{s-1}^{E,u}\right)} \\
&= \sum_{s=t+1}^{T} \frac{(1+g_t)\dots(1+g_{s-1})\widetilde{FCF}_t^u}{\left(1+k_t^{E,u}\right)\dots\left(1+k_{s-1}^{E,u}\right)} \\
&= \widetilde{FCF}_t^u \underbrace{\sum_{s=t+1}^{T} \frac{(1+g_t)\dots(1+g_{s-1})}{\left(1+k_t^{E,u}\right)\dots\left(1+k_{s-1}^{E,u}\right)}}_{=\frac{1}{d_t^u}}.
\end{aligned}$$

But the last equation says exactly that the firm value is a deterministic multiple of the cash flow. The relation between dividends and price d_t^u is deterministic and positive if $g_t > -1$. Using transversality this also applies for $T \to \infty$. Thus the Theorem 3.2 is proven.

L. Kruschwitz, A. Löffler, *Stochastic Discounted Cash Flow*,
Springer Texts in Business and Economics,
https://doi.org/10.1007/978-3-030-37081-7_6

Now we prove Theorem 3.3. The following results from the definition of the cost of equity of the unlevered firm if $t+1<T$

$$\widetilde{V}_t^u = \frac{\mathrm{E}\left[\widetilde{FCF}_{t+1}^u + \widetilde{V}_{t+1}^u|\mathcal{F}_t\right]}{1+k_t^{E,u}} \qquad \text{by Definition 3.1} \tag{6.1}$$

$$= \frac{\mathrm{E}\left[\widetilde{FCF}_{t+1}^u + (d_{t+1}^u)^{-1}\widetilde{FCF}_{t+1}^u|\mathcal{F}_t\right]}{1+k_t^{E,u}} \qquad \text{by Theorem 3.2}$$

$$= \frac{\left(1+(d_{t+1}^u)^{-1}\right)\mathrm{E}\left[\widetilde{FCF}_{t+1}^u|\mathcal{F}_t\right]}{1+k_t^{E,u}}.$$

The following is likewise valid if $t+1<T$

$$\widetilde{V}_t^u = \frac{\mathrm{E}_Q\left[\widetilde{FCF}_{t+1}^u + \widetilde{V}_{t+1}^u|\mathcal{F}_t\right]}{1+r_f} \qquad \text{by Theorem 2.2} \tag{6.2}$$

$$= \frac{\left(1+(d_{t+1}^u)^{-1}\right)\mathrm{E}_Q\left[\widetilde{FCF}_{t+1}^u|\mathcal{F}_t\right]}{1+r_f}. \qquad \text{by Theorem 3.2}$$

The comparison of both terms results in

$$\frac{\mathrm{E}\left[\widetilde{FCF}_{t+1}^u|\mathcal{F}_t\right]}{1+k_t^{E,u}} = \frac{\mathrm{E}_Q\left[\widetilde{FCF}_{t+1}^u|\mathcal{F}_t\right]}{1+r_f}$$

and this also holds for $t+1=T$ from transversality. And that is already the proposition of the theorem for $s=t+1$.

We go back to Eqs. (6.1) and (6.2) and remove the terms already shown to be identical. There then remains

$$\frac{\mathrm{E}\left[\widetilde{V}_{t+1}^u|\mathcal{F}_t\right]}{1+k_t^{E,u}} = \frac{\mathrm{E}_Q\left[\widetilde{V}_{t+1}^u|\mathcal{F}_t\right]}{1+r_f}$$

or

$$\frac{\mathrm{E}\left[\frac{\mathrm{E}\left[\widetilde{FCF}_{t+2}^u+\widetilde{V}_{t+2}^u|\mathcal{F}_{t+1}\right]}{1+k_{t+1}^{E,u}}|\mathcal{F}_t\right]}{1+k_t^{E,u}} = \frac{\mathrm{E}_Q\left[\frac{\mathrm{E}_Q\left[\widetilde{FCF}_{t+2}^u+\widetilde{V}_{t+2}^u|\mathcal{F}_{t+1}\right]}{1+r_f}|\mathcal{F}_t\right]}{1+r_f}.$$

The law of the iterated expectation as well as the fact that the dividend-price relation is deterministic establishes

$$\frac{\mathrm{E}\left[(1+(d^u_{t+2})^{-1})\widetilde{FCF}^u_{t+2}|\mathcal{F}_t\right]}{(1+k^{E,u}_t)(1+k^{E,u}_{t+1})} = \frac{\mathrm{E}_Q\left[(1+(d^u_{t+2})^{-1})\widetilde{FCF}^u_{t+2}|\mathcal{F}_t\right]}{(1+r_f)^2}.$$

After shortening of $\left(1+(d^u_{t+2})^{-1}\right)$, that is the claim of the theorem for $s=t+2$. The propositions for $s=t+3,\ldots$ can now be proven analogously.

6.2 Valuation Formula with Investment Policy Based on Cash Flows (Theorem 3.21)

With the following proof you have to make an effort to keep an overview. We begin with showing the difference between investments and accruals. Because of Definition 3.10 and because there are only non-discretionary accruals, for the time being we could write

$$\widetilde{Inv}_t - \widetilde{Accr}_t = \widetilde{Inv}_t - \frac{1}{n}\left(\widetilde{Inv}_{t-1}+\ldots+\widetilde{Inv}_{t-n}\right).$$

Now it makes sense to use Definition 3.13 and replace $\widetilde{Inv}_s$ with $\alpha_s\widetilde{FCF}^u_s$. That, however, fails in that for investment amounts that are not in the future, we have to take historical real numbers and can only use free cash flows in relation to future investments. With

$$\widetilde{H}_s = \begin{cases} \alpha_s\widetilde{FCF}^u_s, & \text{if } s>0 \\ Inv_s, & \text{else} \end{cases}$$

we get for all $t\geq 1$ equation

$$\widetilde{Inv}_t - \widetilde{Accr}_t = \widetilde{H}_t - \frac{1}{n}\left(\widetilde{H}_{t-1}+\ldots+\widetilde{H}_{t-n}\right). \tag{6.3}$$

Taking advantage of this relation, we get the following for the firm's book value using Theorem 3.17 (operating assets relation) and Assumption 3.9 (subscribed capital) as well as Eq. (3.28)

$$\begin{aligned}
\underline{\widetilde{V}}^l_t &= \underline{V}^l_0 + \underline{e}^l_{0,1} + \ldots + \underline{e}^l_{t-1,t} + \left(\widetilde{Inv}_1 - \widetilde{Accr}_1\right) + \ldots + \left(\widetilde{Inv}_t - \widetilde{Accr}_t\right) \\
&= \underline{V}^l_0 + \underline{e}^l_{0,t} + \left(\widetilde{Inv}_1 - \widetilde{Accr}_1\right) + \ldots + \left(\widetilde{Inv}_t - \widetilde{Accr}_t\right) \\
&= \underline{V}^l_0 + \underline{e}^l_{0,t} + \sum_{s=1}^{t}\left(\widetilde{H}_s - \frac{1}{n}\sum_{r=s-1}^{s-n}\widetilde{H}_r\right)
\end{aligned}$$

$$= \underline{V}_0^l + \underline{e}_{0,t}^l + \sum_{s=1}^{t} \widetilde{H}_s - \frac{1}{n} \sum_{s=1}^{t} \sum_{r=s-n}^{s-1} \widetilde{H}_r$$

$$= \underline{V}_0 + \underline{e}_{0,t}^l + \sum_{s=1}^{t} \widetilde{H}_s - \frac{1}{n} \sum_{s=1}^{t} \sum_{r=0}^{n-1} \widetilde{H}_{r+s-n} \, . \tag{6.4}$$

We will now rearrange the double sum. To this end we determine the number of possibilities to represent a given number a as a sum $a = r + s$ such that the first summand r is between 0 and $n - 1$ and the second summand s is between 1 and t. We first show that $A(a)$ is given by

$$A(a) := \begin{cases} a & \text{if} \quad 0 < a < \min(t,n), \\ \min(t,n) & \text{if} \quad \min(t,n) \leq a \leq \max(t,n), \\ n + t - a & \text{if} \quad \max(t,n) < a < n + t, \\ 0 & \text{else.} \end{cases}$$

To this end write $a = r + s$ as a sum of ones with a separating vertical line between r and s

$$\underbrace{\overbrace{1 \;\; 1 \;\; 1 \;\; 1}^{r} \,|\, \overbrace{1 \;\; 1 \;\; 1 \;\; 1 \;\; 1}^{s}}_{a} \quad .$$

The separating line cannot lie left from the first one (because $r \geq 0$) and cannot lie right from the last one (because $s > 0$). Hence, there are exactly $A(a) = a$ possibilities; this explains the first row of our definition. If a increases by one, the quantity $A(a)$ increases by one as well.

If a gets above $\min(n,t)$, then $A(a)$ remains at its current level. This is so because the vertical line cannot occupy all available positions. If, for example $n \leq t$ and therefore $n < a$, the vertical line cannot be right from the n-th one since we must have $r < n$. The argument is analog for $n > t$. This explains the second line of the definition.

The third line of the definition can be understood as follows. Look at a representation $r + s$ where the vertical line is farthest to the left. Because a is greater than n and t by adding an additional one to the right this representation violates our rules since s gets too large. Hence, increasing a by one decreases the number $A(a)$ by one. This finishes our proof of $A(a)$.

Now (6.4) can be simplified to

$$
\begin{aligned}
\underline{\widetilde{V}}_t &= \underline{V}_0 + \underline{e}^l_{0,t} + \sum_{a=1}^{t} \widetilde{H}_a - \frac{1}{n} \sum_{a=1}^{n+t-1} A(a) \widetilde{H}_{a-n} \\
&= \underline{V}_0 + \underline{e}^l_{0,t} - \sum_{a=1-n}^{0} \frac{A(a+n)}{n} \widetilde{H}_a + \sum_{a=1}^{t} \left(1 - \frac{A(a+n)}{n}\right) \widetilde{H}_a \\
&= \underline{V}_0 + \underline{e}^l_{0,t} - \sum_{s=1-n}^{0} \frac{A(s+n)}{n} Inv_s + \sum_{s=1}^{t} \left(1 - \frac{A(s+n)}{n}\right) \alpha_s \widetilde{FCF}_s . \qquad (6.5)
\end{aligned}
$$

This equation can be simplified even further. To this end we will look at the distinct cases.

First let $n < t$. Then from the definition of $A(s+n)$

$$
\begin{aligned}
A(s+n) &= \begin{cases} s+n & \text{if} \quad 0 < s+n < n \\ n & \text{if} \quad n \le s+n \le t \\ n+t-s-n & \text{if} \quad t < s+n < n+t \end{cases} \\
&= \begin{cases} s+n & \text{if} \quad -n < s < 0 \\ n & \text{if} \quad 0 \le s \le t-n \\ t-s & \text{if} \quad t-n < s < t \end{cases} .
\end{aligned}
$$

We will treat the second and the third summand separately. Because the index s in the first summand runs from $1-n$ to 0 and the index in the second summand runs from 1 to $t-1$ (6.5) simplifies to

$$
\begin{aligned}
\underline{\widetilde{V}}_t &= \underline{V}_0 + \underline{e}^l_{0,t} - \sum_{s=1-n}^{0} \frac{A(s+n)}{n} Inv_s + \sum_{s=1}^{t-n} \left(1 - \frac{A(s+n)}{n}\right) \alpha_s \widetilde{FCF}_s \\
&\quad + \sum_{s=t-n+1}^{t} \left(1 - \frac{A(s+n)}{n}\right) \alpha_s \widetilde{FCF}_s \\
&= \underline{V}_0 + \underline{e}^l_{0,t} - \sum_{s=1-n}^{0} \frac{s+n}{n} Inv_s + \sum_{s=1}^{t-n} \left(1 - \frac{n}{n}\right) \alpha_s \widetilde{FCF}_s \\
&\quad + \sum_{s=t-n+1}^{t} \left(1 - \frac{t-s}{n}\right) \alpha_s \widetilde{FCF}_s \\
&= \underline{V}_0 + \underline{e}^l_{0,t} - \sum_{s=1-n}^{0} \frac{s+n}{n} Inv_s + \sum_{s=t-n+1}^{t} \frac{n-t+s}{n} \alpha_s \widetilde{FCF}_s . \qquad (6.6)
\end{aligned}
$$

Let now $n \geq t$. Then from the definition of $A(s+n)$

$$A(s+n) = \begin{cases} s+n & \text{if } \ 0 < s+n < t \\ t & \text{if } \ t \leq s+n \leq n \\ n+t-s-n & \text{if } \ n < s+n < n+t \end{cases}$$

$$= \begin{cases} s+n & \text{if } \ -n < s < t-n \\ t & \text{if } \ t-n \leq s \leq 0 \\ t-s & \text{if } \ 0 < s < t \end{cases} .$$

Again we will treat the second and the third summand separately. The index s in the first summand runs from $1-n$ to 0 and in the second summand from 1 to $t-1$. Hence, (6.5) simplifies to

$$\begin{aligned} \underline{\widetilde{V}}_t &= \underline{V}_0 + \underline{e}^l_{0,t} - \sum_{s=1-n}^{t-n} \frac{A(s+n)}{n} Inv_s - \sum_{s=t-n+1}^{0} \frac{A(s+n)}{n} Inv_s \\ &+ \quad \sum_{s=1}^{t} \left(1 - \frac{A(s+n)}{n}\right) \alpha_s \widetilde{FCF}_s \\ &= \underline{V}_0 + \underline{e}^l_{0,t} - \sum_{s=1-n}^{t-n} \frac{s+n}{n} Inv_s - \sum_{s=t-n+1}^{0} \frac{t}{n} Inv_s + \sum_{s=1}^{t} \left(1 - \frac{t-s}{n}\right) \alpha_s \widetilde{FCF}_s \\ &= \underline{V}_0 + \underline{e}^l_{0,t} - \sum_{s=1-n}^{0} \frac{\min(s+n,t)}{n} Inv_s + \sum_{s=1}^{t} \frac{n-t+s}{n} \alpha_s \widetilde{FCF}_s \, . \end{aligned} \tag{6.7}$$

Now we are able to rejoin both cases $n < t$ and $n \geq t$. The Eqs. (6.6) and (6.7) yield in compact notation

$$\underline{\widetilde{V}}_t = \underbrace{\underline{V}_0 + \underline{e}^l_{0,t} - \sum_{s=1-n}^{0} \frac{\min(s+n,t)}{n} Inv_s}_{:=\underline{V}_0^{*l}} + \sum_{s=1+\max(t-n,0)}^{t} \frac{n-t+s}{n} \alpha_s \widetilde{FCF}_s \, .$$

The first three summands will be designated as $\underline{V}_0^{*l}$. Economically, this term concerns the amount which the firm's book value would be if up to time t, there are exclusively increases in subscribed capital and no single investment. That leads us to the representation

$$\underline{\widetilde{V}}^l_t = \underline{V}_0^{*l} + \sum_{s=1+\max(t-n,0)}^{t} \frac{n-(t-s)}{n} \alpha_s \widetilde{FCF}^u_s \, .$$

If we use the agreement $\alpha_s = 0$ for $s \leq 0$ (α was up to now only defined for future times), this equation becomes

$$\underline{\widetilde{V}}_t^l = \underline{V}_0^{*l} + \frac{n}{n}\widetilde{FCF}_t^u \alpha_t + \frac{n-1}{n}\widetilde{FCF}_{t-1}^u \alpha_{t-1} + \ldots + \frac{1}{n}\widetilde{FCF}_{1+t-n}^u \alpha_{1+t-n} \tag{6.8}$$

and we will from now on use this form.

The valuation with a policy based on book values is now finally successful by means of this representation. For that purpose we use everything that we have. Look at the valuation Eq. (3.11) which is valid for every conceivable financing policy and onto which we want to fall back now. With means of financing based on book values, we have at all times

$$\underline{\widetilde{D}}_t = \underline{l}_t \underline{\widetilde{V}}_t^l,$$

which with (6.8) and using Assumption 3.7 leads us to

$$\begin{aligned} V_0^l &= V_0^u + \tau r_f \frac{l_0 \underline{V}_0^l}{1+r_f} + \tau r_f \sum_{t=1}^{T-1} \frac{\underline{l}_t}{(1+r_f)^{t+1}} \operatorname{E}_Q\Big[\underline{V}_0^{*l} + \frac{n}{n}\widetilde{FCF}_t^u \alpha_t \\ &\quad + \frac{n-1}{n}\widetilde{FCF}_{t-1}^u \alpha_{t-1} + \ldots + \frac{1}{n}\widetilde{FCF}_{t-n+1}^u \alpha_{t-n+1}\Big] \\ &= \widetilde{V}_0^u + \tau r_f \frac{l_0 \underline{V}_0^l}{1+r_f} + \tau r_f \sum_{t=1}^{T-1} \underline{l}_t \left(\frac{\underline{V}_0^{*l}}{(1+r_f)^{t+1}} + \frac{\operatorname{E}_Q\left[\widetilde{FCF}_t^u\right]}{(1+r_f)^t} \frac{\frac{n}{n}\alpha_t}{1+r_f} \right. \\ &\quad \left. + \frac{\operatorname{E}_Q\left[\widetilde{FCF}_{t-1}^u\right]}{(1+r_f)^{t-1}} \frac{\frac{n-1}{n}\alpha_{t-1}}{(1+r_f)^2} + \ldots + \frac{\operatorname{E}_Q\left[\widetilde{FCF}_{1+t-n}^u\right]}{(1+r_f)^{1+t-n}} \frac{\frac{1}{n}\alpha_{1+t-n}}{(1+r_f)^n} \right). \end{aligned}$$

We are now using the Assumption 3.1 and the Theorem 3.3 based on it. That allows for the representation

$$\begin{aligned} V_0^l &= V_0^u + \tau r_f \frac{l_0 \underline{V}_0^l}{1+r_f} + \tau r_f \sum_{t=1}^{T-1} \underline{l}_t \left(\frac{\underline{V}_0^{*l}}{(1+r_f)^{t+1}} + \frac{\operatorname{E}\left[\widetilde{FCF}_t^u\right]}{(1+k^{E,u})^t} \frac{\frac{n}{n}\alpha_t}{1+r_f} \right. \\ &\quad \left. + \frac{\operatorname{E}\left[\widetilde{FCF}_{t-1}^u\right]}{(1+k^{E,u})^{t-1}} \frac{\frac{n-1}{n}\alpha_{t-1}}{(1+r_f)^2} + \ldots + \frac{\operatorname{E}\left[\widetilde{FCF}_{1+t-n}^u\right]}{(1+k^{E,u})^{1+t-n}} \frac{\frac{1}{n}\alpha_{1+t-n}}{(1+r_f)^n} \right) \\ &= V_0^u + \tau r_f \frac{l_0 \underline{V}_0^l}{1+r_f} + \tau r_f \sum_{t=1}^{T-1} \underline{l}_t \frac{\underline{V}_0^{*l}}{(1+r_f)^{t+1}} \end{aligned}$$

$$+\tau r_f \sum_{t=1}^{T-1} \left(\frac{\alpha_t \operatorname{E}\left[\widetilde{FCF}_t^u\right]}{(1+k^{E,u})^t} \frac{\frac{n}{n} \underline{l}_t}{1+r_f} + \frac{\alpha_{t-1} \operatorname{E}\left[\widetilde{FCF}_{t-1}^u\right]}{(1+k^{E,u})^{t-1}} \frac{\frac{n-1}{n} \underline{l}_t}{(1+r_f)^2} \right.$$

$$\left. + \ldots + \frac{\alpha_{1+t-n} \operatorname{E}\left[\widetilde{FCF}_{1+t-n}^u\right]}{(1+k^{E,u})^{1+t-n}} \frac{\frac{1}{n} \underline{l}_t}{(1+r_f)^n} \right).$$

Lastly, we only have the terms in the last two lines to concentrate on. We are obviously looking at a double sum. To simplify its representation, we have to consider, how often an expected cash flow comes up. It is recognized that the coefficient in front of $\frac{\alpha_t \operatorname{E}\left[\widetilde{FCF}_t^u\right]}{(1+k^{E,u})^t}$ appears with the expressions

$$\frac{\frac{n}{n} \underline{l}_t}{1+r_f}, \frac{\frac{n-1}{n} \underline{l}_{t+1}}{(1+r_f)^2}, \ldots, \frac{\frac{1}{n} \underline{l}_{n+t-1}}{(1+r_f)^n}.$$

Again, this requires that coefficients $\underline{l}_s$ with an index greater than $T-1$ are set to zero. We get

$$V_0^l = V_0^u + \tau r_f \frac{\underline{l}_0 \underline{V}_0^l}{1+r_f} + \tau r_f \sum_{t=1}^{T-1} \underline{l}_t \frac{\underline{V}_0^{*l}}{(1+r_f)^{t+1}} +$$

$$+\tau r_f \sum_{t=1}^{T-1} \frac{\alpha_t \operatorname{E}\left[\widetilde{FCF}_t^u\right]}{(1+k^{E,u})^t} \left(\frac{\frac{n}{n} \underline{l}_t}{1+r_f} + \frac{\frac{n-1}{n} \underline{l}_{t+1}}{(1+r_f)^2} + \ldots + \frac{\frac{1}{n} \underline{l}_{n+t-1}}{(1+r_f)^n} \right),$$

where $\underline{l}_s = 0$ for $s \geq T$. With that Theorem 3.21 is finally proven.

6.3 Adjusted Modigliani–Miller Formula (Theorem 3.22)

Many factors remain constant in the theorem. More than anything, it affects the debt ratio $\underline{l}$, the investment parameter α, and the subscribed capital. Beyond that, it is assumed that the firm to be valued exists without end. By disregarding the time indices with the investment parameter and the debt ratio, we get the following using the sum of a geometric sequence:

$$V_0^l = V_0^u + \tau r_f \frac{\underline{l} \underline{V}_0^l}{1+r_f} + \tau r_f \sum_{t=1}^{\infty} \frac{\underline{l} \underline{V}_0^{*l}}{(1+r_f)^{t+1}} + \tau r_f \sum_{t=1}^{\infty} \frac{\alpha \operatorname{E}\left[\widetilde{FCF}_t^u\right]}{(1+k^{E,u})^t} \left(\frac{\frac{n}{n} \underline{l}}{1+r_f} + \right.$$

$$\left. + \frac{\frac{n-1}{n} \underline{l}}{(1+r_f)^2} + \ldots + \frac{\frac{1}{n} \underline{l}}{(1+r_f)^n} \right)$$

$$= V_0^u + \frac{\tau \underline{l}\left(r_f \underline{V}_0^l + \underline{V}_0^{*l}\right)}{1+r_f} + \frac{\tau r_f \alpha \underline{l}}{n} \sum_{t=1}^{\infty} \frac{\mathrm{E}\left[\widetilde{FCF}_t^u\right]}{\left(1+k^{E,u}\right)^t} \left(\frac{n}{1+r_f} + \frac{n-1}{(1+r_f)^2} + \right.$$

$$\left. + \ldots + \frac{1}{(1+r_f)^n}\right). \tag{6.9}$$

We make the effort now to get a compact representation of the expression

$$\frac{n}{1+r_f} + \frac{n-1}{(1+r_f)^2} + \ldots + \frac{1}{(1+r_f)^n}.$$

To do so we look at the identity

$$(1+r_f)^n + (1+r_f)^{n-1} + \ldots + (1+r_f) = \frac{(1+r_f)((1+r_f)^n - 1)}{r_f}$$

and derive it according to r_f,

$$n(1+r_f)^{n-1} + (n-1)(1+r_f)^{n-2} + \ldots + 1 = \frac{1 + (nr_f - 1)(1+r_f)^n}{r_f^2}.$$

Multiplying by $(1+r_f)^{-n}$ results in

$$n(1+r_f)^{-1} + (n-1)(1+r_f)^{-2} + \ldots + (1+r_f)^{-n} = \frac{nr_f - 1 + (1+r_f)^{-n}}{r_f^2}.$$

Entering this into Eq. (6.9), results in

$$V_0^l = V_0^u + \frac{\tau \underline{l}\left(r_f \underline{V}_0^l + \underline{V}_0^{*l}\right)}{1+r_f} + \frac{\tau r_f \alpha \underline{l}}{n} \frac{nr_f - 1 + (1+r_f)^{-n}}{r_f^2} \sum_{t=1}^{\infty} \frac{\mathrm{E}\left[\widetilde{FCF}_t^u\right]}{(1+k^{E,u})^t}.$$

We recognize that the sum on the right-hand side exactly corresponds to the market value of the unlevered firm. This leads us to

$$V_0^l = V_0^u + \frac{\tau \underline{l}\left(r_f \underline{V}_0^l + \underline{V}_0^{*l}\right)}{1+r_f} + \frac{nr_f - 1 + (1+r_f)^{-n}}{nr_f} \tau \alpha \underline{l} V_0^u.$$

Lastly we turn our attention to the term

$$\frac{\tau \underline{l}\left(r_f \underline{V}_0^l + \underline{V}_0^{*l}\right)}{1+r_f}$$

and consider that at time $t = 0$ the identity

$$\underline{V}_0^{*l} = \underline{V}_0^l - \sum_{s=1-n}^{0} \frac{\min(n-s,t)}{n} Inv_s$$

applies, so long as the influence of depreciation on those assets raised before time $t = 0$ is not excluded. But if we disregard this influence according to the gotten condition, then we get

$$\frac{\tau \underline{l}\left(r_f \underline{V}_0^l + \underline{V}_0^{*l}\right)}{1+r_f} = \frac{\tau \underline{l}\left(r_f \underline{V}_0^l + \underline{V}_0^l\right)}{1+r_f}$$
$$= \tau \underline{l} \underline{V}_0^l .$$

We recognize that the product of debt ratio and book value of the firm corresponds to the book value of the debt, and can close up the proof considering Assumption 3.7.

6.4 Valuation Formula with Financing Based on Cash Flows (Theorems 3.23 and 3.24)

From the definition of financing based on cash flows, the following first results for the amount of debt using the fact that debt is riskless:

$$\widetilde{D}_t = \left((1+\alpha r_f(1-\tau))D_0 - \alpha \widetilde{FCF}_1^u\right)^+ \qquad \forall t \geq 1 .$$

We enter this into Eq. (3.11) and get

$$V_0^l = V_0^u + \frac{\tau \operatorname{E}_Q[Z_1]}{1+r_f} + \sum_{t=1}^{T-1} \frac{\tau r_f \operatorname{E}_Q\left[\left((1+\alpha r_f(1-\tau))D_0 - \alpha \widetilde{FCF}_1^u\right)^+\right]}{(1+r_f)^{t+1}}$$
$$= V_0^u + \frac{\tau r_f D_0}{1+r_f} + \frac{\tau r_f \operatorname{E}_Q\left[\left((1+\alpha r_f(1-\tau))D_0 - \alpha \widetilde{FCF}_1^u\right)^+\right]}{(1+r_f) r_f} \left(1 - \frac{1}{(1+r_f)^{T-1}}\right) .$$

With help of Theorem 3.2, the third summand can be further simplified

$$V_0^l = V_0^u + \frac{\tau r_f D_0}{1+r_f} + \tau \alpha d_1^u \frac{\operatorname{E}_Q\left[\left(\frac{1+\alpha r_f(1-\tau)}{\alpha d_1^u} D_0 - \widetilde{V}_1^u\right)^+\right]}{1+r_f} \left(1 - \frac{1}{(1+r_f)^{T-1}}\right) .$$

Let us now look at a put on the value of the unlevered firm at time $t = 1$ with a strike of $\frac{1+\alpha r_f(1-\tau)}{\alpha d_1^u} D_0$. The bearer of this option receives the difference of the exercise price and the firm value, if this difference is positive. In the opposite case, the payment comes to zero. To determine the value of this put Π, we have to evaluate the expectation $E_Q[\cdot]$ of the payments of the put and discount them with the riskless rate according to the duration of the option. This results exactly in

$$\Pi = \frac{\mathrm{E}_Q\left[\left(\frac{1+\alpha r_f(1-\tau)}{\alpha d_1^u} D_0 - \widetilde{V}_1^u\right)^+\right]}{1+r_f}.$$

But with that applies

$$V_0^l = V_0^u + \frac{\tau r_f D_0}{1+r_f} + \tau\alpha d_1^u \Pi \left(1 - \frac{1}{(1+r_f)^{T-1}}\right),$$

and that was what we wanted to show.

We come to the proof of Theorem 3.24. Since the amount of debt of the first period is positive, expression $(1+\alpha r_f(1-\tau))D_0 - \alpha\, \widetilde{FCF}_1^u$ will not be negative in any case. Therefore we can write

$$\widetilde{D}_t = (1+\alpha r_f(1-\tau))D_0 - \alpha\, \widetilde{FCF}_1^u$$

for all $t \geq 1$. From that we get the simpler valuation equation

$$\begin{aligned} V_0^l &= V_0^u + \frac{\tau r_f D_0}{1+r_f} + \frac{\tau r_f \mathrm{E}_Q\left[(1+\alpha r_f(1-\tau))D_0 - \alpha\, \widetilde{FCF}_1^u\right]}{(1+r_f)r_f}\left(1 - \frac{1}{(1+r_f)^{T-1}}\right) \\ &= V_0^u + \frac{\tau r_f D_0}{1+r_f} + \left(\frac{\tau(1+\alpha r_f(1-\tau))D_0}{1+r_f} - \tau\alpha \frac{\mathrm{E}_Q\left[\widetilde{FCF}_1^u\right]}{1+r_f}\right)\left(1 - \frac{1}{(1+r_f)^{T-1}}\right). \end{aligned}$$

Due to the equivalence of the valuation concepts (Theorem 3.3), there results from that

$$V_0^l = V_0^u + \frac{\tau r_f D_0}{1+r_f} + \left(\frac{\tau(1+\alpha r_f(1-\tau))D_0}{1+r_f} - \tau\alpha \frac{\mathrm{E}\left[\widetilde{FCF}_1^u\right]}{1+k^{E,u}}\right)\left(1 - \frac{1}{(1+r_f)^{T-1}}\right).$$

Lastly we make use of the fact that expected cash flows are constant. With that we end up with

$$\begin{aligned} V_0^l = V_0^u + \frac{\tau r_f D_0}{1+r_f} + \frac{\tau(1+\alpha r_f(1-\tau))D_0}{1+r_f}\left(1 - \frac{1}{(1+r_f)^{T-1}}\right) - \\ - \tau\alpha \frac{V_0^u k^{E,u}}{1+k^{E,u}} \frac{1 - \frac{1}{(1+r_f)^{T-1}}}{1 - \frac{1}{(1+k^{E,u})^{T-1}}}. \end{aligned}$$

That agrees with the claim.

6.5 Valuation with Financing Based on Dividends (Theorem 3.25)

Here we apply a different method to establish the value of the firm. For that we concentrate on the payments, which go to the debt and equity financiers. From the fundamental theorem the following first results for the levered firm:

$$
\begin{aligned}
V_0^l &= \sum_{t=1}^{T} \frac{\mathrm{E}_Q\left[\widetilde{FCF}_t^u + \tau \widetilde{I}_t\right]}{(1+r_f)^t} \\
&= \sum_{t=1}^{T} \frac{\mathrm{E}_Q\left[\widetilde{FCF}_t^u - \widetilde{D}_{t-1} - (1-\tau)\widetilde{I}_t + \widetilde{D}_t\right]}{(1+r_f)^t} + \sum_{t=1}^{T} \frac{\mathrm{E}_Q\left[\widetilde{I}_t + \widetilde{D}_{t-1} - \widetilde{D}_t\right]}{(1+r_f)^t}.
\end{aligned}
$$

The second summand agrees with the sum of the discounted payments to the debt financiers. It should be exactly equal to D_0, which can be easily proven,

$$
\begin{aligned}
\sum_{t=1}^{T} \frac{\mathrm{E}_Q\left[\widetilde{I}_t + \widetilde{D}_{t-1} - \widetilde{D}_t\right]}{(1+r_f)^t} &= \sum_{t=1}^{T} \frac{\mathrm{E}_Q\left[\widetilde{I}_t + \widetilde{D}_{t-1}\right]}{(1+r_f)^t} - \sum_{t=1}^{T} \frac{\mathrm{E}_Q\left[\widetilde{D}_t\right]}{(1+r_f)^t} \\
&= \sum_{t=1}^{T} \frac{\mathrm{E}_Q\left[\widetilde{D}_{t-1}\right]}{(1+r_f)^{t-1}} - \sum_{t=1}^{T} \frac{\mathrm{E}_Q\left[\widetilde{D}_t\right]}{(1+r_f)^t} \\
&= D_0.
\end{aligned}
$$

With that we have the following equation for the value of the levered firm,

$$
V_0^l = \sum_{t=1}^{T} \frac{\mathrm{E}_Q\left[\widetilde{FCF}_t^u - \widetilde{D}_{t-1} - (1-\tau)\widetilde{I}_t + \widetilde{D}_t\right]}{(1+r_f)^t} + D_0.
$$

During the first n periods, the shareholders get exactly the amount Div. Afterwards, the amount of debt remains constant. Using (3.19) that leads to

$$
\begin{aligned}
V_0^l &= D_0 + \sum_{t=0}^{n-1} \frac{Div}{(1+r_f)^{t+1}} + \sum_{t=n}^{T-1} \frac{\mathrm{E}_Q\left[\widetilde{FCF}_{t+1}^u - (1-\tau)\widetilde{I}_{n+1}\right]}{(1+r_f)^{t+1}} - \frac{\mathrm{E}_Q\left[\widetilde{D}_n\right]}{(1+r_f)^T} \\
&= D_0 + \left(1 - \frac{1}{(1+r_f)^n}\right)\frac{Div}{r_f} + \sum_{t=n}^{T-1} \frac{\mathrm{E}_Q\left[\widetilde{FCF}_{t+1}^u\right]}{(1+r_f)^{t+1}} - \\
&\quad - \frac{(1-\tau)r_f\,\mathrm{E}_Q\left[\widetilde{D}_n\right]}{r_f(1+r_f)^n}\left(1 - \frac{1}{(1+r_f)^{T-n}}\right) - \frac{\mathrm{E}_Q\left[\widetilde{D}_n\right]}{(1+r_f)^T}.
\end{aligned}
$$

If we make use of the equivalence of the valuation concepts from (Theorem 3.3) and further consider that the rate of growth of the expected cash flows is constant ($g = \text{const.}$), there then results

$$V_0^l = D_0 + \left(1 - \frac{1}{(1+r_f)^n}\right)\frac{Div}{r_f} + \sum_{t=n}^{T-1} \frac{(1+g)^t \operatorname{E}\left[\widetilde{FCF}_1^u\right]}{(1+k^{E,u})^{t+1}} - \tag{6.10}$$

$$- \frac{\operatorname{E}_Q\left[\widetilde{D}_n\right]}{(1+r_f)^n}\left(1 - \tau\left(1 - \frac{1}{(1+r_f)^{T-n}}\right)\right)$$

$$= D_0 + \left(1 - \frac{1}{(1+r_f)^n}\right)\frac{Div}{r_f} + \frac{\operatorname{E}\left[\widetilde{FCF}_1^u\right]}{k^{E,u} - g}\left[\left(\frac{1+g}{1+k^{E,u}}\right)^n - \left(\frac{1+g}{1+k^{E,u}}\right)^T\right] -$$

$$- \frac{\operatorname{E}_Q\left[\widetilde{D}_n\right]}{(1+r_f)^n}\left(1 - \tau\left(1 - \frac{1}{(1+r_f)^{T-n}}\right)\right). \tag{6.11}$$

We now turn to the amount of debt at time n. Since according to the condition that the credit always remains positive, we can simplify the formation law of the debt. With (3.19) and $r_f{}^* = r_f(1-\tau)$ applies

$$\operatorname{E}_Q\left[\widetilde{D}_t|\mathcal{F}_{t-1}\right] = \operatorname{E}_Q\left[Div - \widetilde{FCF}_t^u|\mathcal{F}_{t-1}\right] + (1+r_f{}^*)D_{t-1} \qquad \forall t \leq n.$$

Taking advantage of the recursion relationship leads to

$$\operatorname{E}_Q\left[\widetilde{D}_n\right] = \operatorname{E}_Q\left[Div - \widetilde{FCF}_n^u\right] + (1+r_f{}^*)\operatorname{E}_Q\left[Div - \widetilde{FCF}_{n-1}^u\right] + \ldots +$$
$$+ (1+r_f{}^*)^{n-1}\operatorname{E}_Q\left[Div - \widetilde{FCF}_1^u\right] + (1+r_f{}^*)^n D_0.$$

This equation can be brought into the form

$$\operatorname{E}_Q\left[\widetilde{D}_n\right] = \frac{(1+r_f{}^*)^n - 1}{r_f{}^*}Div + (1+r_f{}^*)^n D_0 -$$
$$- \operatorname{E}_Q\left[\widetilde{FCF}_n^u\right] - (1+r_f{}^*)\operatorname{E}_Q\left[\widetilde{FCF}_{n-1}^u\right] - \ldots - (1+r_f{}^*)^{n-1}\operatorname{E}_Q\left[\widetilde{FCF}_1^u\right].$$

From that the following is valid under the discounted expectation

$$\frac{\operatorname{E}_Q\left[\widetilde{D}_n\right]}{(1+r_f)^n} = \frac{(1+r_f{}^*)^n - 1}{r_f{}^*(1+r_f)^n}Div + \left(\frac{1+r_f{}^*}{1+r_f}\right)^n D_0 -$$
$$- \frac{\operatorname{E}_Q\left[\widetilde{FCF}_n^u\right]}{(1+r_f)^n} - \frac{1+r_f{}^*}{1+r_f}\frac{\operatorname{E}_Q\left[\widetilde{FCF}_{n-1}^u\right]}{(1+r_f)^{n-1}} - \ldots - \frac{(1+r_f{}^*)^{n-1}}{(1+r_f)^{n-1}}\frac{\operatorname{E}_Q\left[\widetilde{FCF}_1^u\right]}{1+r_f}$$

or due to Theorem 3.3 as well as the constant rate of growth g and with $\gamma = \frac{1+r_f^*}{1+r_f}$ and $\delta = \frac{1+g}{1+k^{E,u}}$

$$\frac{\mathrm{E}_Q\left[\widetilde{D}_n\right]}{(1+r_f)^n} = \frac{(1+r_f^*)^n - 1}{r_f^*(1+r_f)^n} Div + \gamma^n D_0 - \\ - \delta^n \frac{\mathrm{E}\left[\widetilde{FCF}_1^u\right]}{1+g} - \gamma\delta^{n-1}\frac{\mathrm{E}\left[\widetilde{FCF}_1^u\right]}{1+g} - \ldots - \gamma^{n-1}\delta \frac{\mathrm{E}\left[\widetilde{FCF}_1^u\right]}{1+g}.$$

We combine the last summands in the equation and get

$$\frac{\mathrm{E}_Q\left[\widetilde{D}_n\right]}{(1+r_f)^n} = \frac{(1+r_f^*)^n - 1}{r_f^*(1+r_f)^n} Div + \gamma^n D_0 - \left(1 + \frac{\gamma}{\delta} + \ldots + \left(\frac{\gamma}{\delta}\right)^{n-1}\right)\delta^n \frac{\mathrm{E}\left[\widetilde{FCF}_1^u\right]}{1+g}.$$

or, after simplification,

$$\frac{\mathrm{E}_Q\left[\widetilde{D}_n\right]}{(1+r_f)^n} = \frac{(1+r_f^*)^n - 1}{r_f^*(1+r_f)^n} Div + \gamma^n D_0 - \frac{\gamma^n - \delta^n}{\frac{\gamma}{\delta} - 1}\frac{\mathrm{E}\left[\widetilde{FCF}_1^u\right]}{1+g}.$$

We put this into (6.11) and get

$$V_0^l = \left(1 - \gamma^n\left(1 - \tau\left(1 - \frac{1}{(1+r_f)^{T-n}}\right)\right)\right) D_0 + \\ + \left(1 - \gamma^n\left(1 - \tau\left(1 - \frac{1}{(1+r_f)^{T-n}}\right)\right) - \tau\left(1 - \frac{1}{(1+r_f)^T}\right)\right)\frac{Div}{r_f(1-\tau)} + \\ + \left(\delta^n - \delta^T + \frac{\gamma^n - \delta^n}{\frac{\gamma}{\delta} - 1}\frac{k^{E,u} - g}{1+g}\left(1 - \tau\left(1 - \frac{1}{(1+r_f)^{T-n}}\right)\right)\right)\frac{\mathrm{E}\left[\widetilde{FCF}_1^u\right]}{k^{E,u} - g}. \tag{6.12}$$

We now take advantage of the expected cash flow of the unlevered firm showing a constant rate of growth. From that results

$$V_0^u = \sum_{t=1}^{T} \frac{\mathrm{E}\left[\widetilde{FCF}_t^u\right]}{(1+k^{E,u})^t} \\ = \sum_{t=1}^{T} \frac{\mathrm{E}\left[\widetilde{FCF}_1^u\right]}{1+g}\left(\frac{1+g}{1+k^{E,u}}\right)^t \\ = \frac{\mathrm{E}\left[\widetilde{FCF}_1^u\right]}{k^{E,u} - g}\left(1 - \left(\frac{1+g}{1+k^{E,u}}\right)^T\right).$$

Plugging this into equation (6.12) gives

$$V_0^l = \left(1 - \gamma^n \left(1 - \tau \left(1 - \frac{1}{(1+r_f)^{T-n}}\right)\right)\right) D_0 +$$
$$+ \left(1 - \gamma^n \left(1 - \tau \left(1 - \frac{1}{(1+r_f)^{T-n}}\right)\right) - \tau \left(1 - \frac{1}{(1+r_f)^{T}}\right)\right) \frac{Div}{r_f(1-\tau)} +$$
$$+ \left(\delta^n - \delta^T + \frac{\gamma^n - \delta^n}{\frac{\gamma}{\delta} - 1} \frac{k^{E,u} - g}{1+g} \left(1 - \tau \left(1 - \frac{1}{(1+r_f)^{T-n}}\right)\right)\right) \frac{V_0^u}{1-\delta^T}.$$

If we sort the terms around a bit, then we get our desired result.

6.6 Valuation with Debt-Cash Flow Ratio (Theorems 3.26 and 3.27)

From the definition of the dynamic leverage ratio we get

$$\widetilde{D}_s = \widetilde{L}_s^d \left(\widetilde{FCF}_s^u + \tau r_f \widetilde{D}_{s-1}\right),$$

and hence

$$\widetilde{D}_s = \widetilde{L}_s^d \left(\widetilde{FCF}_s^u + \tau r_f \widetilde{L}_{s-1}^d \left(\widetilde{FCF}_{s-1}^u + \tau r_f \widetilde{D}_{s-2}\right)\right).$$

Using induction this gives for $s > t$

$$\widetilde{D}_s = (\tau r_f)^{s-t} \widetilde{L}_s^d \dots \widetilde{L}_{t+1}^d \widetilde{D}_t + \sum_{u=t+1}^{s} \widetilde{L}_s^d \dots \widetilde{L}_u^d (\tau r_f)^{s-u} \widetilde{FCF}_u^u.$$

Plugging this into the general valuation formula (3.11) we get

$$\widetilde{V}_t^l = \widetilde{V}_t^u + \frac{\tau r_f \widetilde{D}_t}{1+r_f} + \sum_{s=t+1}^{T-1} \frac{\tau r_f (\tau r_f)^{s-t} \widetilde{L}_s^d \dots \widetilde{L}_{t+1}^d \widetilde{D}_t}{(1+r_f)^{s-t+1}} +$$
$$+ \sum_{s=t}^{T-1} \sum_{u=t+1}^{s} \frac{\mathrm{E}_Q \left[\tau r_f \left(\widetilde{L}_s^d \dots \widetilde{L}_u^d (\tau r_f)^{s-u} \widetilde{FCF}_u^u\right) | \mathcal{F}_t\right]}{(1+r_f)^{s-t+1}}.$$

This simplifies to (let $\widetilde{L}^d_s \dots \widetilde{L}^d_{t+1} = 1$ if $s = t$)

$$\widetilde{V}^l_t = \widetilde{V}^u_t + \widetilde{D}_t \sum_{s=t}^{T-1} \frac{(\tau r_f)^{s-t+1}}{(1+r_f)^{s-t+1}} \widetilde{L}^d_s \dots \widetilde{L}^d_{t+1} + \\ + \sum_{s=t}^{T-1} \sum_{u=t+1}^{s} \frac{\widetilde{L}^d_s \dots \widetilde{L}^d_u (\tau r_f)^{s+1-u}}{(1+r_f)^{s+1-u}} \frac{\mathrm{E}_Q\left[\widetilde{FCF}^u_u | \mathcal{F}_t\right]}{(1+r_f)^{u-t}}.$$

Changing summation it yields

$$\widetilde{V}^l_t = \widetilde{V}^u_t + \widetilde{D}_t \sum_{s=t}^{T-1} \frac{(\tau r_f)^{s-t+1}}{(1+r_f)^{s-t+1}} \widetilde{L}^d_s \dots \widetilde{L}^d_{t+1} + \\ + \sum_{u=t+1}^{T-1} \frac{\mathrm{E}_Q\left[\widetilde{FCF}^u_u | \mathcal{F}_t\right]}{(1+r_f)^{u-t}} \sum_{s=u}^{T-1} \frac{\widetilde{L}^d_s \dots \widetilde{L}^d_u (\tau r_f)^{s+1-u}}{(1+r_f)^{s+1-u}}$$

or after using Theorem 3.2

$$\widetilde{V}^l_t = \widetilde{V}^u_t + \widetilde{D}_t \sum_{s=t}^{T-1} \frac{(\tau r_f)^{s-t+1}}{(1+r_f)^{s-t+1}} \widetilde{L}^d_s \dots \widetilde{L}^d_{t+1} + \\ + \sum_{u=t+1}^{T-1} \left(\sum_{s=u}^{T-1} \frac{\widetilde{L}^d_s \dots \widetilde{L}^d_u (\tau r_f)^{s+1-u}}{(1+r_f)^{s+1-u}} \right) \frac{\mathrm{E}\left[\widetilde{FCF}^u_u | \mathcal{F}_t\right]}{(1+k^{E,u})^{u-t}}.$$

Changing indices gives Theorem 3.26.

Now let us turn to the case of infinite lifetime (Theorem 3.27) and constant dynamic leverage ratio. In this case

$$\widetilde{V}^l_t = \widetilde{V}^u_t + \widetilde{D}_t \sum_{s=t}^{\infty} \frac{(\tau r_f)^{s-t+1}}{(1+r_f)^{s-t+1}} (\widetilde{L}^d)^{s-t} + \\ + \sum_{s=t+1}^{\infty} \left(\sum_{u=s}^{\infty} \frac{(\widetilde{L}^d)^{u+1-s} (\tau r_f)^{u+1-s}}{(1+r_f)^{u+1-s}} \right) \frac{\mathrm{E}\left[\widetilde{FCF}^u_s | \mathcal{F}_t\right]}{(1+k^{E,u})^{s-t}}.$$

The sum of geometric series gives

$$\widetilde{V}^l_t = \widetilde{V}^u_t + \widetilde{D}_t \frac{\tau r_f}{1+r_f(1-\tau \widetilde{L}^d)} + \frac{\widetilde{L}^d \tau r_f}{1+r_f(1-\tau \widetilde{L}^d)} \sum_{s=t+1}^{\infty} \frac{\mathrm{E}\left[\widetilde{FCF}^u_s | \mathcal{F}_t\right]}{(1+k^{E,u})^{s-t}}.$$

The sum on the right-hand side is just $\widetilde{V}_t^u$ and hence

$$\widetilde{V}_t^l = \widetilde{D}_t \frac{\tau r_f}{1 + r_f(1 - \tau \widetilde{L}^d)} + \widetilde{V}_t^u \left(1 + \frac{\widetilde{L}^d \tau r_f}{1 + r_f(1 - \tau \widetilde{L}^d)}\right).$$

6.7 Fundamental Theorem with Income Tax (Theorem 4.2)

We closely follow Löffler and Schneider (2003). Consider a model in discrete time $t = 0, 1, \ldots, T$ with uncertainty. The probability space is denoted by $(\Omega, \mathcal{F}, P)$. The filtration $\mathcal{F}$ need not be finitely generated, it consists of the σ-algebras $\mathcal{F}_0 \subseteq \mathcal{F}_1 \subseteq \ldots \subseteq \mathcal{F}_T$ that describe the information set of every investor.[1] There are N tradeable risky financial assets that pay dividends (adapted random variables)

$$\widetilde{FCF}_t^1, \ldots, \widetilde{FCF}_t^N.$$

The prices—also called values—of the risky assets at time t are adapted random variables

$$\widetilde{V}_t^1, \ldots, \widetilde{V}_t^N.$$

There is one riskless asset, labeled $n = 0$. The prices of this asset are given by

$$V_t^0 = 1 \tag{6.13}$$

and the cash flows of the risk free asset are given by

$$FCF_t^0 = r_f \tag{6.14}$$

where r_f is the riskless interest rate.[2]

At time $t = 0$ the investor selects a portfolio consisting of the available financial assets. This portfolio will be changed at every trading date $t = 1, \ldots, T$. Immediately after time t the investors form a portfolio $\widetilde{H}_t = \left(\widetilde{H}_t^0, \ldots, \widetilde{H}_t^N\right)$ of all available assets, see Fig. 6.1. $\widetilde{H}_t$ is $\mathcal{F}_t$-adapted. Note that $H_{-1} = \widetilde{H}_T = 0$. At time $t + 1$ her portfolio has a value of

$$\widetilde{H}_t \cdot \widetilde{V}_{t+1} := \sum_{n=0}^{N} \widetilde{H}_t^n \widetilde{V}_{t+1}^n.$$

[1] These are standard assumptions in an uncertain economy, see Duffie (1988).

[2] All our findings are also valid in an economy with a time-dependent interest rate. Therefore, interest is assumed to be constant in time without loss of generality.

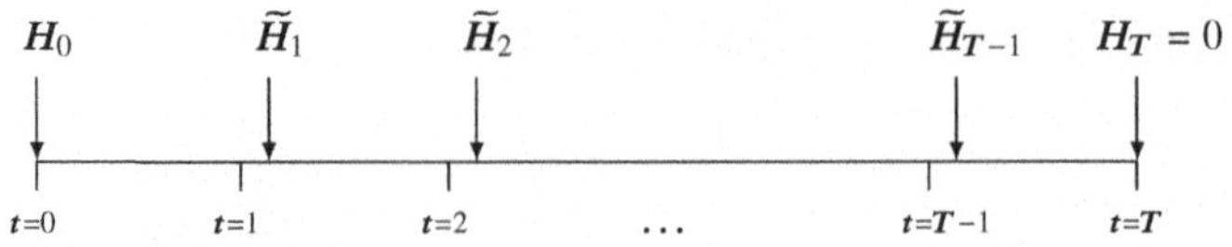

Fig. 6.1 The time structure of the model

We now introduce the tax system. We have to distinguish between the market value of a risky financial asset and the value that will be the underlying for the tax base. The underlying tax base will not be determined by the market alone but by the tax law. We denominate it the book value of a financial asset. The book value of a financial asset n at time t will be denoted by $\underline{\widetilde{V}}_t^n$ and is a random variable. We assume that the book value is an adapted random variable that will be zero at time $t = T$. It is not necessary for our model to incorporate other details from any actual tax law. At time $t + 1$ the portfolio $\widetilde{H}_t$ has the book value

$$\widetilde{H}_t \cdot \underline{\widetilde{V}}_{t+1} = \sum_{n=1}^{N} \widetilde{H}_t^n \underline{\widetilde{V}}_t^n . \tag{6.15}$$

The tax base of the portfolio $\widetilde{H}_t$ at time $t + 1$ now consists of two parts. The first part ("riskless or interest income") is given by the payments of the riskless asset $r_f \widetilde{H}_t^0$. The second part of the tax base ("risky or commercial income") is given by the gains of the remaining risky financial assets

$$\sum_{n=1}^{N} \widetilde{H}_t^n \left(\widetilde{FCF}_{t+1}^n + \underline{\widetilde{V}}_{t+1}^n - \underline{\widetilde{V}}_t^n \right) .$$

Notice that the gain of a financial asset n consists of the cash flow $\widetilde{FCF}_{t+1}^n$ and the capital gain $\underline{\widetilde{V}}_{t+1}^n - \underline{\widetilde{V}}_t^n$. If the tax base is negative, there is an immediate and full loss offset. In $t = 0$ no tax is paid. We assume a proportional tax on both income which is time-independent and deterministic: the tax rate on riskless income ("tax on interest") is τ^I and the tax rate on risky income ("tax on dividend") is τ^D. Therefore, the tax payments in $t + 1$ are given by

$$Tax_{t+1}(\widetilde{H}_t) = \tau^I r_f \widetilde{H}_t^0 + \tau^D \sum_{n=1}^{N} \widetilde{H}_t^n \left(\widetilde{FCF}_{t+1}^n + \underline{\widetilde{V}}_{t+1}^n - \underline{\widetilde{V}}_t^n \right) . \tag{6.16}$$

We now turn to the characterization of the book value of financial assets. Our assumption concerning these book values is motivated by considering a riskless bank account with a closing balance equal to the book value. In every period the interest payment is added to and the cash flow (withdrawal) is subtracted from the opening balance. The evolution of the bank account from t to $t+1$ is as follows:

book value at the beginning of period $t+1$	$\underline{V}_t^0$
+ interest at $t+1$	$r_f \underline{V}_t^0$
− withdrawal at $t+1$	FCF_{t+1}^0
= book value at the end of period $t+1$	$\underline{V}_{t+1}^0$.

We get

$$(1+r_f)\underline{V}_t^0 = FCF_{t+1}^0 + \underline{V}_{t+1}^0, \tag{6.17}$$

which resembles to the fundamental Theorem 4.2. Since at $t = T$ book and market value will be equal to zero we conclude that this equation implies by induction that book value and market value are the same at every time t. Although other rules for the determination of book value could be incorporated, we make the assumption that the tax law requires investors to mark their financial assets to market in each period and the tax law is applied to that measure of value[3]:

Assumption 6.1 *The book value $\widetilde{\underline{V}}_t^n$ of a financial asset is equal to its value $\widetilde{V}_t^n$*

$$\widetilde{V}_t^n = \widetilde{\underline{V}}_t^n. \tag{6.18}$$

We now show that if our tax system has no arbitrage opportunities an equivalent martingale measure exists. To this end let us define when a market is free of arbitrage.

Assumption 6.2 (No Arbitrage with Taxes) *There exists no trading strategy $\widetilde{H}$ that satisfies*

$$\Delta_t\left(\widetilde{H}\right) := \widetilde{H}_t \cdot \left(\widetilde{FCF}_{t+1} + \widetilde{V}_{t+1} - \widetilde{Tax}_{t+1}\right) - \widetilde{H}_{t+1} \cdot \widetilde{V}_{t+1} \geq 0 \tag{6.19}$$

for all t and

$$P\left(\Delta_t\left(\widetilde{H}\right) > 0\right) > 0 \tag{6.20}$$

for at least one t.

Then the following holds.

[3]The existing American tax law states under the Statements of Financial Accounting Standards (SFAS) 115 that "unrealized holding gains and losses for trading securities shall be included in earnings." Hence, the American tax system contains elements similar to our assumption.

Theorem 6.1 *Under Assumptions 6.1 and 6.2 the following holds: There is an equivalent martingale measure Q such that*

$$\widetilde{V}_t = \frac{\mathrm{E}_Q\left[\widetilde{FCF}_{t+1} + \widetilde{V}_{t+1} - Tax_{t+1}|\mathcal{F}_t\right]}{1 + r_f(1-\tau^I)}.$$

The proof of the fundamental theorem uses a result of Kabanov and Kramkov (1994). To this end we first notice that there is no one-period arbitrage in the market, i.e., there is no trading strategy $\widetilde{X}$ such that for one t

$$\widetilde{X}_t \cdot \widetilde{V}_t \leq 0 \quad \text{and} \quad \widetilde{X}_t \cdot \left(\widetilde{FCF}_{t+1} + \widetilde{V}_{t+1} - Tax_{t+1}\right) \geq 0$$

with at least on inequality strict with probability greater than zero and $\widetilde{X}_s = 0$ for all $s \neq t$. But then there is also no random variable $\widetilde{Y}_t$ such that

$$\widetilde{Y}_t \cdot \left(\frac{\widetilde{V}_{t+1} + \widetilde{FCF}_{t+1} - Tax_{t+1}}{1 + r_f(1-\tau^I)} - \widetilde{V}_t\right) \geq 0 \tag{6.21}$$

where the inequality is strict with probability greater than zero. This can be shown as follows: define

$$\widetilde{X}_t := \widetilde{Y}_t - \left(\widetilde{Y}_t \cdot \widetilde{V}_t\right) \begin{pmatrix} 1 \\ 0 \\ \vdots \\ 0 \end{pmatrix}.$$

Using this strategy we get

$$\widetilde{X}_t \cdot \widetilde{V}_t = 0$$

and

$$\begin{aligned} &\widetilde{X}_t \cdot \left(\widetilde{V}_{t+1} + \widetilde{FCF}_{t+1} - Tax_{t+1}\right) = \\ &\quad = \widetilde{Y}_t \cdot \left(\widetilde{V}_{t+1} + \widetilde{FCF}_{t+1} - Tax_{t+1}\right) - \left(1 + r_f\left(1-\tau^I\right)\right)\left(\widetilde{Y}_t \cdot \widetilde{V}_t\right) \\ &\quad \geq 0 \end{aligned}$$

showing that $\widetilde{X}$ would be a one-period arbitrage.

Now apply the theorem 3 of Kabanov and Kramkov (1994), see also Irle (2012, section 5.4). From this there exists a bounded and Almost-everywhere positive Z_{t+1} such that

$$\mathrm{E}\left[Z_{t+1}\frac{\widetilde{V}_{t+1}+\widetilde{FCF}_{t+1}-\widetilde{Tax}_{t+1}}{1+r_f(1-\tau^I)}|\mathcal{F}_t\right]=\widetilde{V}_t\,.$$

The existence of Q follows now from standard arguments, see Kabanov and Kramkov (1994, p. 524) or Irle (2012, section 5.2).

6.8 Valuation Formula with Retention Based on Dividends (Theorem 4.9)

The free cash flows are never lower than the dividend (see Assumption 4.2). From (4.2) and Definition 4.4 it follows

$$\mathrm{E}_Q\left[\widetilde{A}_s|\mathcal{F}_{s-1}\right]=\mathrm{E}_Q\left[\frac{1}{1-\tau^D}\widetilde{FCF}^u_s-Div_s|\mathcal{F}_{s-1}\right]+(1+r_f)\widetilde{A}_{s-1}.$$

Using induction, rule 4 and because dividends are certain, it follows for $s>t$

$$\mathrm{E}_Q\left[\widetilde{A}_s|\mathcal{F}_t\right]=(1+r_f)^{s-t}\widetilde{A}_t+\sum_{v=t+1}^{s}(1+r_f)^{s-v}\left(\frac{\mathrm{E}_Q\left[\widetilde{FCF}^u_v|\mathcal{F}_t\right]}{1-\tau^D}-Div_v\right).$$

We plug this term into (4.4). It yields

$$\begin{aligned}
\widetilde{V}^l_t&=\widetilde{V}^u_t+\left(1-\tau^D\right)\widetilde{A}_t+\sum_{s=t}^{n}\frac{\mathrm{E}_Q\left[\tau^I r_f\left(1-\tau^D\right)\widetilde{A}_s|\mathcal{F}_t\right]}{\left(1+r_f\left(1-\tau^I\right)\right)^{s-t+1}}\\
&=\widetilde{V}^u_t+\left(1-\tau^D\right)\widetilde{A}_t+\sum_{s=t}^{n}\frac{\tau^I r_f\left(1-\tau^D\right)(1+r_f)^{s-t}\widetilde{A}_t}{\left(1+r_f\left(1-\tau^I\right)\right)^{s-t+1}}+\\
&\quad+\sum_{s=t+1}^{n}\sum_{v=t+1}^{s}\frac{\tau^I r_f\,(1+r_f)^{s-v}\left(\mathrm{E}_Q\left[\widetilde{FCF}^u_v|\mathcal{F}_t\right]-\left(1-\tau^D\right)Div_v\right)}{\left(1+r_f\left(1-\tau^I\right)\right)^{s-t+1}}\\
&=\widetilde{V}^u_t+\tau^I\left(1-\tau^D\right)\left(\frac{1+r_f}{1+r_f\left(1-\tau^I\right)}\right)^{n-t+1}\widetilde{A}_t+\\
&\quad+\sum_{v=t+1}^{n}\sum_{s=v}^{n}\frac{\tau^I r_f\,(1+r_f)^{s-v}\left(\mathrm{E}_Q\left[\widetilde{FCF}^u_v|\mathcal{F}_t\right]-\left(1-\tau^D\right)Div_v\right)}{\left(1+r_f\left(1-\tau^I\right)\right)^{s-t+1}},
\end{aligned}$$

the last row by changing summands. Using geometric sums we get

$$\widetilde{V}_u^l = \widetilde{V}_t^u + \tau^I \left(1 - \tau^D\right) \left(\frac{1 + r_f}{1 + r_f \left(1 - \tau^I\right)}\right)^{n-t+1} \widetilde{A}_t$$

$$+\tau^I r_f \sum_{v=t+1}^{n} \frac{\mathrm{E}_Q\left[\widetilde{FCF}_v^u | \mathcal{F}_t\right] - \left(1 - \tau^D\right) Div_v}{\left(1 + r_f \left(1 - \tau^I\right)\right)^{v-t}} \left(1 + \left(\frac{1 + r_f}{1 + r_f \left(1 - \tau^I\right)}\right)^{n+1-v}\right).$$

Lastly, we use Theorem 4.4 and get

$$\widetilde{V}_u^l = \widetilde{V}_t^u + \tau^I \left(1 - \tau^D\right) \left(\frac{1 + r_f}{1 + r_f \left(1 - \tau^I\right)}\right)^{n-t+1} \widetilde{A}_t$$

$$+\tau^I r_f \sum_{v=t+1}^{n} \left(\frac{\mathrm{E}\left[\widetilde{FCF}_v^u | \mathcal{F}_t\right]}{(1 + k^{E,u})^{v-t}} - \frac{\left(1 - \tau^D\right) Div_v}{\left(1 + r_f \left(1 - \tau^I\right)\right)^{v-t}}\right) \cdot \left(1 + \left(\frac{1 + r_f}{1 + r_f \left(1 - \tau^I\right)}\right)^{n+1-v}\right).$$

This was to be shown.

References

Duffie JD (1988) Security markets: stochastic models. Academic, Boston

Harrison JM, Kreps DM (1979) Martingales and arbitrage in multiperiod securities markets. J Econ Theory 20:381–408

Irle A (2012) Finanzmathematik: die bewertung von derivaten, 3rd edn. Springer Spektrum, Wiesbaden

Kabanov YM, Kramkov DO (1994) No-arbitrage and equivalent martingale measures: an elementary proof of the Harrison-Pliska theorem. Theory Probab Appl 39:523–527

Löffler A, Schneider D (2003) Martingales, taxes and neutrality. http://ssrn.com/paper=375060

7 Sketch of Solutions

7.1 Basic Elements

7.1.1 Fundamental Terms

1. (a) We have

$$V_0 = \frac{\mathrm{E}\left[\widetilde{FCF}_1\right]}{1+\kappa_{0,1}} + \frac{FCF_2}{\left(1+r_f\right)^2} = \frac{100}{1.10} + \frac{100}{1.05^2} \approx 181.61\,.$$

The resulting cost of capital is

$$k_0 = \frac{\mathrm{E}\left[\widetilde{FCF}_1 + V_1\right]}{V_0} - 1 \approx \frac{100 + \frac{100}{1.05}}{181.61} \approx 7.5028\,\%\,.$$

(b) We have

$$V_0 = \frac{\mathrm{E}\left[\widetilde{FCF}_1\right]}{1+k_0} + \frac{FCF_2}{(1+k_0)\left(1+r_f\right)} = \frac{100}{1.10} + \frac{100}{1.10\cdot 1.05} \approx 177.49\,.$$

The discount rate is then

$$\kappa_{0,1} = \frac{\mathrm{E}\left[\widetilde{FCF}_1\right]}{V_0 - \frac{FCF_2}{\left(1+r_f\right)^2}} - 1 \approx \frac{100}{177.49 - \frac{100}{1.05^2}} \approx 15.2257\,\%\,.$$

2. Assume we have

$$(1+\kappa_{t,t+1})(1+\kappa_{t+1,t+2}) < (1+\kappa_{t,t+2})^2\,.$$

L. Kruschwitz, A. Löffler, *Stochastic Discounted Cash Flow*,
Springer Texts in Business and Economics,
https://doi.org/10.1007/978-3-030-37081-7_7

Then the investor should do the following. At time t she invests $\frac{1}{(1+\kappa_{t,t+2})^2}$ in the firm to get one dollar of cash flow at time $t+2$.

The amount needed is borrowed in the market: At time $t+1$ (tomorrow) she borrows $\frac{1}{1+\kappa_{t+1,t+2}}$ and has to pay back one dollar at time $t+2$. At time t she again borrows $\frac{1}{(1+\kappa_{t,t+1})(1+\kappa_{t+1,t+2})}$ to pay back $\frac{1}{1+\kappa_{t+1,t+2}}$ at time $t+1$. Mind that both borrowing strategies do not require any net cash flows at time $t+1$ and $t+2$.

The first strategy requires an investment of $\frac{1}{(1+\kappa_{t,t+2})^2}$ and the second one gives a payment of $\frac{1}{(1+\kappa_{t,t+1})(1+\kappa_{t+1,t+2})}$ which is, by assumption, more. By investing again and again the investor will get infinitely rich.

If

$$(1+\kappa_{t,t+1})(1+\kappa_{t+1,t+2}) > (1+\kappa_{t,t+2})^2,$$

a reverse strategy yields the arbitrage opportunity.

7.1.2 Conditional Expectation

1. This is straightforward, see Fig. 7.1.
2. The expectation is evaluated as

$$\mathrm{E}\left[\mathrm{E}_Q\left[\widetilde{FCF}_2|\mathcal{F}_1\right]|\mathcal{F}_0\right] = \frac{1}{2}(0.1\cdot 145.2 + 0.9\cdot 121) + \frac{1}{2}(0.1\cdot 121 + 0.9\cdot 100.6) = 113.03$$

Fig. 7.1 Cash flows in future periods

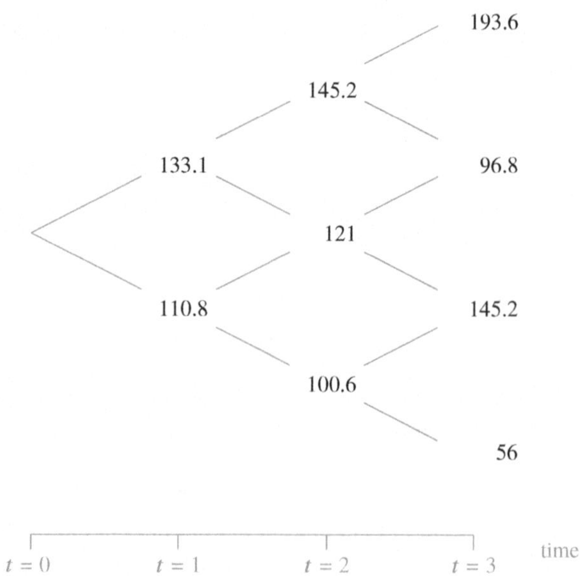

and

$$\mathrm{E}_Q\left[\mathrm{E}\left[\widetilde{FCF}_2|\mathcal{F}_1\right]|\mathcal{F}_0\right] = 0.1\left(\frac{1}{2}\cdot 145.2+\frac{1}{2}\cdot 121\right) + 0.9\left(\frac{1}{2}\cdot 121+\frac{1}{2}\cdot 100.6\right) = 113.03.$$

If we now change the order of expectation, we get

$$\mathrm{E}\left[\mathrm{E}_Q\left[\widetilde{FCF}_2|\mathcal{F}_1\right]|\mathcal{F}_0\right] = \frac{1}{2}(0.1\cdot 145.2+0.9\cdot 120) + \frac{1}{2}(0.1\cdot 122+0.9\cdot 100.6) = 112.63$$

and this does not equal

$$\mathrm{E}_Q\left[\mathrm{E}\left[\widetilde{FCF}_2|\mathcal{F}_1\right]|\mathcal{F}_0\right] = 0.1\left(\frac{1}{2}\cdot 145.2+\frac{1}{2}\cdot 120\right) + 0.9\left(\frac{1}{2}\cdot 122+\frac{1}{2}\cdot 100.6\right) = 113.43.$$

In general, it can be shown that both expectations may be changed if *down–up* and *up–down* yield the same cash flows. Otherwise not. The rule is: If the outcome is independent of the actual path, i.e., if ud yields the same as du and uud yields the same as udu and duu, then expectations may be changed.

3. For the conditional expectation of $\widetilde{FCF}_3$ given $\mathcal{F}_2$ we have four possible realizations: *up–up*, *up–down*, *down–up*, and *down–down*. We start with *up–up* and get

$$\begin{aligned}\mathrm{E}\left[\widetilde{FCF}_3|\mathcal{F}_2\right](uu) &= (u^3+u^2d)FCF_0\\ &= u^2FCF_0\\ &= \widetilde{FCF}_2(uu).\end{aligned}$$

The other equations for ud, du as well as dd follow analogously:

$$\mathrm{E}\left[\widetilde{FCF}_3|\mathcal{F}_2\right] = \widetilde{FCF}_2.$$

4. We have

$$\mathrm{E}\left[\widetilde{FCF}_2|\mathcal{F}_1\right] = \begin{cases} \frac{u+m+d}{3}\,\widetilde{FCF}_1(u) & \text{if } \widetilde{FCF}_1 \text{ is up},\\ \frac{u+m+d}{3}\,\widetilde{FCF}_1(m) & \text{if } \widetilde{FCF}_1 \text{ is middle},\\ \frac{u+m+d}{3}\,\widetilde{FCF}_1(d) & \text{if } \widetilde{FCF}_1 \text{ is down}.\end{cases}$$

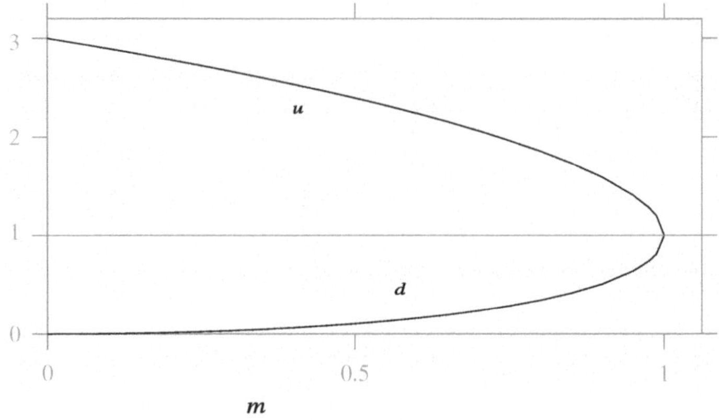

Fig. 7.2 Plot of (u, m, d)

The required relation holds if

$$u + m + d = 3\,.$$

If, for example, $d \in [0,1]$, then this equation jointly with $ud = m^2$ gives the solution

$$d = \frac{1}{2}\left(3 - m + \sqrt{3(3 - 2m - m^2)}\right), \quad u = \frac{m^2}{d}\,.$$

Figure 7.2 shows (u, m, d) for m from $[0,1]$.

7.1.3 A First Glance at Business Values

1. From $s_1 - 1 \geq s_2 - 1 \geq t$ it follows

$$\begin{aligned} \mathrm{E}\left[\widetilde{r}_{s_1}\widetilde{r}_{s_2}|\mathcal{F}_t\right] &= \mathrm{E}\left[\mathrm{E}\left[\widetilde{r}_{s_1}\widetilde{r}_{s_2}|\mathcal{F}_{s_2}\right]|\mathcal{F}_t\right] && \text{by Rule 4} \\ &= \mathrm{E}\left[\widetilde{r}_{s_2}\,\mathrm{E}\left[\widetilde{r}_{s_1}|\mathcal{F}_{s_2}\right]|\mathcal{F}_t\right] && \text{by Rule 5} \\ &= \mathrm{E}\left[\widetilde{r}_{s_2}\,\mathrm{E}\left[\underbrace{\mathrm{E}\left[\widetilde{r}_{s_1}|\mathcal{F}_{s_1-1}\right]}_{:=k_{s_1}}|\mathcal{F}_{s_2}\right]|\mathcal{F}_t\right] && \text{by Rule 4.} \end{aligned}$$

Now using Definition 2.1 and because k_{s_1} is a real number (by assumption) it follows from Rule 2 that

$$\mathrm{E}\left[\widetilde{r}_{s_1}\widetilde{r}_{s_2}|\mathcal{F}_t\right] = k_{s_1}\,\mathrm{E}\left[\widetilde{r}_{s_2}|\mathcal{F}_t\right].$$

Employing Rule 4 yields

$$\begin{aligned} k_{s_1} &= \mathrm{E}\left[\mathrm{E}\left[\widetilde{r}_{s_1}|\mathcal{F}_{s_1-1}\right]|\mathcal{F}_t\right] \\ &= \mathrm{E}\left[\widetilde{r}_{s_1}|\mathcal{F}_t\right] \end{aligned}$$

which gives the desired result.

2. k is constant. We have using Theorem 2.1 as well as (2.5)[1]

$$\begin{aligned} \widetilde{V}_t &= \sum_{s=t+1}^{\infty} \frac{\mathrm{E}\left[\widetilde{FCF}_s|\mathcal{F}_t\right]}{(1+k)^{s-t}} \\ &= \sum_{s=t+1}^{\infty} \frac{(1+g)^{s-t}\widetilde{FCF}_t}{(1+k)^{s-t}} \\ &= \frac{1+g}{k-g}\widetilde{FCF}_t. \end{aligned}$$

Now

$$\widetilde{V}_{t+1} = \begin{cases} u\,\widetilde{V}_t & \text{if up,} \\ d\,\widetilde{V}_t & \text{if down} \end{cases}$$

is an immediate consequence of the fact that $\widetilde{FCF}_t$ follows this pattern. The second part of the solution follows from $\frac{u}{2} + \frac{d}{2} = 0$.

3. We have to show that the firm's value amounts to

$$V_0 = \frac{C}{k-g}.$$

To prove this statement, we use Theorem 2.1 and know that

$$\begin{aligned} V_0 &= \sum_{t=1}^{\infty} \frac{\mathrm{E}\left[\widetilde{FCF}_t\right]}{(1+k)^t} \\ &= \sum_{t=1}^{\infty} \frac{(1+g)^{t-1}\,C}{(1+k)^t} \\ &= \frac{C}{1+g}\sum_{t=1}^{\infty}\left(\frac{1+g}{1+k}\right)^t \\ &= \frac{C}{k-g}. \end{aligned}$$

If $g \geq k$, then the sum does not converge and the value of the firm is infinite.

[1] We have not used $g = 0$ in our proof.

4. We know that

$$\widetilde{V}_t = \frac{\mathrm{E}_Q[\widetilde{V}_{t+1} + \widetilde{FCF}_{t+1}|\mathcal{F}_t]}{1+r_f}$$

holds. Now adding $C(1+r_f)^t$ to both sides

$$\widetilde{V}_t + C(1+r_f)^t = \frac{\mathrm{E}_Q[\widetilde{V}_{t+1} + C(1+r_f)^{t+1} + \widetilde{FCF}_{t+1}|\mathcal{F}_t]}{1+r_f}$$

and replacing $\widetilde{V}_t^* := \widetilde{V}_t + C(1+r_f)^t$ gives the desired result

$$\widetilde{V}_t^* = \frac{\mathrm{E}_Q[\widetilde{V}_{t+1}^* + \widetilde{FCF}_{t+1}|\mathcal{F}_t]}{1+r_f}.$$

Both $\widetilde{V}$ as well as $\widetilde{V}^*$ satisfy the fundamental theorem.

Note that $\widetilde{V}^*$ does not satisfy the transversality condition. We have

$$\lim_{T\to\infty} \frac{\mathrm{E}_Q[\widetilde{V}_T + C(1+r_f)^T|\mathcal{F}_t]}{(1+r_f)^{T-t}} = \lim_{T\to\infty} \frac{\mathrm{E}_Q[\widetilde{V}_T|\mathcal{F}_t]}{(1+r_f)^{T-t}} + C(1+r_f)^t$$

and this cannot be zero for all C.

5. By plugging in the assumption into the expectation under Q we get

$$\begin{aligned}
\frac{\mathrm{E}_Q[\widetilde{V}_{t+1} + \widetilde{FCF}_{t+1}|\mathcal{F}_t]}{1+r_f} &= \frac{\mathrm{E}_Q[\frac{\widetilde{FCF}_0+g}{r_f} + \widetilde{FCF}_0 + \varepsilon_{t+1}|\mathcal{F}_t]}{1+r_f} \\
&= \frac{\frac{\widetilde{FCF}_0+g}{r_f} + \widetilde{FCF}_0 + g}{1+r_f} \\
&= \frac{1}{r_f(1+r_f)}\left(\widetilde{FCF}_0 + g + (\widetilde{FCF}_0 + g)r_f\right) \\
&= \frac{\widetilde{FCF}_0 + g}{r_f} = \widetilde{V}_t
\end{aligned}$$

which is the fundamental theorem.

Also, transversality is easily checked.

$$\lim_{T\to\infty} \frac{\mathrm{E}_Q[\widetilde{V}_T|\mathcal{F}_t]}{(1+r_f)^{T-t}} = \lim_{T\to\infty} \frac{\mathrm{E}_Q\left[\frac{\widetilde{FCF}_0+g}{r_f}|\mathcal{F}_t\right]}{(1+r_f)^{T-t}}$$

$$= \lim_{T\to\infty} \frac{\widetilde{FCF}_0+g}{r_f(1+r_f)^{T-t}} = 0\,,$$

because $r_f > 0$.

7.2 Corporate Income Tax

7.2.1 Unlevered Firms

1. (a) First, if a random variable ε_t can have two values we speak of a binomial structure. In order to get a typical binomial tree from

$$\widetilde{FCF}_t^u = 1 + \varepsilon_1 + \varepsilon_2 + \ldots + \varepsilon_t$$

we have to verify that for any cash flow not the actual movement but only the number of up's and down's is decisive. In other words, "uudd" as well as "uddu," etc. must lead to the same cash flow. But this is evident from the fact that the increments are added.

(b) For the logarithmized cash flows

$$\log(\widetilde{FCF}_t^u) = \log(1+\varepsilon_1) + \log(1+\varepsilon_2)\cdots\log(1+\varepsilon_t)\,.$$

Any $\log(1+\varepsilon_t)$ is binomial as in 1a. Hence, the proposition holds.

2. (a) This follows immediately from the fact that the sum of two standard normally distributed variables is normally distributed again, the variance being the sum of the individual variances.

(b) Following the above solution we have

$$\log(\widetilde{FCF}_t^u) = \log(1+\varepsilon_1) + \log(1+\varepsilon_2)\cdots\log(1+\varepsilon_t)\,.$$

Any summand on the right-hand side is normally distributed with expectation 0 and variance 1. The sum is therefore normally distributed with variance t and the claim is proven.

3. We have

$$\mathrm{E}\left[\widetilde{FCF}_{t+1}^u|\mathcal{F}_t\right] = \mathrm{E}\left[(1+g_t)\widetilde{FCF}_t^u + \varepsilon_{t+1}|\mathcal{F}_t\right]$$

$$= (1+g_t)\widetilde{FCF}_t^u$$

by Rule 5. Furthermore, for $s > t$

$$\begin{aligned}
\operatorname{Cov}[\varepsilon_s,\varepsilon_t] &= \mathrm{E}[\varepsilon_s\,\varepsilon_t] \\
&= \mathrm{E}[\mathrm{E}[\varepsilon_s\,\varepsilon_t|\mathcal{F}_t]] && \text{by Rule 4} \\
&= \mathrm{E}[\varepsilon_t\ \mathrm{E}[\varepsilon_s|\mathcal{F}_t]] && \text{by Rule 5} \\
&= \mathrm{E}\Big[\varepsilon_t\ \mathrm{E}\big[\underbrace{\mathrm{E}[\varepsilon_s|\mathcal{F}_{s-1}]}_{=0}|\mathcal{F}_t\big]\Big] && \text{by Rule 4} \\
&= 0\,.
\end{aligned}$$

4. (a) From Fig. 3.2 we get for the noise term

$$\varepsilon_2 = \begin{cases} \varepsilon(uu) & \text{if development is } uu\,, \\ \varepsilon(ud) & \text{if development is } ud\,, \\ \varepsilon(du) & \text{if development is } du\,, \\ \varepsilon(dd) & \text{if development is } dd\,. \end{cases}$$

The first equation of the problem requires

$$0 = \mathrm{E}[\varepsilon_2] = \mathrm{E}[\varepsilon_2|\mathcal{F}_1]$$

or

$$0 = \frac{\varepsilon(uu)+\varepsilon(ud)+\varepsilon(du)+\varepsilon(dd)}{4} = \begin{cases} \frac{\varepsilon(uu)+\varepsilon(ud)}{2} & \text{if } u\,, \\ \frac{\varepsilon(du)+\varepsilon(dd)}{2} & \text{if } d\,. \end{cases}$$

Hence, we have

$$\frac{\varepsilon(uu)+\varepsilon(ud)}{2} = \frac{\varepsilon(du)+\varepsilon(dd)}{2} = 0\,.$$

This is the only requirement that has to be satisfied for the noise terms. A parametrized solution is

$$\varepsilon = \begin{cases} x & \text{if } uu\,, \\ -x & \text{if } ud\,, \\ y & \text{if } du\,, \\ -y & \text{if } dd\,, \end{cases}$$

for arbitrary x, y.

(b) The second equation of the problem

$$\mathrm{E}[f(\varepsilon_2)] = \mathrm{E}[f(\varepsilon_2)|\mathcal{F}_1]$$

is equivalent to

$$\frac{f(\varepsilon(uu)) + f(\varepsilon(ud)) + f(\varepsilon(du)) + f(\varepsilon(dd))}{4} = \begin{cases} \frac{f(\varepsilon(uu))+f(\varepsilon(ud))}{2} & \text{if } u\,, \\ \frac{f(\varepsilon(du))+f(\varepsilon(dd))}{2} & \text{if } d\,. \end{cases}$$

Since f is an arbitrary function, it is straightforward to see that a sufficient and necessary condition is given by the following cases[2]:
Case 1: The following equations have to be satisfied:

$$\varepsilon(uu) = \varepsilon(du), \quad \text{and} \quad \varepsilon(ud) = \varepsilon(dd)\,.$$

Case 2: The following equations have to be satisfied:

$$\varepsilon(uu) = \varepsilon(dd), \quad \text{and} \quad \varepsilon(ud) = \varepsilon(du)\,.$$

We will from now on only consider case 1.

Since the increments must have expectation zero, we furthermore have to add the requirement

$$\varepsilon(uu) + \varepsilon(ud) = 0, \quad \text{and} \quad \varepsilon(du) + \varepsilon(dd) = 0\,.$$

Hence, there is only one possible solution

$$\varepsilon = \begin{cases} x & \text{if } uu\,, \\ -x & \text{if } ud\,, \\ x & \text{if } du\,, \\ -x & \text{if } dd\,, \end{cases}$$

[2]The formal argument is: if

$$\frac{f(w) + f(x) + f(y) + f(z)}{4} = \frac{f(w) + f(x)}{2} = \frac{f(y) + f(z)}{2}$$

has to hold regardless of what f is, we must have $w = y$ and $x = z$ or $w = z$ and $x = y$. Otherwise, we could change the value $f(w)$ without changing the function f outside w and get a violation of the above assumption.

for arbitrary x. The second case gives us

$$\varepsilon = \begin{cases} x & \text{if } uu\,, \\ -x & \text{if } ud\,, \\ -x & \text{if } du\,, \\ x & \text{if } dd\,, \end{cases}$$

This is far more restrictive than the linear relation from 4a.

Remark The two conditions "independent increments" and "$\widetilde{FCF}_2^u(ud) = \widetilde{FCF}_2^u(du)$" require $\widetilde{FCF}_1^u$ to be chosen properly: The two conditions imply

$$\widetilde{FCF}_1^u(u) + \varepsilon(ud) = \widetilde{FCF}_1^u(d) + \varepsilon(du)$$

and with independent increments and $\widetilde{FCF}_1^u(u) = 133.1$ as well as $\widetilde{FCF}_1^u(d) = 110.8$ this cannot hold.

5. The solution of this problem runs absolutely parallel to the solution of problem 4. Noise terms are zero if and only if

$$\frac{\varepsilon(uu) + \varepsilon(ud)}{2} = \frac{\varepsilon(du) + \varepsilon(dd)}{2} = 0\,.$$

A parametrized solution is

$$\varepsilon = \begin{cases} x & \text{if } uu\,, \\ -x & \text{if } ud\,, \\ y & \text{if } du\,, \\ -y & \text{if } dd\,, \end{cases}$$

for arbitrary x, y.

Noise terms are furthermore independent if

$$\varepsilon = \begin{cases} x & \text{if } uu\,, \\ -x & \text{if } ud\,, \\ x & \text{if } du\,, \\ -x & \text{if } dd\,, \end{cases}$$

or

$$\varepsilon = \begin{cases} x & \text{if } uu\,, \\ -x & \text{if } ud\,, \\ -x & \text{if } du\,, \\ x & \text{if } dd\,, \end{cases}$$

for arbitrary x.

This solution for ε is different from problem 4. In problem 4 the (noise) increments were additive. However, here they are multiplicative.

6. We have

$$\begin{aligned} \text{div}_t &= \frac{\mathrm{E}\left[\widetilde{FCF}^u_{t+1}|\mathcal{F}_t\right]}{\widetilde{V}^u_t} \\ &= \frac{(1+g_t)\widetilde{FCF}^u_t}{\widetilde{V}^u_t} = (1+g_t)d^u_t \end{aligned}$$

and

$$\begin{aligned} \text{gain}_t &= \frac{\mathrm{E}\left[\widetilde{V}^u_{t+1} - \widetilde{V}^u_t|\mathcal{F}_t\right]}{\widetilde{V}^u_t} \\ &= \frac{\mathrm{E}\left[\frac{\widetilde{FCF}^u_{t+1}}{d^u_{t+1}} - \frac{\widetilde{FCF}^u_t}{d^u_t}|\mathcal{F}_t\right]}{\frac{\widetilde{FCF}^u_t}{d^u_t}} \\ &= \frac{\frac{1+g_t}{d^u_{t+1}}\widetilde{FCF}^u_t - \frac{\widetilde{FCF}^u_t}{d^u_t}}{\frac{\widetilde{FCF}^u_t}{d^u_t}} \\ &= (1+g_t)\frac{d^u_t}{d^u_{t+1}} - 1\,. \end{aligned}$$

7. (a) In this case

$$\begin{aligned} \widetilde{V}^u_t &= \sum_{s=t+1}^{\infty} \frac{\mathrm{E}\left[\widetilde{FCF}^u_s|\mathcal{F}_t\right]}{(1+k^{E,u})^{s-t}} \\ &= \sum_{s=t+1}^{\infty} \frac{(1+g)^{s-t}\widetilde{FCF}^u_t}{(1+k^{E,u})^{s-t}} \end{aligned}$$

$$= \widetilde{FCF}_t^u \sum_{s=t+1}^{\infty} \left(\frac{1+g}{1+k^{E,u}} \right)^{s-t}$$

$$= \widetilde{FCF}_t^u \frac{1+g}{k^{E,u}-g},$$

if $g < k^{E,u}$.

The dividend-price ratio is $\frac{k^{E,u}-g}{1+g}$.
Using this relation the dividend ratio is

$$\begin{aligned} \mathrm{div}_t &= \frac{\mathrm{E}\left[\widetilde{FCF}_{t+1}^u | \mathcal{F}_t\right]}{\widetilde{V}_t^u} \\ &= \frac{(1+g)\widetilde{FCF}_t^u}{\widetilde{FCF}_t^u} \frac{k^{E,u}-g}{1+g} \\ &= k^{E,u}-g \end{aligned}$$

and the capital gains ratio is

$$\begin{aligned} \mathrm{gain}_t &= \frac{\mathrm{E}\left[\widetilde{V}_{t+1}^u - \widetilde{V}_t^u | \mathcal{F}_t\right]}{\widetilde{V}_t^u} \\ &= \frac{\mathrm{E}\left[\frac{(1+g)\widetilde{FCF}_{t+1}^u}{k^{E,u}-g} - \frac{(1+g)\widetilde{FCF}_t^u}{k^{E,u}-g} | \mathcal{F}_t\right]}{\frac{(1+g)\widetilde{FCF}_t^u}{k^{E,u}-g}} \\ &= \frac{g\,\widetilde{FCF}_t^u}{\widetilde{FCF}_t^u} \\ &= g. \end{aligned}$$

(b) In this case the firm value is infinite.
(c) From the fundamental theorem we have

$$\begin{aligned} \widetilde{V}_t^u &= \frac{\mathrm{E}_Q\left[\widetilde{FCF}_{t+1}^u + \widetilde{V}_{t+1}^u | \mathcal{F}_t\right]}{1+r_f} \\ \widetilde{FCF}_t^u \frac{1+g}{k^{E,u}-g} &= \frac{\mathrm{E}_Q\left[\widetilde{FCF}_{t+1}^u + \widetilde{FCF}_{t+1}^u \frac{1+g}{k^{E,u}-g} | \mathcal{F}_t\right]}{1+r_f} \\ \mathrm{E}_Q\left[\widetilde{FCF}_{t+1}^u | \mathcal{F}_t\right] &= \frac{(1+g)\left(1+r_f\right)}{1+k^{E,u}} \widetilde{FCF}_t^u. \end{aligned}$$

8. (a) First we have by Rule 4

$$\begin{aligned}
\mathrm{E}\left[\widetilde{FCF}^u_{t+2}|\mathcal{F}_t\right] &= \mathrm{E}\left[\mathrm{E}\left[\widetilde{FCF}^u_{t+2}|\mathcal{F}_{t+1}\right]|\mathcal{F}_t\right] \\
&= \mathrm{E}\left[\widetilde{FCF}^u_{t+1} + X_{t+1}|\mathcal{F}_t\right] \\
&= \mathrm{E}\left[\widetilde{FCF}^u_{t+1}|\mathcal{F}_t\right] \\
&= \widetilde{FCF}^u_t + X_t
\end{aligned}$$

and hence for $s > t$

$$\mathrm{E}\left[\widetilde{FCF}^u_s|\mathcal{F}_t\right] = \widetilde{FCF}^u_t + X_t.$$

The value of the company is given by

$$\begin{aligned}
\widetilde{V}^u_t &= \sum_{s=t+1}^{\infty} \frac{\mathrm{E}\left[\widetilde{FCF}^u_s|\mathcal{F}_t\right]}{(1+k^{E,u})^{s-t}} \\
&= \sum_{s=t+1}^{\infty} \frac{\widetilde{FCF}^u_t + X_t}{(1+k^{E,u})^{s-t}} \\
&= \frac{\widetilde{FCF}^u_t}{k^{E,u}} + \frac{X_t}{k^{E,u}}.
\end{aligned}$$

Since $\widetilde{FCF}^u_t$ and X_t are uncorrelated the variance of the firm is greater than the variance of the cash flows (if $k^{E,u} < 100\,\%$),

$$\begin{aligned}
\mathrm{Var}\left[\widetilde{V}^u_t\right] &= \mathrm{Var}\left[\frac{\widetilde{FCF}^u_t}{k^{E,u}} + \frac{X_t}{k^{E,u}}\right] \\
&= \frac{\mathrm{Var}\left[\widetilde{FCF}^u_t\right]}{(k^{E,u})^2} + \frac{\mathrm{Var}\left[X_t\right]}{(k^{E,u})^2} \\
&> \frac{\mathrm{Var}\left[\widetilde{FCF}^u_t\right]}{(k^{E,u})^2} > \mathrm{Var}\left[\widetilde{FCF}^u_t\right].
\end{aligned}$$

(b) Now

$$\mathrm{E}\left[\widetilde{V}^u_{t+1}|\mathcal{F}_t\right] = \mathrm{E}\left[\frac{\widetilde{FCF}^u_{t+1}}{k^{E,u}} + \frac{X_{t+1}}{k^{E,u}}|\mathcal{F}_t\right]$$

$$= \frac{\mathrm{E}\left[\widetilde{FCF}^u_{t+1} | \mathcal{F}_t\right]}{k^{E,u}}$$

$$= \frac{\widetilde{FCF}^u_t + X_t}{k^{E,u}} = \widetilde{V}^u_t$$

and the expected capital gains rate is zero.

(c) This is harder to show and we closely follow the proof of Theorem 3.3.

$$\frac{\mathrm{E}\left[\widetilde{FCF}^u_{t+1} + \widetilde{V}^u_{t+1} | \mathcal{F}_t\right]}{1 + k^{E,u}} = \frac{\mathrm{E}_Q\left[\widetilde{FCF}^u_{t+1} + \widetilde{V}^u_{t+1} | \mathcal{F}_t\right]}{1 + r_f} = \widetilde{V}^u_t$$

$$\frac{\mathrm{E}\left[\widetilde{FCF}^u_{t+1} + \frac{\widetilde{FCF}^u_{t+1} + X_{t+1}}{k^{E,u}} | \mathcal{F}_t\right]}{1 + k^{E,u}} = \frac{\mathrm{E}_Q\left[\widetilde{FCF}^u_{t+1} + \frac{\widetilde{FCF}^u_{t+1} + X_{t+1}}{k^{E,u}} | \mathcal{F}_t\right]}{1 + r_f}$$

$$\frac{(1 + \frac{1}{k^{E,u}})\,\mathrm{E}\left[\widetilde{FCF}^u_{t+1} | \mathcal{F}_t\right]}{1 + k^{E,u}} = \frac{(1 + \frac{1}{k^{E,u}})\,\mathrm{E}_Q\left[\widetilde{FCF}^u_{t+1} | \mathcal{F}_t\right]}{1 + r_f}$$

$$\frac{\mathrm{E}\left[\widetilde{FCF}^u_{t+1} | \mathcal{F}_t\right]}{1 + k^{E,u}} = \frac{\mathrm{E}_Q\left[\widetilde{FCF}^u_{t+1} | \mathcal{F}_t\right]}{1 + r_f}$$

which is the first part of the claim.

The second part follows from

$$\frac{\mathrm{E}\left[\widetilde{FCF}^u_{t+1} + \widetilde{V}^u_{t+1} | \mathcal{F}_t\right]}{1 + k^{E,u}} = \frac{\mathrm{E}_Q\left[\widetilde{FCF}^u_{t+1} + \widetilde{V}^u_{t+1} | \mathcal{F}_t\right]}{1 + r_f} = \widetilde{V}^u_t$$

$$\frac{\mathrm{E}\left[\widetilde{V}^u_{t+1} | \mathcal{F}_t\right]}{1 + k^{E,u}} = \frac{\mathrm{E}_Q\left[\widetilde{V}^u_{t+1} | \mathcal{F}_t\right]}{1 + r_f}$$

$$\frac{\mathrm{E}\left[\frac{\mathrm{E}\left[\widetilde{FCF}^u_{t+2} + \widetilde{V}^u_{t+2} | \mathcal{F}_{t+1}\right]}{1 + k^{E,u}} | \mathcal{F}_t\right]}{1 + k^{E,u}} = \frac{\mathrm{E}_Q\left[\frac{\mathrm{E}_Q\left[\widetilde{FCF}^u_{t+2} + \widetilde{V}^u_{t+2} | \mathcal{F}_{t+1}\right]}{1 + r_f} | \mathcal{F}_t\right]}{1 + r_f}$$

$$\frac{\mathrm{E}\left[\widetilde{FCF}^u_{t+2} + \widetilde{V}^u_{t+2} | \mathcal{F}_t\right]}{(1 + k^{E,u})^2} = \frac{\mathrm{E}_Q\left[\widetilde{FCF}^u_{t+2} + \widetilde{V}^u_{t+2} | \mathcal{F}_t\right]}{(1 + r_f)^2}$$

$$\frac{\mathrm{E}\left[\widetilde{FCF}^u_{t+2} + \frac{\widetilde{FCF}^u_{t+2} + X_{t+2}}{k^{E,u}} | \mathcal{F}_t\right]}{(1 + k^{E,u})^2} = \frac{\mathrm{E}_Q\left[\widetilde{FCF}^u_{t+2} + \frac{\widetilde{FCF}^u_{t+2} + X_{t+2}}{k^{E,u}} | \mathcal{F}_t\right]}{(1 + r_f)^2}$$

and since $\mathrm{E}\left[X_{t+2}|\mathcal{F}_{t+1}\right] = \mathrm{E}_Q\left[X_{t+2}|\mathcal{F}_{t+1}\right] = 0$,

$$\frac{\left(1+\frac{1}{k^{E,u}}\right)\mathrm{E}\left[\widetilde{FCF}^u_{t+2}|\mathcal{F}_t\right]}{(1+k^{E,u})^2} = \frac{\left(1+\frac{1}{k^{E,u}}\right)\mathrm{E}_Q\left[\widetilde{FCF}^u_{t+2}|\mathcal{F}_t\right]}{\left(1+r_f\right)^2}$$

which is almost the claim.

9. (a) First we have

$$\mathrm{E}\left[\widetilde{FCF}^u_s|\mathcal{F}_t\right] = (s-t)C + \widetilde{FCF}^u_t$$

by induction. But then

$$\begin{aligned}
\widetilde{V}^u_t &= \sum_{s=t+1}^{\infty} \frac{\mathrm{E}\left[\widetilde{FCF}^u_s|\mathcal{F}_t\right]}{(1+k^{E,u})^{s-t}} \\
&= \sum_{s=t+1}^{\infty} \frac{\widetilde{FCF}^u_t + (s-t)C}{(1+k^{E,u})^{s-t}} \\
&= \sum_{s=t+1}^{\infty} \frac{\widetilde{FCF}^u_t}{(1+k^{E,u})^{s-t}} + \sum_{s=t+1}^{\infty} \frac{(s-t)C}{(1+k^{E,u})^{s-t}} \\
&= \frac{\widetilde{FCF}^u_t}{k^{E,u}} + \frac{1+k^{E,u}}{(k^{E,u})^2}C
\end{aligned}$$

using an algebraic formula.[3] In particular, the price-dividend ratio is not deterministic any more. Compare this to problem 3.

[3]Note that

$$\sum_{s=1}^{\infty} \frac{1}{(1+x)^s} = \frac{1}{x}.$$

Differentiating this relation yields

$$\sum_{s=1}^{\infty} \frac{-s}{(1+x)^{s+1}} = -\frac{1}{x^2}$$

or after multiplying by $-(1+x)$

$$\sum_{s=1}^{\infty} \frac{s}{(1+x)^s} = \frac{1+x}{x^2}.$$

(b) We have

$$\begin{aligned}\mathrm{E}\left[\widetilde{V}^u_{t+1}|\mathcal{F}_t\right] &= \mathrm{E}\left[\frac{\widetilde{FCF}^u_{t+1}}{k^{E,u}} + \frac{1+k^{E,u}}{(k^{E,u})^2}\,C|\mathcal{F}_t\right]\\ &= \frac{\widetilde{FCF}^u_t + C}{k^{E,u}} + \frac{1+k^{E,u}}{(k^{E,u})^2}\,C\\ &= \widetilde{V}^u_t + \frac{C}{k^{E,u}}\end{aligned}$$

and hence the expected capital gains rate is not zero.

(c) We use

$$\frac{\mathrm{E}\left[\widetilde{FCF}^u_{t+1} + \widetilde{V}^u_{t+1}|\mathcal{F}_t\right]}{1+k^{E,u}} = \frac{\mathrm{E}_Q\left[\widetilde{FCF}^u_{t+1} + \widetilde{V}^u_{t+1}|\mathcal{F}_t\right]}{1+r_f} = \widetilde{V}^u_t\,.$$

Employing the above result this implies

$$\frac{\mathrm{E}\left[\widetilde{FCF}^u_{t+1} + \frac{\widetilde{FCF}^u_{t+1}}{k^{E,u}} + \frac{1+k^{E,u}}{(k^{E,u})^2}\,C|\mathcal{F}_t\right]}{1+k^{E,u}} = \frac{\mathrm{E}_Q\left[\widetilde{FCF}^u_{t+1} + \frac{\widetilde{FCF}^u_{t+1}}{k^{E,u}} + \frac{1+k^{E,u}}{(k^{E,u})^2}\,C|\mathcal{F}_t\right]}{1+r_f}$$

and after rearranging and multiplying by $\frac{k^{E,u}}{1+k^{E,u}}$,

$$\frac{\mathrm{E}\left[\widetilde{FCF}^u_{t+1}|\mathcal{F}_t\right] + \frac{1}{k^{E,u}}\,C}{1+k^{E,u}} = \frac{\mathrm{E}_Q\left[\widetilde{FCF}^u_{t+1}|\mathcal{F}_t\right] + \frac{1}{k^{E,u}}\,C}{1+r_f}\,. \tag{7.1}$$

Rearranging once again gives

$$\mathrm{E}_Q\left[\widetilde{FCF}^u_{t+1}|\mathcal{F}_t\right] = \frac{1+r_f}{1+k^{E,u}}\,\mathrm{E}\left[\widetilde{FCF}^u_{t+1}|\mathcal{F}_t\right] + \frac{1+r_f}{k^{E,u}}\left(\frac{1}{1+k^{E,u}} - \frac{1}{1+r_f}\right)C$$

which is, after using the assumption,

$$\mathrm{E}_Q\left[\widetilde{FCF}^u_{t+1}|\mathcal{F}_t\right] = \frac{1+r_f}{1+k^{E,u}}(\widetilde{FCF}^u_t + C) + \frac{C}{k^{E,u}}\left(\frac{1+r_f}{1+k^{E,u}} - 1\right).$$

Summarizing the terms with C gives the required result.

Now consider Theorem 3.3. Since C does not cancel in (7.1) this intermediate result shows that our weak auto-regressive assumption will violate Theorem 3.3. We have

$$\frac{C}{k^{E,u}(1+k^{E,u})} \neq \frac{C}{k^{E,u}\,(1+r_f)} \quad\Longrightarrow\quad \frac{\mathrm{E}\left[\widetilde{FCF}^u_{t+1}|\mathcal{F}_t\right]}{1+k^{E,u}} \neq \frac{\mathrm{E}_Q\left[\widetilde{FCF}^u_{t+1}|\mathcal{F}_t\right]}{1+r_f}\,.$$

Hence, using this assumption about cash flows we can still use cost of capital as discount rates but we have to add a correction term due to the fact that $C \neq 0$.

10. (a) From the definition of discount rates (Definition 3.2) we have

$$\frac{\mathrm{E}_Q\left[\widetilde{FCF}^u_{t+2}|\mathcal{F}_t\right]}{\left(1+r_f\right)^2} = \frac{\mathrm{E}\left[\widetilde{FCF}^u_{t+2}|\mathcal{F}_t\right]}{(1+\kappa_t)(1+\kappa_{t+1})}.$$

From Rule 4 it follows that

$$\frac{1}{1+r_f}\frac{\mathrm{E}_Q\left[\mathrm{E}_Q\left[\widetilde{FCF}^u_{t+2}|\mathcal{F}_{t+1}\right]|\mathcal{F}_t\right]}{1+r_f} = \frac{\mathrm{E}\left[\mathrm{E}\left[\widetilde{FCF}^u_{t+2}|\mathcal{F}_{t+1}\right]|\mathcal{F}_t\right]}{(1+\kappa_t)(1+\kappa_{t+1})}.$$

Independence and (2.5) implies that the outer expectation can be neglected,

$$\frac{1}{1+r_f}\frac{\mathrm{E}_Q\left[\widetilde{FCF}^u_{t+2}|\mathcal{F}_{t+1}\right]}{1+r_f} = \frac{1}{1+\kappa_t}\frac{\mathrm{E}\left[\widetilde{FCF}^u_{t+2}|\mathcal{F}_{t+1}\right]}{1+\kappa_{t+1}}.$$

The term on the right-hand side is by definition of a discount rate equal to

$$\frac{1}{1+r_f}\frac{\mathrm{E}_Q\left[\widetilde{FCF}^u_{t+2}|\mathcal{F}_{t+1}\right]}{1+r_f} = \frac{1}{1+\kappa_t}\frac{\mathrm{E}_Q\left[\widetilde{FCF}^u_{t+2}|\mathcal{F}_{t+1}\right]}{1+r_f}$$

implying $r_f = \kappa_t$. This argument will apply to all κ_t.

(b) If all discount rates κ_t are equal to the riskless rate, then the firm value is given by

$$V_0 = \sum_{t=1}^{T}\frac{\mathrm{E}[\widetilde{FCF}_t]}{(1+\kappa_1)\dots(1+\kappa_t)} = \sum_{t=1}^{T}\frac{\mathrm{E}[\widetilde{FCF}_t]}{\left(1+r_f\right)^t}$$

and this obviously violates the fact that $\mathrm{E}[\widetilde{FCF}_t] \neq \mathrm{E}_Q\left[\widetilde{FCF}_t\right]$ and the fundamental theorem

$$V_0 = \sum_{t=1}^{T}\frac{\mathrm{E}_Q\left[\widetilde{FCF}_t\right]}{\left(1+r_f\right)^t}.$$

There is no other conclusion to be drawn from this problem than that in this case the definition of discount rate $\kappa_t^{r\to s}$ cannot be simplified by omitting r and s from κ_t. It is necessary to specify the time s when the cash flow is paid and the time r when the cash flow is valued as well.

7.2.1.1 Basics About Levered Firms

1. We start with (3.19) and get for $s > t$

$$\mathrm{E}_Q\left[\widetilde{D}_s|\mathcal{F}_t\right] = \frac{\mathrm{E}_Q\left[\widetilde{I}_{s+1} + \widetilde{D}_{s+1} + \widetilde{R}_{s+1}|\mathcal{F}_t\right]}{1+r_f}.$$

At time $s+1$ we similarly have

$$\mathrm{E}_Q\left[\widetilde{D}_{s+1}|\mathcal{F}_t\right] = \frac{\mathrm{E}_Q\left[\widetilde{I}_{s+2} + \widetilde{D}_{s+2} + \widetilde{R}_{s+2}|\mathcal{F}_t\right]}{1+r_f}.$$

Plugging this into the first equation gives

$$\mathrm{E}_Q\left[\widetilde{D}_s|\mathcal{F}_t\right] = \frac{\mathrm{E}_Q\left[\widetilde{I}_{s+1} + \frac{\mathrm{E}_Q\left[\widetilde{I}_{s+2}+\widetilde{D}_{s+2}+\widetilde{R}_{s+2}|\mathcal{F}_t\right]}{1+r_f} + \widetilde{R}_{s+1}|\mathcal{F}_t\right]}{1+r_f}$$

$$= \frac{\mathrm{E}_Q\left[\widetilde{I}_{s+1} + \widetilde{R}_{s+1}|\mathcal{F}_t\right]}{1+r_f} + \frac{\mathrm{E}_Q\left[\widetilde{I}_{s+2} + \widetilde{R}_{s+2}|\mathcal{F}_t\right]}{(1+r_f)^2} + \frac{\mathrm{E}_Q\left[\widetilde{D}_{s+2}|\mathcal{F}_t\right]}{(1+r_f)^2}$$

Continuing this approach we get for $s = t$

$$\mathrm{E}_Q\left[\widetilde{D}_t|\mathcal{F}_t\right] = \sum_{s=t+1}^{T} \frac{\mathrm{E}_Q\left[\widetilde{I}_s + \widetilde{R}_s|\mathcal{F}_t\right]}{(1+r_f)^{s-t}} + \frac{\mathrm{E}_Q\left[\widetilde{D}_T|\mathcal{F}_t\right]}{(1+r_f)^{T-t}}.$$

Financing is always such that $\widetilde{D}_T = 0$ and $D_t = \mathrm{E}_Q\left[\widetilde{D}_t|\mathcal{F}_t\right]$ (Rule 5). This proves the claim.

2. The tax shield satisfies

$$\widetilde{V}_0^l - \widetilde{V}_0^u = \sum_{t=0}^{2} \frac{\tau r_f\, \mathrm{E}_Q\left[\widetilde{D}_t\right]}{\left(1+r_f\right)^t}.$$

Hence, we have to evaluate the expectations $\mathrm{E}_Q\left[\widetilde{D}_t\right]$. We get

$$\mathrm{E}_Q\left[D_0\right] = 100,$$

since D_0 is certain. It follows that

$$\mathrm{E}_Q\left[\widetilde{D}_1\right] = 120 \cdot 0.25 + 110 \cdot 0.75 = 112.5.$$

At time $t = 2$ we get similarly

$$\mathrm{E}_Q\left[\widetilde{D}_2\right] = 150 \cdot 0.25^2 + 145 \cdot 2 \cdot 0.25 \cdot 0.75 + 100 \cdot 0.75^2 = 120.$$

Using both equations gives us

$$\widetilde{V}_0^l - \widetilde{V}_0^u = \frac{0.1 \cdot 0.5 \cdot 100}{1+0.1} + \frac{0.1 \cdot 0.5 \cdot 112.5}{(1+0.1)^2} + \frac{0.1 \cdot 0.5 \cdot 120}{(1+0.1)^3}$$
$$\approx 13.702.$$

3. Equation (3.11) implies

$$\widetilde{V}_{t+1}^l = \widetilde{V}_{t+1}^u + \frac{\mathrm{E}_Q\left[\tau r_f \widetilde{D}_{t+1} | \mathcal{F}_{t+1}\right]}{1+r_f} + \ldots + \frac{\mathrm{E}_Q\left[\tau r_f \widetilde{D}_{T-1} | \mathcal{F}_{t+1}\right]}{\left(1+r_f\right)^{T-t-1}}.$$

Rule 4 gives

$$\mathrm{E}_Q\left[\widetilde{V}_{t+1}^l - \widetilde{V}_{t+1}^u | \mathcal{F}_t\right] = \frac{\mathrm{E}_Q\left[\tau r_f \widetilde{D}_{t+1} | \mathcal{F}_t\right]}{1+r_f} + \ldots + \frac{\mathrm{E}_Q\left[\tau r_f \widetilde{D}_{T-1} | \mathcal{F}_t\right]}{\left(1+r_f\right)^{T-t-1}}$$

or

$$\frac{\mathrm{E}_Q\left[\widetilde{V}_{t+1}^l - \widetilde{V}_{t+1}^u | \mathcal{F}_t\right]}{1+r_f} = \frac{\mathrm{E}_Q\left[\tau r_f \widetilde{D}_{t+1} | \mathcal{F}_t\right]}{\left(1+r_f\right)^2} + \ldots + \frac{\mathrm{E}_Q\left[\tau r_f \widetilde{D}_{T-1} | \mathcal{F}_t\right]}{\left(1+r_f\right)^{T-t}}.$$

Adding $\frac{\tau r_f \widetilde{D}_t}{1+r_f}$ and taking into account that $\widetilde{D}_t$ is known at time t (Rule 5) gives

$$\frac{\mathrm{E}_Q\left[\widetilde{V}_{t+1}^l - \widetilde{V}_{t+1}^u | \mathcal{F}_t\right]}{1+r_f} + \frac{\tau r_f \widetilde{D}_t}{1+r_f} = \frac{\mathrm{E}_Q\left[\tau r_f \widetilde{D}_t | \mathcal{F}_t\right]}{1+r_f} + \ldots + \frac{\mathrm{E}_Q\left[\tau r_f \widetilde{D}_{T-1} | \mathcal{F}_t\right]}{\left(1+r_f\right)^{T-t}}$$
$$= \widetilde{V}_t^l - \widetilde{V}_t^u$$

and this is the claim.

We have shown that the value of the tax shield in $t+1$ and the value of the tax shield in t are related by the above equation. Such a relation is sometimes called recursive. If Q is unknown still an evaluation of the tax shield is possible if all $\widetilde{D}_t$ are known using this recursive equation.

4. From (3.11) we have

$$\widetilde{V}_t^l = \widetilde{V}_t^u + \sum_{s=t}^{T-1} \frac{\tau r_f \, \mathrm{E}_Q\left[\widetilde{D}_s | \mathcal{F}_t\right]}{(1+r_f)^{s+1-t}}$$
$$= \widetilde{V}_t^u + \sum_{s=t}^{T-1} \frac{\tau \, \mathrm{E}_Q\left[\widetilde{D}_s | \mathcal{F}_t\right]}{(1+r_f)^{s-t}} \left(1 - \frac{1}{1+r_f}\right)$$

and from this

$$\begin{aligned}
\widetilde{V}_t^l &= \widetilde{V}_t^u + \sum_{s=t}^{T-1} \frac{\tau \operatorname{E}_Q\left[\widetilde{D}_s|\mathcal{F}_t\right]}{(1+r_f)^{s-t}} - \sum_{s=t}^{T-1} \frac{\tau \operatorname{E}_Q\left[\widetilde{D}_s|\mathcal{F}_t\right]}{(1+r_f)^{s+1-t}} \\
&= \widetilde{V}_t^u + \tau \widetilde{D}_t + \sum_{s=t+1}^{T-1} \frac{\tau \operatorname{E}_Q\left[\widetilde{D}_s|\mathcal{F}_t\right]}{(1+r_f)^{s-t}} - \sum_{s=t}^{T-1} \frac{\tau \operatorname{E}_Q\left[\widetilde{D}_s|\mathcal{F}_t\right]}{(1+r_f)^{s+1-t}} \\
&= \widetilde{V}_t^u + \tau \widetilde{D}_t + \sum_{s=t}^{T-1} \frac{\tau \operatorname{E}_Q\left[\widetilde{D}_{s+1}|\mathcal{F}_t\right]}{(1+r_f)^{s+1-t}} - \sum_{s=t}^{T-1} \frac{\tau \operatorname{E}_Q\left[\widetilde{D}_s|\mathcal{F}_t\right]}{(1+r_f)^{s+1-t}}
\end{aligned}$$

which was to be shown (note that $\widetilde{D}_T = 0$).

7.2.2 Autonomous Financing

1. We have

$$\begin{aligned}
\operatorname{E}\left[\widetilde{FCF}_{t+1}^l|\mathcal{F}_t\right] &= \operatorname{E}\left[\widetilde{FCF}_{t+1}^u + \tau r_f \widetilde{D}_t|\mathcal{F}_t\right] \\
&= \operatorname{E}\left[\widetilde{FCF}_{t+1}^u|\mathcal{F}_t\right] + \tau r_f \widetilde{D}_t \\
&= (1+g_t)\widetilde{FCF}_t^u + \tau r_f \widetilde{D}_t \\
&\neq (1+g_t)\underbrace{\left(\widetilde{FCF}_t^u + \tau r_f \widetilde{D}_{t-1}\right)}_{=\widetilde{FCF}_t^l}.
\end{aligned}$$

For weak auto-regressive levered cash flows debt $\widetilde{D}_{t-1}$ must increase with the growth rate

$$\widetilde{D}_t = (1+g_t)\widetilde{D}_{t-1} = \ldots = (1+g_t)\ldots(1+g_1)D_0$$

and is therefore deterministic.

2. In the infinite example the value of the firm can be rearranged as follows:

$$\begin{aligned}
\widetilde{V}_t^l &= \widetilde{V}_t^u + \sum_{s=t+1}^{\infty} \frac{\tau r_f D_s}{\left(1+r_f\right)^{s-t}} \\
&= \frac{\widetilde{FCF}_t^u}{k^{E,u}} + \tau r_f D_t \sum_{s=t+1}^{\infty} \frac{1}{\left(1+r_f\right)^{s-t}} \\
&= \frac{\widetilde{FCF}_t^u}{k^{E,u}} + \tau r_f D_t \frac{1}{r_f} \\
&= \frac{\widetilde{FCF}_t^u}{k^{E,u}} + \tau D_t.
\end{aligned}$$

3. The dividend-price ratio of the levered firm is

$$\begin{aligned} d_t^l &= \frac{\widetilde{FCF}_t^l}{\widetilde{V}_t^l} \\ &= \frac{\widetilde{FCF}_t^u + \tau r_f D_{t-1}}{\widetilde{V}_t^u + \tau D_t} \\ &= k^{E,u} \frac{\widetilde{V}_t^u + \frac{r_f}{k^{E,u}} \tau D_{t-1}}{\widetilde{V}_t^u + \tau D_{t-1}}. \end{aligned}$$

To verify that this dividend ratio is stochastic we first realize that $\frac{r_f}{k^{E,u}} \neq 1$ since the cash flows are uncertain. Then, the function

$$f(x) := \frac{x + \frac{r_f}{k^{E,u}} \tau D_{t-1}}{x + \tau D_{t-1}}$$

is strictly monotone and hence $f(\widetilde{V}_t^u)$ will again be a random variable, i.e., if for two different states $\widetilde{V}_t^u(\omega)$ is different from $\widetilde{V}_t^u(\omega')$, it will be true that $d_t^l(\omega) \neq d_t^l(\omega')$ and hence the dividend-price ratio is stochastic.

4. The conditional Q-probabilities are as in Fig. 3.1. From this, the unconditional probabilities can easily be evaluated: see Table 7.1.

This yields the following Q-expected cash flows:

$$\mathrm{E}_Q\left[\widetilde{FCF}_1^l\right] = 96.6667, \qquad \mathrm{E}_Q\left[\widetilde{FCF}_2^l\right] = 97.4306, \qquad \mathrm{E}_Q\left[\widetilde{FCF}_3^l\right] = 95.7008.$$

From this, immediately

$$V_0 = \frac{\mathrm{E}_Q\left[\widetilde{FCF}_1^l\right]}{1+r_f} + \frac{\mathrm{E}_Q\left[\widetilde{FCF}_2^l\right]}{(1+r_f)^2} + \frac{\mathrm{E}_Q\left[\widetilde{FCF}_3^l\right]}{(1+r_f)^3} \approx 240.30$$

as was to be shown.

Table 7.1 Unconditional Q-probabilities

Time	$Q(\cdot)$
$t=1$	$Q_1(u) = 0.0833,\ Q_1(d) = 0.9167$
$t=2$	$Q_2(uu) = 0.00347,\ Q_2(ud) = 0.07986,\ Q_2(du) = 0.11458,\ Q_2(dd) = 0.80208$
$t=3$	$Q_3(uuu) = 0.00130,\ Q_3(uud) = 0.00217,\ Q_2(udu) = 0.05657,\ Q_2(duu) = 0.08116,$
	$Q_3(udd) = 0.02329,\ Q_3(dud) = 0.08116,\ Q_3(ddu) = 0.33420,\ Q_3(ddd) = 0.46788$

5. Due to (3.19),

$$(1+r_f)\,D_2 = \left(1+\widetilde{k}_2^{D,nom}(dd)\right) D_2\,(1-Q_3(\mathrm{d}|\mathrm{dd})) + \frac{\widetilde{FCF}_3^u(ddd)-\tau D_2}{1-\tau}\,Q_3(\mathrm{d}|\mathrm{dd})$$

$$1.1\cdot D_2 \approx \left(1+\widetilde{k}_2^{D,nom}(dd)\right)\cdot D_2\cdot(1-0.5833) + \frac{48.4-0.5\cdot D_2}{1-0.5}\,0.5833$$

$$\widetilde{k}_2^{D,nom}(dd) \approx 3.04024 - \frac{135.531}{D_2}\,.$$

From this equation it is clear that there will be default if $D_2 \geq 46.09$, otherwise $\widetilde{k}_2^{D,nom}(dd) = 10\,\%$.

The cost of debt is given by its definition as an expected return under the subjective probability,

$$\widetilde{k}_2^D(dd) = \frac{\left(1+\widetilde{k}_2^{D,nom}\right) D_2\,(1-P_3(\mathrm{d}|\mathrm{dd})) + \frac{1}{1-\tau}\left(\widetilde{FCF}_3^u(ddd)-\tau D_2\right) P_3(\mathrm{d}|\mathrm{dd})}{D_2} - 1$$

$$\widetilde{k}_2^D(dd) \approx \frac{\left(1+3.04024-\frac{135.531}{D_2}\right)\cdot D_2\cdot(1-0.5) + \frac{1}{1-0.5}\,(48.4-0.5D_2)\cdot 0.5}{D_2} - 1$$

$$\approx 0.52012 - \frac{19.3654}{D_2}$$

for $D_2 \geq 46.09$, otherwise $\widetilde{k}_2^D(dd) = 10\,\%$.

Remark For very large D_2 there will be a default at state $\omega = duu$ (and probably uud, udu as well) which requires a more complicated evaluation that we will not present here.

7.2.3 Financing Based on Market Values

1. (a) We start with the value of the levered firm at $t = 0$,

$$V_0^l = \frac{\mathrm{E}\left[\widetilde{FCF}_1^u\right]}{1+WACC} + \frac{\mathrm{E}\left[\widetilde{FCF}_2^u\right]}{(1+WACC)^2} + \frac{\mathrm{E}\left[\widetilde{FCF}_3^u\right]}{(1+WACC)^3}$$

$$= \frac{100}{1+0.18} + \frac{110}{(1+0.18)^2} + \frac{121}{(1+0.18)^3} \approx 237.39.$$

The value at $t = 1$ depends on the state of nature. We get

$$\widetilde{V}_1^l = \frac{\mathrm{E}\left[\widetilde{FCF}_2^u|\mathcal{F}_1\right]}{1+WACC} + \frac{\mathrm{E}\left[\widetilde{FCF}_3^u|\mathcal{F}_1\right]}{(1+WACC)^2}$$

$$= \begin{cases} \frac{121}{1+0.18} + \frac{133.1}{(1+0.18)^2} \approx 198.13 & \text{if up,} \\ \frac{99}{1+0.18} + \frac{108.9}{(1+0.18)^2} \approx 162.11 & \text{if down.} \end{cases}$$

(b) This debt schedule implies the following leverage ratios:

$$l_0 = \frac{D_0}{V_0^l} = \frac{50}{237.39} \approx 21.06\,\%$$

and

$$\widetilde{l}_1 = \frac{\widetilde{D}_1}{\widetilde{V}_1^l} = \begin{cases} \frac{60}{198.13} \approx 30.28\,\% & \text{if up,} \\ \frac{40}{162.11} \approx 24.67\,\% & \text{if down.} \end{cases}$$

The Miles–Ezzell formula must not be applied.

(c) The WACC textbook formula will give us the cost of equity of the levered firm since

$$\widetilde{WACC}_1(u) = \widetilde{k}_1^{E,l}(u)\left(1 - \widetilde{l}_1(u)\right) + r_f\,(1-\tau)\,\widetilde{l}_1(u)$$

$$0.18 \approx \widetilde{k}_1^{E,l}(u) \cdot (1 - 0.3028) + 0.1 \cdot (1 - 0.5) \cdot 0.3028$$

implying

$$\widetilde{k}_1^{E,l}(u) \approx 23.65\,\%.$$

Analogously one gets

$$\widetilde{k}_1^{E,l}(d) \approx 22.26\,\%.$$

The weighted average cost of capital type 1 can be evaluated using the TCF textbook formula

$$\widetilde{k}_1^{\varnothing}(u) = \widetilde{k}_1^{E,l}(u)\left(1 - \widetilde{l}_1(u)\right) + r_f\,\widetilde{l}_1(u)$$

$$\widetilde{k}_1^{\varnothing}(u) \approx 0.2365 \cdot (1 - 0.3028) + 0.1 \cdot 0.3028 \approx 19.52\,\%$$

and again

$$\widetilde{k}_1^{\varnothing}(d) = \widetilde{k}_1^{E,l}(d)\left(1 - \widetilde{l}_1(d)\right) + r_f\,\widetilde{l}_1(d)$$

$$\widetilde{k}_1^{\varnothing}(d) \approx 0.2226 \cdot (1 - 0.2467) + 0.1 \cdot 0.2467 \approx 19.24\,\%.$$

Note that we did all calculations using EXCEL and rounded the numbers only after all calculations were done.

2. We have

$$\begin{aligned}\mathrm{WACC} - k^{E,u}(1-\tau l_0) &= (1+\mathrm{WACC}) - \left(1 + k^{E,u}(1-\tau l)\right)\\ &= (1+k^{E,u})\left(1 - \frac{\tau r_f}{1+r_f} l\right) - \left(1 + k^{E,u}(1-\tau l)\right)\\ &= \frac{(k^{E,u} - r_f)\tau l}{1+r_f} > 0\end{aligned}$$

which was to be shown.

3. In this case we have

$$\begin{aligned}\widetilde{V}_t^l &= \sum_{s=t+1}^{\infty} \frac{\mathrm{E}\left[\widetilde{FCF}_s^u | \mathcal{F}_t\right]}{(1+WACC)^{s-t}}\\ &= \sum_{s=t+1}^{\infty} \frac{\widetilde{FCF}_t^u}{(1+WACC)^{s-t}}\\ &= \frac{\widetilde{FCF}_t^u}{WACC}.\end{aligned}$$

Since

$$\widetilde{V}_t^u = \frac{\widetilde{FCF}_t^u}{k^{E,u}}$$

using the Miles–Ezzell formula gives

$$\widetilde{V}_t^l = \frac{\widetilde{FCF}_t^u}{k^{E,u}} \frac{k^{E,u}}{(1+k^{E,u})\left(1 - \frac{\tau r_f}{1+r_f} l\right) - 1}$$

which gives the result after some rearranging.

4. We have

$$1 + WACC_t = \left(1 + k_t^{E,u}\right)\left(1 - \frac{\tau r_f}{1+r_f} l_t\right)$$

according to Miles–Ezzell. Now plug in

$$1+r_f+(\mathrm{E}\left[\tilde{r}_M\right]-r_f)\beta_t^{WACC} = \left(1 + r_f + (\mathrm{E}\left[\tilde{r}_M\right] - r_f)\beta_t^{E,u}\right)\left(1 - \frac{\tau r_f}{1+r_f} l_t\right)$$

and this can be rearranged to

$$\beta_t^{WACC} = \beta_t^{E,u}\left(1 - \frac{\tau r_f}{1+r_f}\, l_t\right) - \frac{\tau r_f}{\mathrm{E}\left[\tilde{r}_M\right] - r_f}\, l_t\,.$$

7.2.4 Financing Based on Book Values

1. (a) First, since

$$\widetilde{FCF}^u_{t+1} = FCF^u_0 + \varepsilon_1 + \ldots + \varepsilon_t$$

and using the hint we know that the cash flows are normally distributed. They have expectation FCF^u_0 and variance t.

(b) This is easy, since

$$\widetilde{V}^u_t = \frac{\widetilde{FCF}^u_t}{k^{E,u}}$$

the value of the firm is normally distributed and has expectation $\frac{FCF^u_0}{k^{E,u}}$ and variance $\frac{t}{(k^{E,u})^2}$.

(c) For the book value we have using (6.8) and the assumptions on the past of the firm

$$\underline{\widetilde{V}}^l_t = \underline{V}^l_0 + \sum_{s=t-n+1}^{t} \frac{n-(t-s)}{n}\, \alpha\, \widetilde{FCF}^u_s\,.$$

Every summand $\frac{n-(t-s)}{n}\, \alpha\, \widetilde{FCF}^u_s$ is normally distributed with expectation $\frac{n-(t-s)}{n} \alpha FCF^u_0$ and variance $\left(\frac{n-(t-s)}{n}\alpha\right)^2 t$. Hence, the whole sum is again normally distributed. It has expectation

$$\underline{V}^l_0 + \sum_{s=t-n+1}^{t} \frac{n-(t-s)}{n} \alpha FCF^u_0 = \underline{V}^l_0 + \frac{n+1}{2} \alpha FCF^u_0\,.$$

When evaluating the variance we have to take into account that the $\widetilde{FCF}^u_s$ are correlated. We assume $t > n$ for simplicity and get

$$\mathrm{Var}\left[\sum_{s=t-n+1}^{t} \frac{n-(t-s)}{n}\, \alpha\, \widetilde{FCF}^u_s\right] = \alpha^2\, \mathrm{Var}\left[\sum_{s=t-n+1}^{t} \frac{n-(t-s)}{n} \sum_{r=1}^{s} \varepsilon_r\right]$$

$$= \alpha^2\, \mathrm{Var}\left[\frac{1}{n}\sum_{s=1}^{t-n+1} \varepsilon_s + \frac{2}{n}\sum_{s=1}^{t-n+2} \varepsilon_s + \ldots + \frac{n}{n}\sum_{s=1}^{t} \varepsilon_s\right]$$

$$= \alpha^2 \operatorname{Var}\left[\sum_{s=1}^{t-n+1} \left\{\frac{1}{n} + \frac{2}{n} + \ldots + \frac{n}{n}\right\} \varepsilon_s + \left\{\frac{2}{n} + \ldots + \frac{n}{n}\right\} \varepsilon_{t-n+2} + \ldots + \left\{\frac{n}{n}\right\} \varepsilon_t\right]$$

$$= \alpha^2 \operatorname{Var}\left[\sum_{s=1}^{t-n+1} \frac{n(n+1)}{2n} \varepsilon_s + \frac{(n+2)(n+1-2)}{2n} \varepsilon_{t-n+2}\right.$$

$$\left. + \frac{(n+3)(n+1-3)}{2n} \varepsilon_{t-n+3} + \ldots + \frac{(n+n)(n+1-n)}{2n} \varepsilon_t\right].$$

Since the ε are pairwise independent it follows that the variance is equal to

$$\alpha^2 \left[\sum_{s=1}^{t-n+1} \operatorname{Var}[\varepsilon_s] \frac{n^2(n+1)^2}{4n^2} + \frac{(n+2)^2(n+1-2)^2}{4n^2} \operatorname{Var}[\varepsilon_{t-n+2}] + \right.$$

$$\left. + \frac{(n+3)^2(n+1-3)^2}{4n^2} \operatorname{Var}[\varepsilon_{t-n+3}] + \ldots + \frac{(n+n)^2(n+1-n)^2}{4n^2} \operatorname{Var}[\varepsilon_t]\right].$$

Since the variance of all noise terms is 1, this can be simplified to

$$\alpha^2 \left[\frac{n^2(n+1)^2(t-n)}{4n^2} + \frac{(n+1)^2(n+1-1)^2}{4n^2} + \frac{(n+2)^2(n+1-2)^2}{4n^2}\right.$$

$$\left. + \frac{(n+3)^2(n+1-3)^2}{4n^2} + \ldots + \frac{(n+n)^2(n+1-n)^2}{4n^2}\right].$$

Although this is a complicated sum it can nevertheless be evaluated (for example, using Mathematica) and we get

$$\alpha^2 \left[\frac{n^2(n+1)^2(t-n)}{4n^2} + \frac{(n+1)(1+2n)\left(1+2n+2n^2\right)}{30n}\right]$$

and after simplification,

$$\alpha^2 \frac{(1+n)(2+15tn(n+1)+8n-3n^2-7n^3)}{60n}.$$

This is the variance of the book value of the firm.

These evaluations show two interesting things:

- The expectation of the future book value does not depend on time. It stays constant at a level above the book value today.
- The variance does depend on time. With higher t the variance increases, the increase is linear with slope $\alpha \frac{(n+1)^2}{4}$.

2. The value of the firm that is financed by book value is given by

$$V_0^l(\text{finan. book value}) = V_0^u + \tau D_0 + \frac{nr_f - 1 + \left(1 + r_f\right)^{-n}}{nr_f} \tau \alpha \underline{l} V_0^u$$
$$= \frac{100}{0.15} + 0.34 \cdot 500$$
$$+ \frac{4 \cdot 0.05 - 1 + (1 + 0.05)^{-4}}{4 \cdot 0.05} \cdot 0.34 \cdot 0.5 \cdot 0.7 \cdot \frac{100}{0.15}$$
$$\approx 845.672\,.$$

The Miles–Ezzell formula for infinite lifetime (see problem 3 in Sect. 3.4.7) can be applied, but l_0 is not known (if l_0 were equal to $\underline{l}$, then book and market value would coincide). Hence,

$$V_0^l(\text{finan. market value}) = \frac{\mathrm{E}\left[\widetilde{FCF}_t^u\right]}{(1 + k^{E,u})\left(1 - \frac{\tau r_f}{1+r_f} l_0\right) - 1}$$
$$= \frac{\widetilde{FCF}_t^u}{(1 + k^{E,u})\left(1 - \frac{\tau r_f}{1+r_f} \frac{D_0}{V_0^l(\text{finan. market value})}\right) - 1}.$$

This can be rearranged to

$$V_0^l(\text{finan. market value}) = \frac{\mathrm{E}\left[\widetilde{FCF}_t^u\right]}{k^{E,u}} + \frac{\tau r_f}{1 + r_f} \frac{1 + k^{E,u}}{k^{E,u}} D_0$$
$$= \frac{100}{0.15} + \frac{0.34 \cdot 0.05}{1 + 0.05} \frac{1 + 0.15}{0.15} 500$$
$$\approx 728.73\,.$$

Obviously, the difference is very big.

7.2.5 Other Financing Policies

1. First, if $n \to \infty$ and $T \to \infty$

$$\lim_{n \to \infty} \delta^n = \lim_{T \to \infty} \delta^T = 0$$

since $\delta < 1$. The same holds for γ and $\frac{1}{1+r_f}$. Now Theorem 3.25 reduces to

$$\begin{aligned}\lim_{T,n\to\infty} V_0^l &= (1 - 0\,(1 - \tau\,(1 - 0)))\, D_0 \\ &\quad + (1 - 0\,(1 - \tau\,(1 - 0)) - \tau\,(1 - 0))\,\frac{Div}{r_f(1-\tau)} \\ &\quad + \left(0 - 0 + \frac{0}{\frac{\gamma}{\delta}-1}\,\frac{k^{E,u}-g}{1+g}\right)\frac{V_0^u}{1-0}\end{aligned}$$

which was to be shown.

2. In a binomial model, the individual probabilities Q can be determined (see Fig. 3.1).
   (a) Using (3.11) this gives

$$\begin{aligned}V_0^l &= V_0^u + (\widetilde{D}_1(u)Q_1(u) + \widetilde{D}_1(d)Q_1(d))\frac{\tau r_f}{(1+r_f)^2} \\ &= 159.72 + (\widetilde{D}_1(u)\cdot 0.083 + \widetilde{D}_1(d)\cdot 0.917)\cdot 0.0281.\end{aligned}$$

   (b) Since

$$100 = \mathrm{E}\left[\widetilde{D}_1\right] = \frac{1}{2}\left(\widetilde{D}_1(d) + \widetilde{D}_1(u)\right)$$

   and since debt cannot be negative, the highest value of V_0^l is achieved for

$$\widetilde{D}_1(d) = 200, \qquad \widetilde{D}_1(u) = 0\,.$$

   This yields a firm value of 164.87.

7.3 Personal Income Tax

7.3.1 Unlevered and Levered Firms

1. Due to Theorem 4.4, we get

$$\begin{aligned}\frac{\mathrm{E}_Q\left[\widetilde{FCF}_1^u\right]}{1+r_f(1-\tau)} &= \frac{\mathrm{E}\left[\widetilde{FCF}_1^u\right]}{1+k^{E,u}} \\ \frac{Q_1(u)\widetilde{FCF}_1^u(u) + Q_1(d)\widetilde{FCF}_1^u(d)}{1+r_f(1-\tau)} &= \frac{\mathrm{E}\left[\widetilde{FCF}_1^u\right]}{1+k^{E,u}} \\ \frac{Q_1(u)\cdot 110 + Q_1(d)\cdot 90}{1.05} &= \frac{100}{1.2},\end{aligned}$$

and from this

$$Q_1(u) \approx -0.125, \qquad Q_1(d) \approx 1.125\,.$$

Any claim that pays one dollar after tax if *up* and nothing after tax if *down* must have a price of

$$V_0^u = \frac{Q_1(u)}{1 + r_f(1-\tau)} < 0$$

and this is an arbitrage opportunity. If $k^{E,u} = 15\%$ we get

$$Q_1(u) \approx 0.0652, \qquad Q_1(d) \approx 0.9348\,. \tag{7.2}$$

To evaluate $Q_2(dd), \ldots$ we concentrate on $t = 1$. Analogously, we must have

$$\frac{Q_2(u|u) \cdot 132 + Q_2(d|u) \cdot 110}{1.05} = \frac{121}{1.15},$$

which gives

$$Q_2(u|u) \approx 0.0217, \quad Q_2(d|u) \approx 0.9783\,.$$

Now

$$Q_2(uu) = Q_1(u)Q_2(u|u) \approx 0.0014$$
$$Q_2(ud) = Q_1(u)Q_2(u|d) \approx 0.0638$$

and analogously

$$Q_2(du) \approx 0.1016, \qquad Q_2(dd) \approx 0.8332\,.$$

2. Equation (4.4) implies

$$\widetilde{V}_{t+1}^l = \widetilde{V}_{t+1}^u + (1-\tau^D)\widetilde{A}_{t+1} + \frac{\mathrm{E}_Q\left[\tau^I r_f (1-\tau^D)\widetilde{A}_{t+1}|\mathcal{F}_{t+1}\right]}{1 + r_f(1-\tau^I)} + \ldots$$
$$+ \frac{\mathrm{E}_Q\left[\tau^I r_f (1-\tau^D)\widetilde{A}_{T-1}|\mathcal{F}_{t+1}\right]}{(1 + r_f(1-\tau^I))^{T-t-1}}.$$

Rule 4 gives

$$\mathrm{E}_Q\left[\widetilde{V}_{t+1}^l - \widetilde{V}_{t+1}^u|\mathcal{F}_t\right] = \mathrm{E}_Q\left[(1-\tau^D)\widetilde{A}_{t+1}|\mathcal{F}_t\right] +$$
$$+ \frac{\mathrm{E}_Q\left[\tau^I r_f (1-\tau^D)\widetilde{A}_{t+1}|\mathcal{F}_t\right]}{1 + r_f(1-\tau^I)} + \ldots + \frac{\mathrm{E}_Q\left[\tau^I r_f (1-\tau^D)\widetilde{A}_{T-1}|\mathcal{F}_t\right]}{(1 + r_f(1-\tau^I))^{T-t-1}}$$

or

$$\frac{\mathrm{E}_Q\left[\widetilde{V}^l_{t+1}-\widetilde{V}^u_{t+1}-(1-\tau^D)\widetilde{A}_{t+1}|\mathcal{F}_t\right]}{1+r_f(1-\tau^I)}=\frac{\mathrm{E}_Q\left[\tau^I r_f(1-\tau^D)\widetilde{A}_{t+1}|\mathcal{F}_t\right]}{(1+r_f(1-\tau^I))^2}+\ldots+\frac{\mathrm{E}_Q\left[\tau^I r_f(1-\tau^D)\widetilde{A}_{T-1}|\mathcal{F}_t\right]}{(1+r_f(1-\tau^I))^{T-t}}.$$

Now adding $\frac{\mathrm{E}_Q\left[\tau^I r_f(1-\tau^D)\widetilde{A}_t|\mathcal{F}_t\right]}{1+r_f(1-\tau^I)}$ results in

$$\frac{\mathrm{E}_Q\left[\widetilde{V}^l_{t+1}-\widetilde{V}^u_{t+1}|\mathcal{F}_t\right]}{1+r_f(1-\tau^I)}+\frac{\mathrm{E}_Q\left[\tau^I r_f(1-\tau^D)\widetilde{A}_t-(1-\tau^D)\widetilde{A}_{t+1}|\mathcal{F}_t\right]}{1+r_f(1-\tau^I)}=$$
$$\frac{\mathrm{E}_Q\left[\tau^I r_f(1-\tau^D)\widetilde{A}_t|\mathcal{F}_t\right]}{1+r_f(1-\tau^I)}+\frac{\mathrm{E}_Q\left[\tau^I r_f(1-\tau^D)\widetilde{A}_{t+1}|\mathcal{F}_t\right]}{(1+r_f(1-\tau^I))^2}+\ldots$$
$$+\frac{\mathrm{E}_Q\left[\tau^I r_f(1-\tau^D)\widetilde{A}_{T-1}|\mathcal{F}_t\right]}{(1+r_f(1-\tau^I))^{T-t}}=\widetilde{V}^l_t-\widetilde{V}^u_t-(1-\tau^D)\widetilde{A}_t\,.$$

Reshuffling gives

$$\widetilde{V}^l_t-\widetilde{V}^u_t=\frac{\mathrm{E}_Q\left[\widetilde{V}^l_{t+1}-\widetilde{V}^u_{t+1}|\mathcal{F}_t\right]}{1+r_f(1-\tau^I)}+\frac{(1+r_f)(1-\tau^D)}{1+r_f(1-\tau^I)}\widetilde{A}_t-\frac{\mathrm{E}_Q\left[(1-\tau^D)\widetilde{A}_{t+1}|\mathcal{F}_t\right]}{1+r_f(1-\tau^I)}.$$

3. We have

$$\widetilde{V}^l_t=\widetilde{V}^u_t+\left(1-\tau^D\right)\widetilde{A}_t+\sum_{s=t}^{T}\frac{\tau^I\left(1-\tau^D\right)r_f\,\mathrm{E}_Q\left[\widetilde{A}_s|\mathcal{F}_t\right]}{(1+r_f\left(1-\tau^I\right))^{s-t+1}}$$
$$=\widetilde{V}^u_t+\left(1-\tau^D\right)\widetilde{A}_t+\frac{\tau^I\left(1-\tau^D\right)r_f\widetilde{A}_t}{1+r_f\left(1-\tau^I\right)}+\sum_{s=t+1}^{T}\frac{\tau^I\left(1-\tau^D\right)r_f\,\mathrm{E}_Q\left[\widetilde{A}_s|\mathcal{F}_t\right]}{(1+r_f\left(1-\tau^I\right))^{s-t+1}}$$
$$=\widetilde{V}^u_t+\frac{(1+r_f)(1-\tau^D)}{1+r_f(1-\tau^I)}\widetilde{A}_t+\sum_{s=t+1}^{T}\frac{\tau^I\left(1-\tau^D\right)r_f\,\mathrm{E}_Q\left[\widetilde{A}_s|\mathcal{F}_t\right]}{(1+r_f\left(1-\tau^I\right))^{s-t+1}}$$
$$=\widetilde{V}^u_t+\frac{(1+r_f)(1-\tau^D)}{1+r_f(1-\tau^I)}\widetilde{A}_t+\frac{\tau^I\left(1-\tau^D\right)}{1-\tau^I}\sum_{s=t+1}^{T}\frac{\mathrm{E}_Q\left[\widetilde{A}_s|\mathcal{F}_t\right]}{(1+r_f\left(1-\tau^I\right))^{s-t}}\frac{(1-\tau^I)r_f}{1+r_f(1-\tau^I)}$$

$$
\begin{aligned}
&= \widetilde{V}_t^u + \frac{(1+r_f)(1-\tau^D)}{1+r_f(1-\tau^I)}\widetilde{A}_t + \frac{\tau^I\left(1-\tau^D\right)}{1-\tau^I}\sum_{s=t+1}^{T}\frac{\mathrm{E}_Q\left[\widetilde{A}_s|\mathcal{F}_t\right]}{\left(1+r_f\left(1-\tau^I\right)\right)^{s-t}} \\
&\quad + \left(1 - \frac{1}{1+r_f(1-\tau^I)}\right) \\
&= \widetilde{V}_t^u + \frac{(1+r_f)(1-\tau^D)}{1+r_f(1-\tau^I)}\widetilde{A}_t + \frac{\tau^I\left(1-\tau^D\right)}{1-\tau^I}\sum_{s=t+1}^{T}\frac{\mathrm{E}_Q\left[\widetilde{A}_s|\mathcal{F}_t\right]}{\left(1+r_f\left(1-\tau^I\right)\right)^{s-t}} \\
&\quad - \frac{\tau^I\left(1-\tau^D\right)}{1-\tau^I}\sum_{s=t+1}^{T}\frac{\mathrm{E}_Q\left[\widetilde{A}_s|\mathcal{F}_t\right]}{\left(1+r_f\left(1-\tau^I\right)\right)^{s-t+1}} \\
&= \widetilde{V}_t^u + \frac{(1+r_f)(1-\tau^D)}{1+r_f(1-\tau^I)}\widetilde{A}_t + \frac{\tau^I\left(1-\tau^D\right)}{1-\tau^I}\sum_{s=t+1}^{T}\frac{\mathrm{E}_Q\left[\widetilde{A}_s|\mathcal{F}_t\right]}{\left(1+r_f\left(1-\tau^I\right)\right)^{s-t}} \\
&\quad - \frac{\tau^I\left(1-\tau^D\right)}{1-\tau^I}\sum_{s=t+2}^{T}\frac{\mathrm{E}_Q\left[\widetilde{A}_{s-1}|\mathcal{F}_t\right]}{\left(1+r_f\left(1-\tau^I\right)\right)^{s-t}}
\end{aligned}
$$

using $\widetilde{A}_T = 0$. Rearranging gives

$$
\begin{aligned}
\widetilde{V}_t^l &= \widetilde{V}_t^u + \frac{(1+r_f)(1-\tau^D)}{1+r_f(1-\tau^I)}\widetilde{A}_t + \frac{\tau^I\left(1-\tau^D\right)}{1-\tau^I}\sum_{s=t+1}^{T}\frac{\mathrm{E}_Q\left[\widetilde{A}_s|\mathcal{F}_t\right]}{\left(1+r_f\left(1-\tau^I\right)\right)^{s-t}} \\
&\quad - \frac{\tau^I\left(1-\tau^D\right)}{1-\tau^I}\sum_{s=t+1}^{T}\frac{\mathrm{E}_Q\left[\widetilde{A}_{s-1}|\mathcal{F}_t\right]}{\left(1+r_f\left(1-\tau^I\right)\right)^{s-t}} + \frac{\tau^I\left(1-\tau^D\right)}{1-\tau^I}\frac{\widetilde{A}_t}{1+r_f(1-\tau^I)}
\end{aligned}
$$

and this is equivalent to

$$
\widetilde{V}_t^l = \widetilde{V}_t^u + \frac{1-\tau^D}{1-\tau^I}\widetilde{A}_t + \frac{\tau^I\left(1-\tau^D\right)}{1-\tau^I}\sum_{s=t+1}^{T}\frac{\mathrm{E}_Q\left[\widetilde{A}_s - \widetilde{A}_{s-1}|\mathcal{F}_t\right]}{\left(1+r_f\left(1-\tau^I\right)\right)^{s-t}}.
$$

7.3.2 Excursus: Cost of Equity and Tax Rate

1. This follows from

$$
\begin{aligned}
k^{\text{post-tax}} &= \frac{\mathrm{E}\left[\widetilde{GCF}_{t+1} + \widetilde{V}_{t+1}^u - \tau(\widetilde{GCF}_{t+1} + \widetilde{V}_{t+1}^u - \widetilde{V}_t^u)|\mathcal{F}_t\right]}{\widetilde{V}_t^u} \\
&= (1-\tau)\frac{\mathrm{E}\left[\widetilde{GCF}_{t+1} + \widetilde{V}_{t+1}^u|\mathcal{F}_t\right]}{\widetilde{V}_t^u} \\
&= (1-\tau)k^{\text{pre-tax}}.
\end{aligned}
$$

2. We have

$$\widetilde{V}_t^u = \sum_{s=t+1}^{\infty} \frac{\mathrm{E}_Q\left[\widetilde{GCF}_s(1-\tau)|\mathcal{F}_t\right]}{(1+r_f(1-\tau))^{s-t}}$$

$$= \sum_{s=t+1}^{\infty} \frac{\mathrm{E}_Q\left[\widetilde{GCF}_s|\mathcal{F}_t\right]}{\left(1+r_f\right)^{s-t}} \frac{(1-\tau)\left(1+r_f\right)^{s-t}}{(1+r_f(1-\tau))^{s-t}}$$

$$= \sum_{s=t+1}^{\infty} \frac{\mathrm{E}\left[\widetilde{GCF}_s|\mathcal{F}_t\right]}{(1+k^{\text{pre-tax}})^{s-t}} \frac{(1-\tau)\left(1+r_f\right)^{s-t}}{(1+r_f(1-\tau))^{s-t}}$$

$$= \sum_{s=t+1}^{\infty} \frac{\widetilde{GCF}_t}{(1+k^{\text{pre-tax}})^{s-t}} \frac{(1-\tau)\left(1+r_f\right)^{s-t}}{(1+r_f(1-\tau))^{s-t}}$$

$$= \frac{(1-\tau)\widetilde{GCF}_t}{\frac{(1+k^{\text{pre-tax}})(1+r_f(1-\tau))}{1+r_f} - 1}$$

and this is obviously different from

$$\frac{(1-\tau)\widetilde{GCF}_t}{k^{\text{pre-tax}}(1-\tau)}.$$

3. (a) As in Sect. 3.6.1 we get

$$\frac{\mathrm{E}_Q\left[\widetilde{GCF}_1\right]}{1+r_f} = \frac{\mathrm{E}\left[\widetilde{GCF}_1\right]}{1+k}$$

$$\frac{Q_1(u)\widetilde{GCF}_1(u) + Q_1(d)\widetilde{GCF}_1(d)}{1+r_f} = \frac{\mathrm{E}\left[\widetilde{GCF}_1\right]}{1+k}$$

$$\frac{Q_1(u)\cdot 110 + Q_1(d)\cdot 90}{1.05} = \frac{100}{1.15},$$

and hence

$$Q_1(u) \approx 0.0652, \qquad Q_1(d) \approx 0.93478\,.$$

(b) If we look at the second company, the gross cash flows are different and we get

$$\frac{\mathrm{E}_Q\left[\widetilde{GCF}'_1\right]}{1+r_f} = \frac{\mathrm{E}\left[\widetilde{GCF}'_1\right]}{1+k'}$$

$$\frac{Q_1(u)\widetilde{GCF}'_1(u) + Q_1(d)\widetilde{GCF}'_1(d)}{1+r_f} = \frac{\mathrm{E}\left[\widetilde{GCF}'_1\right]}{1+k'}$$

$$\frac{0.0652 \cdot 120 + 0.93478 \cdot 80}{1.05} \approx \frac{100}{1+k'},$$

and hence

$$k' \approx 27.105\,\%\,.$$

(c) This is the same calculation except that we have to add taxes:

$$\frac{\mathrm{E}_Q\left[(1-\tau)\widetilde{GCF}_1\right]}{1+r_f(1-\tau)} = \frac{\mathrm{E}\left[(1-\tau)\widetilde{GCF}_1\right]}{1+k(1-\tau)}$$

$$\frac{Q_1(u)(1-\tau)\widetilde{GCF}_1(u) + Q_1(d)(1-\tau)\widetilde{GCF}_1(d)}{1+r_f(1-\tau)} = \frac{\mathrm{E}\left[(1-\tau)\widetilde{GCF}_1\right]}{1+k(1-\tau)}$$

$$\frac{Q_1(u)(1-\tau)110 + Q_1(d)(1-\tau)90}{1+0.05(1-\tau)} = \frac{100(1-\tau)}{1+0.15(1-\tau)},$$

and hence

$$Q_1(u) \approx 2.8333\,\frac{(0.176471+\tau)}{7.6667-\tau}, \qquad Q_1(d) = 1 - Q_1(u)\,.$$

(d) The calculation is as above,

$$\frac{\mathrm{E}_Q\left[(1-\tau)\widetilde{GCF}_1\right]}{1+r_f(1-\tau)} = \frac{\mathrm{E}\left[(1-\tau)\widetilde{GCF}_1\right]}{1+k'(1-\tau)}$$

$$\frac{Q_1(u)(1-\tau)\widetilde{GCF}_1(u) + Q_1(d)(1-\tau)\widetilde{GCF}_1(d)}{1+r_f(1-\tau)} = \frac{\mathrm{E}\left[(1-\tau)\widetilde{GCF}_1\right]}{1+k'(1-\tau)}$$

$$\frac{Q_1(u)(1-\tau)120 + Q_1(d)(1-\tau)80}{1+0.05(1-\tau)} = \frac{100(1-\tau)}{1+15.5\,\%(1-\tau)},$$

and hence

$$Q_1(u) \approx 1.1667 \frac{(1.85714 + \tau)}{7.6667 - \tau}, \qquad Q_1(d) = 1 - Q_1(u)\,.$$

This is different from the result in 3c.

7.3.3 Retention Policies

1. From (4.4) it follows that the market value is maximized if the retentions are as large as possible. Since necessarily

$$\widetilde{A}_3 = 0,$$

we only look at $\widetilde{A}_1$ and $\widetilde{A}_2$. We will determine the highest possible retention and evaluate the corresponding market value of the firm.

If the company maintains its highest possible retention, the cash flows to the shareholders are zero. From this

$$\widetilde{A}_1 := \frac{1}{1-\tau^D}\widetilde{FCF}^u_1, \qquad \widetilde{A}_2 := \left(1+r_f\right)\widetilde{A}_1 + \frac{1}{1-\tau^D}\widetilde{FCF}^u_2\,.$$

We put this into (4.4) and get, using Theorem 4.4,

$$\begin{aligned}
V^l_0 &= V^u_0 + \frac{\tau^I r_f(1-\tau^D)\,\mathrm{E}_Q\left[\widetilde{A}_1\right]}{(1+r_f(1-\tau^I))^2} + \frac{\tau^I r_f(1-\tau^D)\,\mathrm{E}_Q\left[\widetilde{A}_2\right]}{(1+r_f(1-\tau^I))^3}\\
&= V^u_0 + \frac{\tau^I r_f(1-\tau^D)\,\mathrm{E}_Q\left[\frac{\widetilde{FCF}^u_1}{1-\tau^D}\right]}{(1+r_f(1-\tau^I))^2} + \frac{\tau^I r_f(1-\tau^D)\,\mathrm{E}_Q\left[\frac{(1+r_f)\widetilde{FCF}^u_1+\widetilde{FCF}^u_2}{1-\tau^D}\right]}{(1+r_f(1-\tau^I))^3}\\
&= V^u_0 + \frac{\tau^I r_f\,\mathrm{E}_Q\left[\widetilde{FCF}^u_1\right]}{(1+r_f(1-\tau^I))^2} + \frac{\tau^I r_f(1+r_f)\,\mathrm{E}_Q\left[\widetilde{FCF}^u_1\right]}{(1+r_f(1-\tau^I))^3} + \frac{\tau^I r_f\,\mathrm{E}_Q\left[\widetilde{FCF}^u_2\right]}{(1+r_f(1-\tau^I))^3}\\
&= V^u_0 + \frac{\tau^I r_f\,\mathrm{E}\left[\widetilde{FCF}^u_1\right]}{(1+k^{E,u})(1+r_f(1-\tau^I))} + \frac{\tau^I r_f(1+r_f)\,\mathrm{E}\left[\widetilde{FCF}^u_1\right]}{(1+k^{E,u})(1+r_f(1-\tau^I))^2}\\
&\qquad + \frac{\tau^I r_f\,\mathrm{E}\left[\widetilde{FCF}^u_2\right]}{(1+k^{E,u})^2(1+r_f(1-\tau^I))}
\end{aligned}$$

$$
\begin{aligned}
&\approx 249.692 + \frac{0.5 \cdot 0.1 \cdot 100}{(1+0.15) \cdot (1+0.1 \cdot (1-0.5))} \\
&\qquad + \frac{0.5 \cdot 0.1 \cdot (1+0.1) \cdot 100}{(1+0.15) \cdot (1+0.1 \cdot (1-0.5))^2} \\
&\qquad\qquad + \frac{0.5 \cdot 0.1 \cdot 110}{(1+0.15)^2 \cdot (1+0.1 \cdot (1-0.5))} \\
&\approx 260.061\,.
\end{aligned}
$$

2. With retention in riskless assets (4.3) reads

$$
\mathrm{E}_Q\left[\widetilde{FCF}_t^l - \widetilde{FCF}_t^u|\mathcal{F}_{t-1}\right] = \left(1-\tau^I\right)\left(1+r_f\right)\widetilde{A}_{t-1} - \left(1-\tau^I\right)\mathrm{E}_Q\left[\widetilde{A}_t|\mathcal{F}_{t-1}\right].
$$

Following Eq. (4.4) we get

$$
\begin{aligned}
\widetilde{V}_t^l = \widetilde{V}_t^u &+ \frac{(1-\tau^I)\,\mathrm{E}_Q\left[(1+r_f)\,\widetilde{A}_t - \widetilde{A}_{t+1}|\mathcal{F}_t\right]}{1+r_f\,(1-\tau^I)} + \dots \\
&+ \frac{(1-\tau^I)\,\mathrm{E}_Q\left[(1+r_f)\,\widetilde{A}_{T-2} - \widetilde{A}_{T-1}|\mathcal{F}_t\right]}{1+r_f\,(1-\tau^I)^{T-t-1}} \\
&+ \frac{(1-\tau^I)\,\mathrm{E}_Q\left[(1+r_f)\,\widetilde{A}_{T-1}|\mathcal{F}_t\right]}{\left(1+r_f\,(1-\tau^I)\right)^{T-t}}\,.
\end{aligned}
$$

After some minimal reshuffling the following results:

$$
\begin{aligned}
\widetilde{V}_t^l = \widetilde{V}_t^u &+ \frac{(1-\tau^I)\,(1+r_f)\,\widetilde{A}_t}{1+r_f\,(1-\tau^I)} \\
&+ \frac{\mathrm{E}_Q\left[\frac{(1+r_f)(1-\tau^I)}{1+r_f(1-\tau^I)}\widetilde{A}_{t+1} - (1-\tau^I)\,\widetilde{A}_{t+1}|\mathcal{F}_t\right]}{1+r_f\,(1-\tau^I)} + \dots \\
&+ \frac{\mathrm{E}_Q\left[\frac{(1+r_f)(1-\tau^I)}{1+r_f(1-\tau^I)}\widetilde{A}_{T-1} - (1-\tau^I)\,\widetilde{A}_{T-1}|\mathcal{F}_t\right]}{\left(1+r_f\,(1-\tau^I)\right)^{T-t}}\,.
\end{aligned}
$$

This brings us to the conclusion,

$$\widetilde{V}_t^l = \widetilde{V}_t^u + \left(1 - \tau^I\right) \widetilde{A}_t + \frac{\tau^I \left(1 - \tau^I\right) r_f \operatorname{E}_Q\left[\widetilde{A}_t | \mathcal{F}_t\right]}{1 + r_f \left(1 - \tau^I\right)} + \ldots$$

$$+ \frac{\tau^I \left(1 - \tau^I\right) r_f \operatorname{E}_Q\left[\widetilde{A}_{T-1} | \mathcal{F}_t\right]}{\left(1 + r_f \left(1 - \tau^I\right)\right)^{T-t}}.$$

In case of autonomous retention, with an eternally living firm this simply yields

$$\widetilde{V}_t^l = \widetilde{V}_t^u + A.$$

7.4 Corporate and Personal Income Tax

1. We get

$$\begin{aligned} \widetilde{V}_t^l &= \widetilde{V}_t^u + \frac{\left(1 - \tau^D\right)\left(1 - \tau^C\right)}{1 - \tau^I} A + \tau^C D \\ &= 500 + \frac{(1 - 0.5) \cdot (1 - 0.5)}{1 - 0.5} 10 + 0.5 \cdot 100 \\ &= 555. \end{aligned}$$

Index

L. Kruschwitz, A. Löffler, *Stochastic Discounted Cash Flow*,
Springer Texts in Business and Economics,
https://doi.org/10.1007/978-3-030-37081-7

The manufacturer's authorised representative in the EU is Springer Nature Customer Service Centre GmbH, Europaplatz 3, 69115 Heidelberg, Germany. If you have any concerns regarding our products, please contact ProductSafety@springernature.com

Printed and bound by CPI Group (UK) Ltd, Croydon, CR0 4YY
30/09/2026
02225645-0016